Slow Dust Rising

Ron Cogdill

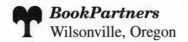

BookPartners
Wilsonville, Oregon

Library of Congress Cataloging-in-Publication Data

Cogdill, Ron, 1942-
　　Slow Dust Rising / Ron Cogdill.
　　　　p.　　cm.
　　　　ISBN 1-58151-019-5 (softcover　: alk. paper)
　　　　I. Title.
　　PS3553. 041524S58　　1999
　　813' .54--dc21　　　　　　　　　　　　　　　　　　　　99-34257
　　　　　　　　　　　　　　　　　　　　　　　　　　　　　　CIP

Copyright © 2001 by Ron Cogdill
All rights reserved
Printed in U.S.A.
Library of Congress Catalog 98-73996
ISBN 1-58151-019-5

Cover design by Richard Ferguson
Text design by Sheryl Mehary

BookPartners, Inc.
P. O. Box 922
Wilsonville, Oregon 97070

In memory of my mother,
who read my work
when it was unreadable.
To my dad, who lived the real-life
bear stories,
and to my wife, who has worked
beside me the entire way.

The last relics of what is wild in the world struggle at the rear of a traveling herd, their ribs growing sharper, their pace slower, and they live the lie that they can make it. But the herd does not turn. It moves along with a slow dust rising and white bones bleaching in its wake.

Chapter 1

I sometimes think back on that terrible year and wonder if it turned out badly because of the blunders my family made, or if it was out of our hands from the start—if we were just in the wrong place at the wrong time, like the passenger pigeons. The big push to save the last few remaining pockets of wildness was in full swing by then. The country was wringing its hands over disappearing salmon and spotted owls and old-growth forests and god only knows what other parts of nature that were getting steamrolled by "progress." There was a long list of "endangered" species that kept growing. But I'm not sure one creature didn't get left off that list—us! The steamroller came up from the valley, twisted through the pine forest on the red cinder road, and turned up the mile of potholes that was our driveway to level our way of life as flat as a clear-cut forest. I'm not sure that my family and our farm and poor old Rooster weren't endangered species, too (that merely got overlooked). I don't know...I do know this, though: our lives took a sad turn that year. And for me, at least, the part about Rooster was the saddest of all.

I was nine that year, and my mom swore up and down that the stork had gotten its wires crossed when it made me and had accidentally put a boy inside a girl's skin. My brother Percy agreed with her. But my dad had the opposite opinion on the matter. He said I was "girl" clean through and that my being a "tomboy" had less to do with how the stork had made me than which chimney it had dropped me down. He said it was common practice among storks to drop "girly" girls (the kind Mom wanted) down city chimneys, and when they had babies they wanted to grow up with scabs on their knees and dirty fingernails, they dropped them down country chimneys like ours. He was happy with me like I was, and I was, too. I was thankful the stork had dropped me where it had.

The only thing I would have changed about the chimney where the stork dropped me was the house the chimney belonged to. We had a good chimney, but a bad house. It was a relic, and that's putting it kindly. It was an old two-story box with a steep roof to shed the snow and a porch on the front that was so tilted you needed one long leg to stand on it. There wasn't a shred of insulation in the whole place, so when the wind blew, you'd swear you were living in a sieve. It was cold as sin. We spent our winters sticking rags around the doors and windows and burning the stove so hot the pipe glowed red. We had water piped down to the back door from a spring, and we carried it from there in buckets. Our lights ran on gas that was delivered to us in metal cylinders that looked like bombs. There was power at the road a mile away, but it cost too much to bring in, so we did without.

We also did without a bathroom. We took our baths on the kitchen floor in a metal tub we filled and emptied by hand, and when we had to do our duty, we took a hike out the back door and across the garden to the outhouse. Mom was always naming things. She had names for cows, chickens, cars, tractors, and even the outhouse. She named the outhouse "Heaven" and hung a sign above the door. When we had to go to the bathroom, we said were going to Heaven. Trouble was, it wasn't a pleasant place. Sitting down on that frosty toilet seat in the dead of winter with the temperature below zero was pure torture, and it wasn't much better any other time. I suspect that a good part of the questionable behavior my brother and I unleashed on the world during those years had to do with our determination to make sure we never made it to the real Heaven. By our logic, who would want to spend eternity in a place that smelled like that?

One time when Percy, was just a little boy, Heaven blew over in a windstorm with him in it. It landed face down so the door wouldn't open, and he spent the whole afternoon pounding on the sides to get someone's attention. When Mom finally found him, he had his head sticking out through the toilet hole, yelling at the top of his lungs. After that, Dad anchored Heaven to a tree with a cable, but for a long time, Percy wouldn't go to the bathroom if the wind was blowing.

If the house under the chimney where the stork dropped me wasn't much to brag on, the farm that the house stood on was something special. At least it was to my family and me. It was surrounded by miles of what most people would call "nothing" (meaning, of course, a lot of everything but people). That suited us fine. You could have stood in our yard and shot your rifle in any direction and not hit anything but a tree in the endless forest.

To the north, the dome of South Peak towered above a roadless wilderness. To the east, Mount Thompson held up our sunrise each morning with its graceful cone. And to the south and west, the forest rolled off to the horizons, with a drainage so befuddled by countless lava flows that the streams were still learning their way to the ocean. Lakes and pools cupped in depressions behind basalt outpourings, reflecting the sky and trees.

Our pasture was a natural meadow which, as best we could figure, had once been one of these old lake-bottoms. It was as flat and green as a billiard table, and looking across it, you would swear you were not seeing a pasture at all, but a green lake. From a distance the cattle looked like some strange kind of horned waterfowl floating on the grassy surface. Up close, our cattle were less picturesque. In fact, they were downright motley. They weren't like the herds you'd see down on the big ranches in the lowlands, where every animal was the same shape and hue. We had a rainbow mix of every breed under the sun, including some that were out-and-out weird-looking. But, as Mom put it, "Beauty is on the inside. When cows are ground up and between a bun, they all look alike, anyway."

If our herd wasn't much to look at, the ranch itself was. It was as pretty as a picture, and there was something about it that nurtured us the way the grass nurtured the livestock. The trouble was, as good as it looked, it was a hard place to turn a penny. It would have made a nice postcard or movie set, but since you can't eat scenery, it didn't provide us with much of an income. It was only with a lot of skimping that we made ends meet at all, and the truth was that, skimping or not, we usually came up short.

I suppose if we'd had any sense at all, we would have sold the ranch and moved down to lower country where the growing seasons were longer and profits were easier to come by. The Forest Service, in fact, had tried to buy it from us for years, and for a good price. They wanted to turn it into a campground. It was probably more suited for that purpose, anyway. Surrounded by National Forest land, it was the only private parcel for miles, and I'm sure campers would have loved it. But we loved it, too—far too much ever to part with it. Mom, who was born in the city and had never even set foot in the woods until she met my dad, said she wouldn't leave it for anything less than a castle in Florida. And Dad, who had been born on this very land, said he wouldn't leave it for anything—not for all of Florida. He meant it, too. Percy and I felt the same way about it. The two of us were raised in accord with Dad's intense love for the wild, and when it came right down to it, the ranch was as much a part of us as our arms or toes. We knew every inch of it.

That year when I was nine, Percy and I had one friend. He was a boy named Jon Pindar. If we had lived anywhere else, I doubt we would have called him our friend. But except for the week-enders who came up to the cabins at Russ Lake a mile or so away, he was the only kid our age for fifteen miles. We were friends by necessity. Jon Pindar and Percy were both eleven that year, but they looked like Mutt and Jeff. Percy was tall for his age, and stronger and faster than most boys several years older. Jon, on the other hand, was almost as short as me. He said he'd rather be short than ugly, but I thought he was both. He hated girls, but tolerated me for the same reason I tolerated him. I was all there was. The peace between the two of us was always uneasy, to say the least. Deep down, I think he was afraid of me. The only time we ever got into a real fight that came to blows, I nearly beat him to a pulp before Percy finally pulled us apart.

Jon Pindar was what you would call "the stick that kept the pot stirred." He came to us that way. He had grown up on the other side of the mountains in Portland. His parents were business people and they cared more about earning money than taking care of Jon. As a result, he had grown up doing pretty much what he pleased. Now, I wouldn't say that Percy and I didn't have a free rein ourselves, but there was a difference. Jon had freedom because his parents didn't care; we had freedom because ours did care. Anyway, Jon was always telling us stories about the mischief he had gotten into back in the city before his parents bought the Russ Lake Lodge. They were enough to make your hair stand on end. Percy and I were pretty naive about things like that. We didn't know a lot about the city, and we listened to his tales with our mouths gaping open.

Jon Pindar hated work, and he bragged that he knew tricks to get out of any kind of work there was. For that matter, he knew how to get out of just about anything he didn't want to do, work or not. He bragged about that, too. In school, he got the teacher's goat, and there wasn't a whole lot she could do about it. He handed in an assignment about as often as a cow lays an egg. Every day or two our teacher sent him upstairs to the principal. The principal also taught the seventh and eighth grade room, and he had a big paddle hanging beside his door that he liked to use. Sometimes when discipline was getting ragged, he'd just walk around the room slapping the thing against his leg loud enough to make a good pop, and everyone's behavior took a noticeable turn for the better. But Jon's parents had sent a letter to school saying something to the effect that if he laid a hand or paddle or anything else on their son's bottom, they'd sue him for everything but his underwear...and maybe those, too. Jon had a copy of the letter that he kept in his desk, just in case. So when he got in trouble, there wasn't much anyone could do to him. A few times they sent him home as punishment, but they soon learned that this was more like a reward. He liked getting sent home, and in a few days he'd always come back wearing a nice tan and telling us about all the fun he'd had. Eventually they quit sending him home and just sat him in the hall all day. He didn't mind that, either. He said it was better than doing schoolwork. In the end, our teacher gave up trying to get work out of Jon and told him that if he wanted to be dumb all his life, it was OK with her. Of course, it was OK with Jon, too. He enjoyed learning to be dumb a lot more than the rest of us were enjoying learning to be smart. They kept him two years in the fourth grade, though. In a word, he flunked. And after that, even though he never did exactly set the world on fire with his work habits, he at least began to dribble an assignment in now and then.

Jon's parents had pretty much the same defeated attitude toward him as his teachers did. They were always busy, so as long as he stayed out of their hair, they didn't care much what he did. He had a free run of the pop and ice cream machines in the lodge (which was a fact that caught Percy's and my attention right off the bat). So, when there was play to be done, which was pretty much all the time, we did it as close to those pop and ice cream machines as was humanly possible. Those play sessions usually degenerated into pop and ice cream orgies, and we'd drag home with our stomachs so bloated we'd be in misery. It was a wonder our teeth didn't rot and fall out.

The Redbone Rod and Gun Club cabin across the end of Russ Lake from the lodge was our special hideout that year. When the club built it two years earlier, they came up from the town of Redbone in a long caravan of cars, trucks, and trailers that stretched halfway around the end of the lake. The hammer-and-beer-toting club members swarmed the site like so many maggots on road kill, mainly getting in one another's way and falling off things. But they had a good time at it, and the cabin gradually rose up out of the pine needles and lava rock.

Dad wasn't impressed. "Won't last through the winter," he said. And he pointed out how the roof was too flat and the spans too long and the timbers too small. "They don't know what four feet of snow looks like, much less what it can do," he said.

I secretly hoped a four-foot snow would come along and teach the Redbone Rod and Gun Club a lesson in construction. Like Dad, I didn't have much use for towns or town people, and it was my firm opinion that (along with rattlesnakes, scorpions, and possibly slugs) the world would be better off without them.

Well, the Rod and Gun Club made what looked like a good building. It was long, with big windows in the front that faced out over the lake. It got more than its share of use that fall. But that winter we had a big snow in November, and we didn't see the sun again until mid-January. My dad measured a little over four feet of snow on the flat of the meadow, and the road was out for days on end. When things melted that spring, the roof of the cabin was resting on the floor and the walls were folded out like banana peels. The only part left standing was a little porch-like kitchen at the back. The Rod and Gun Club never rebuilt the cabin or cleaned up the remains, and two years later it didn't look much different from the day it fell. For Percy, Jon Pindar, and me, the kitchen was "the hideout," and though we didn't know it at the time, it was the place where events of that year began their turn to the bad.

Chapter 2

By the time our diapers had moved from our bottoms to the rag drawer, Dad had filled Percy's and my heads with what he called "common sense," and he expected us to use it. He wanted us to grow up independent and tough. We had chores to do, which contributed greatly to our toughness, but very little to our independence, and when they were finished, he trusted us to head off alone to the woods or lakes and rivers. He didn't like to see us loafing around the house. It was "sitting on their rears," he claimed, that made people sick. He himself hadn't been under the weather in over twenty years, and he swore it was because he had spent every day of those twenty years outdoors working.

Mom and Dad didn't always see eye to eye about this matter of independence for Percy and me. Dad was the third generation of Simpsons to grow up in this wild and beautiful place, and "independence" was his middle name. Mom, on the other hand, had lived the better part of her life as a city girl where you didn't step out the door or head for the bathroom without leaving a phone message or note for someone, telling your whereabouts, your route of travel, estimated times of arrival and departure, and the name of your doctor in case something unexpected happened. It was no surprise that Mom didn't like the idea of two kids running around the woods alone, and thinking of them near bodies of water scared her spitless. So when we wanted to do anything like that, it was always Dad we asked.

"Go ahead," Dad said one day in April when Percy and I asked to go fish Russ Lake. "But don't let your Mom know. Season ain't open yet. You know how she is about fishin' outa season."

We assured him she'd never find out, and headed off. It was mid-morning. The ground was soft from the recent thaw, and muddy where snow patches were running meltwater. We went across the meadow, then through the forest and over the ridge to Russ Lake. Percy was walking in front, leaving footprints in the soft dirt, and I was taking giant steps to plant my feet in his tracks. I'd heard or read somewhere that this trick of stepping in each other's prints was how Indians threw off white guys who might be after them. We were big into Indians that year, and especially Indian tricks.

Just as we got below the top of the ridge where the trail snuggled under some rimrock, a scream ripped the air, and Jon Pindar dropped down from a ledge. He had a whittled piece of wood that was supposed to be a knife clenched in his teeth and was spread-eagled in flight like a skydiver. Percy disappeared under him. The two of them rolled in the dirt until they finally came to a stop with Percy on top and Jon pinned flat on his back.

"I got you suckers that time," Jon said, peering up at Percy with a big grin on his face.

"Whadda ya mean?" Percy said.

"If I was an Indian, I'd've killed you both," Jon said.

"If you was an Indian you'd be the dead one," Percy said, releasing his arms. "And if you do that again, I'm gonna smash your face in."

I stepped up beside Jon and poked him in the ribs with the toe of my boot. "I hate it when you do that," I snapped. "You're gonna hurt somebody some day. You're lucky we ain't in the mood or we'd beat you up." I poked him again with my boot, a little harder this time.

With Percy still sitting across his hips, Jon propped himself up on his elbows. He turned his head and spit out on the ground, then licked his lips and spit again. "I ain't big, but I'm tougher 'n both of you," he said. "And you two don't know nothin' about walkin' these woods. I coulda killed you both if I'd wanted."

Percy let him up and beat the dirt off and gave himself a quick once-over for damage. His pole and can of worms were scattered out in the trees, and the worms were breaking for freedom in the pine needles. We gathered them up.

Jon Pindar was always ambushing us that year. He was reading Indian stories and got kicks out of dropping down from trees or jumping off rocks or out from behind logs at us. He must have spent a good part of his time waiting in hiding places for us to come along. I hated it.

"Let's go to the hideout."

"Goin' fishin'," I answered. "Who'd want to play with you, anyway?"

"When you see what I've got you'll say different," he said.

We traded "will not's" and "will so's," then Percy asked, "What you got?"

"I ain't tellin' unless you come see for yourself."

Percy mulled it over for a moment, then said, "Naw...some other time."

"Suit yourself," Jon said, but then he pulled something out of his pocket and cupped it in his hands. He moved his eyes back and forth between Percy and me with his eyebrows raised and his lips puckered out.

"What's that, smarty pants?" I asked. I didn't like it when he looked like that.

"Thought you didn't care," he said.

"What is it?"

He started to put it back in his pocket, but I grabbed his hands and tried to pry them apart. He wrestled away.

"Promise you'll come with me?" he asked.

"Show us what you got and we'll decide," Percy said.

Jon thought for a moment, still shifting his eyes back and forth to play up the drama. Then, about as slow as a clam opening its shell, he unfolded his fingers from around a metal waterproof match container.

"Full of matches," he said. "Dry as a bone."

"That's nothin'," Percy said.

"You won't think it's nothin' when I tell you I found this an' a lot of other stuff that's even better. You wouldn't believe what I found."

"Liar," I said.

"Call me a liar if you want, but it's true." He looked at Percy and beckoned with his head. "Come on..."

He started off down the trail. Percy and I hesitated a moment then followed him.

We hadn't gone very far before I started having trouble keeping up. I had a big, long pole with a wooden bobber tied a couple feet above the hook. The line kept coming undone and catching on branches. I yelled for the boys to wait up, but that was like throwing gas on a fire to put it out. They took off running. By the time I came to Russ Lake, my line was raveled up like spaghetti and the boys were nowhere in sight. I was so mad you could have fried an egg on my head.

What was left of the Rod and Gun Club cabin lay in a heap at the end of a dirt driveway on a little isolated beach about fifty yards past the last vacation cabin. The closer I got to it, the blacker my mood grew. Running off and leaving me gave the boys a kick, but I was tired of it. When I was close enough to hear their voices I decided there was no way I was going to give them the pleasure of seeing me straggle in like that, so I turned off into the trees behind the cabin and climbed up on a rock outcropping to brood. "Dopes," I muttered. I picked at my line to try to get it untangled. But it was such a mess even Houdini couldn't have figured it out. Finally I ripped it off and put the bobber and hook in my pocket. This is happening too darn much, I thought to myself, getting left behind and treated like dirt. I tried to think of ways to get even. But I was even too mad to think. All I could come up with was suicide, and that didn't especially appeal to me.

It was about then that I noticed the back door of the old kitchen easing open. The boys were still out front, so I knew it wasn't them. As I watched, an old dirty-looking guy came inching out. I shuddered and slid back against the rocks. He had a pack slung over one shoulder. It was a pretty messed up pack. I remember that, because it was lopsided, like maybe it had been run over by something big. Anyway, he eased the door shut and hunched up the trail straight toward me. I held as still as I could, but it was like in the movies when the monster comes directly into the camera, getting bigger and bigger, and the last thing you see is its gigantic eyeball or nostril filling the whole screen. That's how it was with the bum. I could see his yellow old rotten teeth through his open lips and the whiskers on his face. He jerked quick, nervous glances behind him, and as he waddled closer I could see twigs and pine needles stuck in his stringy hair where it hung down from under his stocking cap.

Then he was directly below me, still coming on a beeline. By this time I was plastered against the rocks, not breathing a breath or blinking a blink. He was so close I could have spit on him, if I could have made spit. Finally, when he was so close I could almost smell his breath, he saw me. His eyes were small and dull, and they riveted on me like a cat's eyes rivet on a mouse when it's ready to pounce. I don't know how long we stayed frozen there. It was probably only a second or two, but it seemed like forever. I'm not sure who flinched first, him or me. I think it must have been me, though, and I think I must have screamed or maybe kicked at him, because he took a big swipe at me with his pack and let out a half grunt, half yell, then sprinted off into the forest.

The next thing I knew, I was running, too, as fast as my legs could move. I ran down around the old kitchen, hurdled some debris and scrambled over to where Percy and Jon were. They didn't know what was going on, of course. I was screaming and crying all at the same time, and the two of them just stood there with their mouths open.

"He was in the kitchen! He was in the kitchen!" I kept yelling.

They hunched down with their noses in my face and began peppering me with questions. "What's wrong? What's wrong?" they kept asking.

"There's a killer back there, an' he's gettin' away!" I shouted.

"Killer?"

"Liar," Jon said.

"I ain't a liar!" I yelled at him. "There's an ol' bum back there, an' he snuck outa the hideout an' came at me."

"When?" Percy asked.

"Just now, just a few seconds ago!"

Then Jon looked over at Percy and his face turned baby's-bottom white. "The stuff!" he blurted.

Percy gasped and clamped his hand over his mouth.

They stood there looking at each other with strange expressions on their faces for a long moment, then Jon bellowed, "Run!" You've never seen two guys run so fast, and of course I took off after them. We ran like dogs were chasing us, all the way around the north end of the lake. We didn't stop until we were hidden down in Jon's room at the lodge with his door locked shut and the curtains pulled. When we had breath enough to talk, I gave them the gory details of my encounter with the bum, and they told me about the stuff.

Later that day, after we had bolstered our nerves with a good dose of pop and candy from the machines, the three of us sneaked back to the Rod and Gun Club cabin. We watched it from hiding for a long time to make sure the bum hadn't come back. When we were finally satisfied that he wasn't there, we inched our way up front to the collapsed part, where the boys pulled up a board in the old floor and showed me the stuff.

"Don't ever tell anybody about this, Susie," Jon warned. He leveled his eyes right at me when he said it. "Promise?"

"I promise," I said. "I won't tell as long as I live."

"You tell an' you'll wish you hadn't."

"I won't. Cross my heart."

Jon looked around one more time to make sure the bum still hadn't appeared, then reached down into the hole and began pulling stuff up. He pulled up a box of .22 shells and sat it in front of us. They were Remington long rifles, a whole box with none missing. He slid it all the way open to show us, and carefully pulled one out to pass around.

"Blow a crow's head right off," he said.

"Where they from?" I asked.

"Right here," he said. "I was just pokin' around an' found 'em. There's more."

He reached back down and pulled out more things. There was a canteen that'd hang on your belt, a compass, a flashlight, a fly reel full of fly line, a creel with a leather shoulder strap, two nice galvanized buckets with hardly any dents in them, a silver belt buckle, a Swiss army knife that was missing only the toothpick, a blanket, and a whole box of Big Hunk candy bars. He laid them out in front of us one at a time. Our eyes bugged out.

"What if they're the bum's?" Percy asked.

"Yeah, and what if he comes back to get 'em?" I said. "I bet a zillion dollars he's killed people before. I bet he stole this stuff, and he'd kill us if he got a chance."

"I ain't afraid," Jon said. "I ain't afraid of an ol' bum. I'll shoot him if he comes after me!"

We spent a lot of time the next week, watching the Rod and Gun Club cabin from hiding on the hillside. Every day after school we raced home to check under the loose board to see if the stuff had been taken, but it hadn't. The bum had simply disappeared.

Percy and I didn't tell our parents about either the bum or the stuff, for fear Mom would use them as reason to keep us close to home. We did ask casual questions about bums in general, though. Dad told us he didn't figure we would ever see one out here in the country, but in the cities there were more bums than fleas on a dog. He told us how they lived in abandoned houses and under bridges and ate things from garbage cans, which sounded pretty sick to me.

I asked if they ever killed kids.

"What makes you ask a question like that?" Mom asked.

"I was just wonderin'," I said. I figured I hadn't better ask any more questions.

The next Saturday Jon Pindar tried to ambush us from a low-hanging tree limb along the trail to Mallard Lake, but we spotted him spraddled down in the foliage and just about knocked him out of the tree with pine cones. When he came down he told us he had something that would make our eyes pop out. This time we followed him eagerly to the old Rod and Gun Club cabin, and when he reached down into the hole he pulled out a .22 rifle. It was a single shot, bolt action with a nice leather sling on it.

"Did you see him hide it?" Percy asked.

"No," he said. "But why's that matter, anyway? Who else would've? Wasn't the tooth fairy."

We all nodded agreement.

"The way I see it, he stole all this stuff," Jon said, talking with a low, huffy voice, like he was giving us a lecture. "And he stole this gun to shoot somebody with. I think we oughta take it all an' hide it someplace safe, so he can't hurt anybody, especially the gun."

"Wouldn't that be stealin'?" I asked.

Jon rolled his eyes. "You can't steal stuff that's already stolen," he said. "Anyway, we're just doin' it to save lives. Nothin' wrong with that."

We all nodded.

Percy said he knew where there was a cave nobody would ever find. Jon said it sounded good to him, so we cleaned everything out of the hole and headed off toward Mallard Lake with Percy leading the way. The cave he led us to was plenty tall enough to stand up in. It burrowed fifteen or twenty feet back into a low cliff in an old lava flow. Some big rocks at its mouth made it hard to spot from the lake, unless you knew it was there. We spent what was left of the day clearing the rest of our things out of the Rod and Gun Club kitchen, figuring they weren't safe there any longer, and we put them in the cave, also. Just before we left for home we smashed a bottle of Nehi Orange on one of the boulders at the cave's entrance and christened it our new hideout.

As the days passed, we kept a careful eye out for the bum, but we didn't see hide nor hair of him. But here's the odd thing: every day or so when we went back to the Rod and Gun Club cabin to check under the loose board, we would reach down inside and pull out some new treasure. And unlike the first batch of loot, which was mainly made up of harmless and useful things which a cold and hungry person might have used to keep himself alive and comfortable, the new things were more exotic and dangerous—things like the .22 rifle, an ax that was so sharp you could have peeled potatoes with it, a hunting knife, a bayonet, and even a high-caliber rifle complete with shells. We had no proof they had been put there by the bum, of course, but down inside we knew it had to have been him. I was a little scared, but at the same time there was something exciting going on, and I liked it. It was like playing Indians, except it wasn't play. It was the real thing.

Chapter 3

Percy and I met our school bus each morning at the head of the driveway. The driveway was a mile long, with two gates and some mud puddles you could almost lose a car in. Lodgepole pine grew so closely along its length you had the feeling you were passing through a long green tunnel. There was a little stream and a nice meadow at the second gate, and you could always see deer there in the mornings, and sometimes elk. In good weather we walked out to wait for the bus. If we got there early we would throw rocks or torture the salamanders that lived in a weedy little pond at one end of the culvert. If the weather was bad, or if it was still dark, as it usually was in the winter, Dad or Mom would take us out in the truck, and we would wait in a little A-frame hut Dad had built for us.

The highway through this section of country was paved with red cinder, and it cut a red swath through the pines. It didn't have many curves, so standing at our mail box you could see a half mile in one direction and twice as far in the other. The school bus always came at 7:37 in the morning, and you could spot it a minute or so before it arrived. The driver was an old white-haired guy named Mr. Peters, who was also the custodian at school. Rain or snow or sunshine, he was never late and never early. You could set your watch by him. He was a gruff old guy, and if you messed around when he was at the wheel you'd find yourself hiking to school for a long time. It was the joke going around that he stayed on schedule by keeping the bus half full. Mr. Peters got fired two years later for drinking on the job. They found a whole case of whiskey hidden away down in the furnace room, and we came to learn that his main motivation for being so punctual on his bus rounds was that he and our principal had a standing appointment for a drink or two before school each morning. It wasn't long after Mr. Peters lost his job that we also got a new principal.

Jon Pindar usually sat alone on the bus. Nobody else would sit with him, because when you did, you usually ended up in trouble. It was a kind of preventive isolation. But one morning not long after we found the hunting rifle, we climbed on board and Jon motioned us to his seat. He was at the back of the bus, which was also a good place to avoid.

As we squashed in beside him, he announced the big news: his mom had seen the bum going through the dumpster that stood just inches from Jon's very bedroom window. It was big news, all right. But in those days I had a nose that bent out of shape easily, and as far as I was concerned, Jon was overly impressed by the dumpster's nearness to his window. Glass or no glass, he was convinced he'd had a near-death experience, and he was too proud of it for my taste.

I suppose I should have kept quiet or said something tactful, but doing so most likely would have made me vomit, so what came out of my mouth was "Bull."

Jon gave me a hard look to let me know what he thought of my lack of reverence for someone who had almost met his maker, then said, "You guys have lived out here in the sticks too long. In the city, guys like this bum go through windows like they're cobwebs. They'd as soon kill a kid in his sleep as pick their nose. There was this one lady we knew back in Portland who got stabbed by one of 'em right in broad daylight. Used a big ol' switchblade, 'bout like this." He held his hands out about two feet apart. "He came up to her an' grabbed her purse. Didn't even give her a chance to hand it over. Ain't that somethin'?"

It was an impressive story, all right, but I was feeling one-upped and not too happy about that living in the sticks. "I was as close as from me to you from this ol' bum," I said. "An' there wasn't any piece of glass between us, just plain ol' air. He coulda switched his blade an' stuck me easy as pie."

"You ain't the only one in this world that's seen an ol' bum, miss smarty-pants," Jon said. "Percy an' me were right there just a few feet from him before you even got there, miss slowpoke." He put his face right up in mine when he said "slow-poke." "He was probably lookin' through a crack in the door right at Percy an' me all the time. We were takin' his stuff right out from under his nose, you know. I bet he was sneakin' off to get his weapon so's he could come back and get us."

"Well, I seen him, an' you didn't," I huffed.

"Big deal," Jon said. He had this talent of being able to burp any time he wanted. He took a gulp of air, worked it down, and let out a big one right in my face.

"I'm leavin'," I sputtered. "Anyway, your breath stinks." I slid off the seat and moved toward the front of the bus.

"What's going on back there?" yelled old Mr. Peters.

I folded down into the nearest seat, but the bus was pulling to a hard stop and I could see Mr. Peters' eyes fastened on me in the mirror. He stopped at the side of the road, then racheted the brake on and pulled himself up to his feet on the rail you use to get up the steps. "What are you doing moving around when the bus is going?" His voice was like a bullhorn and he was looking right at me. Everybody was looking right at me. "You want to ride on my bus you keep your little fanny planted in that seat. Hear? I see you up like that again and I'll give you walking papers. Understand?"

I was looking down at my feet.

"Understand?" he bellowed again.

I gave a weak nod, then slid down in my seat as far as the laws of physics allowed.

Finally the bus jerked into motion again. Mr. Peters shifted through the gears with more than his usual amount of grinding. Behind me I could hear the boys snickering, and Jon's voice in a loud whisper saying, "Keep that fanny planted, Susie—long walk home."

I steamed all the way to school.

I was mad all morning about the bus incident, and I worked hard at letting Jon and Percy know it. By afternoon, though, my anger was losing its fizz, and the boys were showing signs of wanting peace. The thing was, I'd learned early on that peace didn't have much in the way of material value when it came time to cash it in, and if I could at least act mad long enough, Percy would usually get antsy and start trying to bribe me back into a good mood. Sometimes these bribes were worth the effort. He knew that if I went home mad, there was no telling what I'd blab to Mom and Dad about him, so he usually did his best to get any disagreements ironed out before school was over.

At morning recess I stayed on the other side of the school from where the boys were and played marbles. When I went back in, there was a piece of candy stuck down in my inkwell hole with a note from them saying they wanted to see me in our hideout at the afternoon recess. It was Percy's writing. When I glanced across the room they were both peering over at me from behind their spelling books. I was careful not to smile or look too friendly, but I could tell things were looking up.

At school the three of us had a hideout down by the creek back in a jungle of blackberry bushes. A lot of kids knew about it, but none of them ever came in. They were afraid we'd beat them up. To get to it you had to crawl quite a ways through a tunnel we'd cut, and then you came to a hollowed-out place back in the middle that was so big you could actually stand up in it. We had a secret password. It was "wappato." It was the only real Indian word we knew. Dad said it was a Yakima tribe word that meant "big potato." It didn't matter what it meant, anyway. It sounded good, so we used it.

At noon recess I went crawling in.

"Wappato," I whispered.

Jon answered in his low Indian chief voice, "Wappato."

They were sitting cross-legged with their arms folded across their chests, wearing headbands cut from innertubes with a half dozen big goose feathers sticking out the back.

"Where'd you get those feathers?" I asked.

"Found 'em," Percy said.

"Got a naked goose at your place?" Jon said. He thought his quip was funny and poked Percy to make sure he'd gotten it.

"Well, it looks stupid," I said. "No real Indian would wear a piece of car tire around his head."

"Modern-day Indians," Jon said.

"Here, we have one for you," Percy said. He handed me one of the slices of inner tube and a handful of the rattiest feathers you've ever seen. If this was my reward for a half day of pouting, I was suddenly feeling cheated.

"These feathers look like they came from a pillow," I said. "I want some big ones like you guys."

The boys rolled their eyes, then Percy said, "Just the braves wear the big feathers. Squaws wear little ones. That's how it is with Indians."

"I'm no squaw," I said. "I'm a girl brave and you can't say I ain't." I kept up a fuss until they finally gave me some of their big feathers.

Jon was reading a library book about Indians. He fished down in his hip pocket and pulled out a folded-up page from the book. It was about tracking animals.

"You'll get in big trouble tearing pages out like that," Percy told him.

"I oughta tell," I said.

"Teacher'll never know," he said. "Nobody looks at that book, anyway." He laid the page on the ground and smoothed it out. "It shows a trick, here. Says that if you take a tree bough and brush a piece of trail clean, you can see the new tracks if anything walks over it—and I mean anything, deer, coon, bear—even a bum." He paused to let the word "bum" sink in.

"So what?" I asked.

"So it's a good way to track down this bum. We know he's around someplace, but we never see him. Must be comin' at night or when we're in school or somethin'. If we're gonna find him we're gonna have to be sneaky. All we gotta do is dust off a little piece of all the trails an' then check 'em for tracks."

"I don't know why we don't just leave him alone," I said. "I seen him once, and that's plenty for me. Anyway, how do we know what his tracks look like? Didn't think about that, did you. One person's tracks look like anybody else's. Really—you could be trackin' your dad or even the president for all you know. Them Indian tricks don't work, anyway. If they worked, the white people'd be livin' on reservations an' the Indians'd own the country."

Jon gave the page a long, blank look. "Well, it sounds like a good idea to me. Anyway, they wouldn't put it in a book if it didn't work."

"You know?" Percy asked. You could see the wheels in his head starting to turn.

"Know what?" Jon asked.

"Well..." Percy paused, and you could tell he was still figuring out what he had on his mind. "I was just thinkin'. I bet we could catch this bum. I don't mean catch him like grabbin' him or capturin' him, but I bet we could find where he's stayin' an' spy on him till he breaks the law." He looked at Jon and then at me with his eyebrows raised so high his forehead was wrinkled.

"Wouldn't that be somethin'?" Jon grinned. He punched his fist into his palm. "Heck, we know he's stealin' stuff right and left. We could follow him and catch him an' turn him in."

"Would we get a reward?" I asked.

"Sure," Jon said. "There's always a reward for stuff like that. Probably a medal, too." The grin on this face was spreading toward his ears. "Wouldn't it be neat if we could turn him in an' get a thousand dollars or somethin'?" He clapped his hands. "Let's do it!"

When we went back into the school after recess, Jon got in trouble about the torn-out page. He had it laid out in his desk under his books, and one of the other kids saw it and told on him.

Our teacher's name was Mrs. Woods. She was real old and had a wart on her chin with a hair growing out of it, like a witch. She could be as mean as a witch, too—especially to Jon. She made him stand at the blackboard with his nose in a circle all afternoon, and she wrote a letter to his parents saying that if Jon was going to rip up her book, he was darn well going to pay for it. The trouble was, Jon's mom and dad did what they always did. Instead of having Jon pay for it out of his own money, they just forked over the fifteen ninety-five out of their pockets. Of course, this was great for Jon, because the next day when he turned the money in, the school gave him the Indian book to take home with the page taped back in.

We saw a lot of the Indian book the rest of that year. Jon carried it with him the way some churchgoers carry their Bibles. By June it looked like it had been through a war, and by the Fourth of July it had been reduced to a loose stack of muddy pages.

The rest of that particular week was a whirlwind of preparation for the upcoming weekend, when we intended to start tracking the bum in earnest. Jon's plan for sweeping trails with pine boughs still didn't make a lot of sense to me, but what the heck. We spent every recess in the hideout drawing maps of the trail and cabins we would sweep on Saturday. On the bus ride home that Friday we put in writing that we would divide the reward money evenly, just to make things legal. Then we declared ourselves ready to go. I've never looked forward to a weekend so much in my life.

Chapter 4

April weather up in the mountains was something you could count on to foul up a kid's plans. You could be be planting the garden one day and shoveling wet snow the next. Through most of that week when we were doing our planning, you could have sworn summer had come. There were bees out and robins pulling worms in the grass, and it was so warm the kids came in from recess looking like sweat balls. It even smelled like summer. But that Friday it turned cold. There was ice on the puddles in the driveway that morning, and the wash Mom left hanging on the line was frozen stiff. About dusk, clouds settled in from the west, and by night it was snowing. It wasn't like winter snow. We only got six inches or so, and it was wet and heavy. But it was enough that when Saturday morning came, Mom wouldn't let Percy or me out of sight of the house. Getting hurt or lost in the woods in normal weather was one thing as far as she was concerned, but with snow on the ground it was a whole different matter.

Normally that was no problem. There was plenty for a couple of kids to do within sight of the house, but this time, with a bum to track, it was torture. I was worried sick that Jon might be out there catching the bum without us. "What if Jon gets the whole reward all by himself?" I moaned.

"Plan's shot, anyway," Percy said. "Ever tried sweeping a trail with a pine bough when there's snow on the ground?"

"Never thought of that," I said, and I began feeling better.

The sky cleared not long after dawn, and it got almost warm again. Melt water poured from the eaves like waterfalls, and tree limbs catapulted up as their loads slid off. Percy and I sledded down the hill below the orchard until midday, when our runners began cutting through the slush and digging into the mud. We spent the rest of the day playing in the barn. There was a long flight of steps that climbed the back wall of the hayloft and ended at a landing near the roof. When the loft was full, we used the stairs to get to the top of the hay. Now, at the end of winter with the hay supply shrunk to a mound against one wall, it was our launching pad. Hanging from a rope we had tied to a rafter, we could swing down off the landing and drop into the hay.

We swung every way we could think of. We swung alone and two at a time. We had distance-swinging contests and accuracy drops. We had "crazy drop" contests and "dramatic drop" contests. We did swings with the dogs and cats and chickens, and even tied Herman, our goat, to the rope and gave him a ride.

Herman was our only failure. We tied the end of the rope around his belly and pushed him off the landing. The problem was, there was no way he could release himself to drop into the hay. So Herman swung in big pendulum sweeps back and forth across the loft, each sweep growing shorter than the one before, until he finally hung motionless from the rafter with his legs stiff as boards. We howled, but then fell dumb when we realized we had a problem.

"How we gonna get Herman down?" Percy half whispered. You could see miscalculation all over his face.

"Cripe...I thought you knew," I said.

Herman didn't make a sound and didn't move a muscle.

"Dad'll skin us alive," I said.

Percy didn't answer, but you could tell he was feeling skinned already.

We tried everything. We tried a ladder. We tried lassoing his horns and pulling him back to the stairs. We tried stacking the hay up under him. Finally Percy looked over at me and said he'd have to cut him down.

"It'll kill him," I said.

"There's a lotta hay under him. I think he'll be okay," he said. But he didn't seem too certain. Anyway, he climbed back up in the rafters with his pocket knife between his teeth and cut the rope. Herman disappeared into the hay. There was a brief thrashing. I stood paralyzed. Then Herman came stumbling out. With hay hanging from his horns and sticking in his ears, and with the rope still dragging from his belly, he wandered over and lay down against the wall as though nothing had happened.

A little later, poor Herman found himself in the wrong place a second time. Percy was standing in the open loft door looking down, and he said, "That snow looks soft. I bet we could jump down into it and not even get hurt." There was a pile of old snow below the door where Dad had pushed it off the driveway with the dozer through the winter. It was covered with new snow and a lot of hay we had kicked out the door.

"I ain't jumpin'," I said. "You might wanta break your leg, but not me."

"Chicken," he said.

"Chicken, yourself. I'm just smart. You'd have to be dumb to jump out there."

Herman was standing nearby. Percy gave him a long stare, then looked over at me and grinned the way he always did when he knew better than to do something but intended to do it, anyway.

"Don't you dare," I said.

But he did. Percy heaved against Herman's rump. His hooves skidded across the wood floor. At the lip of the opening he disappeared.

I leaned out, looking down.

Herman's lower parts had dissolved into the snowbank. He looked like a slug with hair and horns, buried up to his chest. We raced down to dig him out before his bleating attracted Mom or Dad, and we laughed so hard we couldn't stand up.

Later that evening, the whole family went to the barn loft to watch the sunset. We did this fairly often. Mom had named the loft the "art gallery," because she said the view of the peaks to the north above the forest the loft doorway framed was the prettiest picture in the world, especially at sunset. Looking out across the sweep of forest to the big, white hulk of South Peak hung up against the golden sky was breathtaking. I can't imagine a picture anywhere as lovely. Percy and I liked sunsets. Dad did, too. But Mom loved them. She was always taking us off someplace to see flowers or sunsets or something the rest of us saw as "things" but she saw as "beautiful." It was just how she was.

Dad first met Mom when she was vacationing over at a cabin at Russ Lake with friends. As the story goes, she fell out of a sailboat and Dad rescued her. But according to Mom, she had already swum halfway across the lake, and his rescue took place when she was in water shallow enough to put her feet down. She said she wasn't so much rescued as absconded with. The details don't really matter, because it resulted in Mom and Dad's marriage a few months later, and ultimately in Percy and me, which, as far as I was concerned, was the most important detail. It was an odd match from the first, though, and it took a lot of adjusting on Mom's part. She was taken in by the beauty of this place she was moving to, and Dad says to this day that she married him as much for the scenery as for him. Adapting to the hard life on an isolated mountain farm didn't take her long. She pitched right in and in no time at all she was looking like a farm girl, Dad said.

When I came along, I found myself with a Mom who had learned to pitch hay and slop hogs and cook on a wood stove that should have been outlawed years earlier, but who was still gentle and lovely, and who couldn't get the need to find beauty in the world out of her blood.

Mom was a beauty to look at, too. She had long blond hair and never lost her athletic build. Inside, she radiated the same beauty. She was a joy to be around. When she was upset about something, she wouldn't get mad. She'd just get quiet. The quieter she was, the bigger trouble you were in. If she had to get after you about something that wasn't especially earth-shattering, she would usually do it with some sort of tease. There was always a message in her teasing, and it was in your best interest to heed it. I got sent a lot of messages.

"Well, Susie," she'd say. "How are things up in the pigsty?" That meant I'd better get up and clean out my room. If she said, "I didn't know you had a rat's nest hat," she was telling me it was time I tried to pull a brush through my hair.

Mom teased my dad a lot, too—often about our old house. "When are we going to move into the barn, Sam?" she'd ask him. She'd raise her eyebrows in an impish way, and she'd usually tweak his nose or pinch his cheek. Then she'd say something like, "If we lived in the barn we'd at least have an inside bathroom. If the cows can piddle on the floor, we could too. Right?"

Dad would have given his right arm to build Mom a new house with electricity and phones and an inside bathroom, but we just didn't have the money for it. Mom understood this, but she never gave up hope. She even had a site picked out in the grove of trees beside the barn. Sometimes you'd see her standing on the spot looking up to the north across the pasture and forest to the mountains. The view from the spot was almost the same as the one from the loft door, so I'm sure all the sunsets she took us to the loft to see had something to do with her craving for a new house.

On that particular evening, she had a thermos of hot chocolate for us and a blanket to put over us if we got cold. Of course, just going up to the loft started Percy and me laughing again. In our minds we could still see Herman dangling from the rope. And when Dad threw the loft doors open and we looked down at the spot where Herman's legs had drilled four holes into the snow, we broke up again.

Even by Mom's standards, that evening's sunset was special. I don't know if it was the snow or the cloud formations or just what it was, but we all agreed it was one of the best we had seen. We had been watching a while and had our hot chocolate nearly finished, when Dad pointed across the alfalfa field to a dark spot coming through the dusk down across the snow toward the orchard.

"It's a bear," Dad said. "I'm seein' him pretty regular, lately. Comes 'bout the same time each evenin'."

Mom reached over and felt Dad's forehead. "Feels hot," she said. A slow grin spread across her face. "Is the great white hunter getting bear-hunting fever?" She pinched his cheek. "And of course, it is bear season, isn't it?" Mom knew it wasn't bear season, but she also knew Dad never paid much attention to any of the game seasons. He said those laws were for city people who just hunted for sport.

He looked over at us. "What do you say we all go out tomorrow and shoot this guy?"

"You don't mean what I think you mean, do you?" Mom asked with a disbelieving look on her face.

"What do you think I mean?" he asked.

"I think you mean you want a woman and a couple of kids to go bear hunting."

He looked at her blankly. "Objection?"

"Well, I've heard better ideas."

You could tell Mom didn't like the idea, but she also knew Dad and how he was always coming up with schemes that weren't exactly sane, to her way of thinking anyway.

By the next evening most of the snow had melted, and after dinner the four of us went out to shoot the bear. The air was a shady silence around us as we walked across the field. Dad had his rifle, and Mom strode along beside him with her hand in his. Percy and I had sticks and we were beating the tops off mole hills.

"Hunter afraid?" Mom asked Dad, trying to sound like an Indian.

He smiled and shook his head. "No." She was baiting him and he liked it.

"Squaw scared," she said. "Squaw's knees knocking."

"Hunter brave. No worry," Dad said.

"Hunter big liar," she said. She grinned at him.

Dad leaned over and gave Mom a kiss on the side of her head. "Isn't this fun?" he said.

"Oh, good fun," she said. "Squaw like to go to woods with two papooses and get eaten by bear for bedtime snack." She tweaked his cheek.

"Squaw big chicken-liver," he said.

We came to a shelf of rimrock above the draw where we had seen the bear the night before. The spring where the bear was coming to drink was off to our left and below us.

"Wind's right," Dad said. "It's blowin' toward us, so ol' mister bear won't smell us. We'll just keep down behind these rocks an' he won't know what hit him."

"Do you like to shoot bears?" I asked.

Dad was looking for a place to plant himself for the best shot. As he looked he said, "We don't kill for pleasure, Susie—not anything—not unless there's a reason. The reason we shoot bears is the mess they make of our fruit trees."

"They're just hungry," Mom said.

Dad reached down into his pocket and pulled out a handful of cartridges. "But so are we," he said. "You three have clothes an' food just as long as I provide it. Every tree one of these buggers rips apart's food off our table and clothes off our backs. An' bear meat's pretty good stuff, to boot. Anyway, bears an' people don't mix. Out in the wilds they eat what they're supposed to an' don't bother nothin', but get 'em around people an' they turn into beggars real fast. It's easier for 'em to swipe apples than to scrounge around the woods for an honest meal."

"Do they ever eat people?" I asked.

Mom looked over at Dad with her eyebrows raised and said, "Just when people use bad judgment...like when they take their whole family out to shoot one. Wounded bears will do anything."

We waited quietly, then. With our eyes we scoured the hillside across from us where the wall of evergreens bounded the sterile rows of fruit trees. The leafless orchard stood in stark contrast to the forest that stretched off thick and green to the horizon. Overhead, a cluster of crows trudged across the sky. In the draw below us, sporadic frog croaks drifted up through the cool air.

Shortly before dark, the bear emerged from the forest.

One moment it was not there and the next it was. It didn't so much come as simply appear.

Dad clicked the safety off and eased his gun up. He rested his elbow on the rock and cupped the front stock in his palm.

The bear moved along, not so much a bear in detail as in shape. It seemed close and big but at the same time far away. I looked over at Dad. I could see him calculating his shot, judging distance and elevation and picking out the spot to aim for. The bear angled down the opposite hillside toward the orchard, coming closer. Finally it was directly below us and had become more than a shape or movement. It was now all bear, and we were quiet.

Dad sighted.

I put my fingers in my ears.

The shot ripped through the silence and echoed across the hillside. It was so loud you could feel the air jump. The bear lurched, and a puff of dirt spurted up from the slope above its back. Dad worked the bolt and the shell flew out in front of where we were crouched. The bear was moving fast now, back toward the woods with huge, loping strides. Dad shot again and worked the bolt again. Another shell kicked out in front of us. We were standing now, Mom and Percy and I, but Dad was still on his knees with his elbow on the rock and the gun to this shoulder, following the black shape through his sights as it disappeared into the trees.

"Shot high," he said. He gave his head a disbelieving shake.

"That's OK," Mom said. She put her arm around Dad's shoulder as he knelt there. "My heart's pounding," she said. She squeezed him. "I'm glad you missed, though. It was beautiful."

"Woulda been meat," Dad said. He emptied the remaining shells from the gun and put them back in his pocket, one by one.

"Will it come back?" Percy asked.

"Hard to tell," Dad said.

"Well, I hope he doesn't," Mom said. "I hope he takes the hint and stays away."

We turned and walked back toward the house. The sunlight was still touching the tops of the mountains, but fading fast. When we came in sight of the house a thin line of smoke was coming from the chimney. The cattle were grazing in the meadow, and I could see our milk cow coming up to the barn to be milked. It was mild and pleasant out, and I was thinking to myself that, like Mom, I was glad Dad had missed. And I was also thinking that it was too bad bears couldn't just stay back in the forests and eat what they were supposed to eat and leave people's orchards alone.

Chapter 5

I dreaded seeing Jon Pindar at school that Monday. Bear hunt or not, I wasn't sure I could take it if he'd had some big adventure with the bum over the weekend while we were stuck back on the ranch.

Well, he wasn't on the bus. He and Mr. Peters, the bus driver, had had a lopsided parting of the ways the previous Friday, so he was finding other transportation to and from school "until hell freezes over," as Mr. Peters had put it. When we got to school, Jon wasn't there, either, but about ten minutes after class began, he came wandering in with his hair messed up and his shirttail hanging out. He had obviously overslept.

We were doing the weather report when he came in, and I was over at the window looking to see which way the smoke was blowing from the house across the road. As he brushed by me on his way to his desk he whispered, "Guess what?"

I knew right then that my worst fears were probably coming true. I left him standing there.

All morning, up to spelling time, Jon kept looking over at me, giving me signals, but I ignored him. There was no way I was going to let him get me in trouble with his signaling—especially when I didn't want to hear what he had to tell me anyway. Mrs. Woods had a warped sense of justice when it came to the punishment of innocent bystanders. If you were anywhere near mischief when it happened, to her way of thinking, you were involved in it. I knew that all I had to do was look over at Jon Pindar just once when he was flashing a signal and that would be it.

Sure enough, pretty soon I heard her screech, "Jon Pindar, who you signaling to?"

Jon had his geography book standing up on his desk so he could hunch down behind it. He raised his head above it and said, "What signalin'?"

She turned her owl eyes my way. All the kids on my side of the room were shaking their heads "no" as earnestly as they could.

"Susie?" I could feel her eyes on me.

"Not me," I said. "I didn't even know he was here." I was sitting so straight and tall I felt like a rock.

She stuck her pencil in her hair, then took a slow stroll down our aisle. She turned around at the globe and came back down the same aisle. It was so quiet in the room her heels hitting against the floor sounded like war drums. Every kid sat motionless.

Well, nothing happened to me, but Mrs. Woods sent Jon to the hall for the rest of the morning with two pages from the Funk & Wagnall Encyclopedia to copy.

At recess Percy and I went to the blackberry patch hideout.

"I think he's got somethin' big," Percy said to me.

"I know," I said. "I think he might've got the reward."

We crawled in the tunnel, figuring we would be there alone, but when we came to the main part, there was Jon sitting cross-legged with his headband on and his big I'm-better-than-you grin that made me want to puke spread across his face.

"I thought you had to sit in the hall," I said.

He shrugged. "For a while," he said. Then he said, "You'll never guess what I found at the Kiwanis cabin."

Neither of us said anything.

Jon kept smiling. "You ain't gonna believe it," he said.

"Just tell us what it is," I said. "Don't make a production out of it."

He looked at each of us separately, again, then made us promise we wouldn't tell. "You tell about this an' you'll wish you hadn't. Understand?"

"Don't act like a big shot," I told him. "Percy an' me do what we say. If we say we won't tell, we won't tell. Anyway...maybe we don't wanta know what you got. We probably have fifty dozen of 'em already."

"Nobody has what I found. You could go clear up to Portland an' you wouldn't find another kid that has one."

"Show us," Percy said.

Jon checked to see if there was anyone coming, then pulled his pants leg up and fished down in his boot. He pulled out a pistol.

Our mouths dropped open. Jon held it up in front of him, cupped in his two hands the way you'd hold up a fish you had caught to show how big it was. I was impressed, but it made my stomach turn to see him gloating.

"Is it real?" Percy asked.

"Yep."

"You'll shoot your leg off carryin' it in your boot like that," I said.

"No bullets," he said.

"What kind's it take?" Percy asked.

"Don't know. I stuck one of the .22 shells in, but it was too small, an' the rifle shells are way too big."

"You know..." Percy said, and he stopped to think a minute. "Maybe we should tell somebody about this. If this is the bum's gun, he's dangerous. I mean, who'd have a gun like this? Bad guy, that's who. And if he hid this one, he probably has another one. He probably hid this one because he couldn't carry two around all the time."

"Look," Jon said. "Who knows these woods better'n the three of us? An' we're learnin' more every day. We're startin' to think like Indians. Right?"

We nodded.

"We don't have to catch this guy," he went on. "All we gotta do is find him an' spy on him for a while till we catch him at somethin'. Anyway, we have knives an' rifles, too, you know. Somethin' goes wrong, we'll be able to take care of ourselves. I'm not sayin' we'd ever use a weapon, but we have 'em if we need 'em. He won't dare mess with us."

"You don't even know how to shoot a gun," I said. "Anyway, what you gonna do without bullets—pull the trigger an' say bang?"

"Look, if you're afraid, Percy an' me can do it by ourselves," Jon sneered. "We don't need you."

"I didn't say I was afraid," I said.

Jon poked the gun back in his boot and pulled the leg of his pants down over it. He stood up and gave his leg a shake to settle the gun in his boot, then said, "Is the plan back on for next weekend?"

"Sure," Percy said. "Just like before. Just hope it don't snow this time."

When we got home that evening Mom was in the kitchen frying chicken for a picnic.

"Dad's burning the limb pile down in the orchard," she said. "We'll eat by the fire."

Eating by the pruning fire had become an annual tradition with us, like fireworks on the Fourth of July or cutting trees on Christmas. Burning the limbs from the winter's pruning was our rite of spring.

Percy and I did our chores as quickly as we could, then headed off with Mom along the dirt rut that led to the orchard. We could see the tire prints Dad's tractor had pressed into the soil. There were muddy places where water was running from patches of melting snow. As we came into view of the orchard, we could see Dad working. He had a mountain of limbs heaped in an open area between the fruit trees and the forest, and flames were working their way through it. A column of smoke stood up above it and bent off to the east. A fine blue haze hung above the ridge, and the smell of wood smoke was sweet in the air.

When we got to Dad, Percy and I helped him flip limbs into the flames while Mom laid out the meal on an old bedspread she stretched out on the ground. She placed it close enough to the fire that we could feel the good heat. When she had everything ready, she called us to eat.

"Guess that means us," Dad said. "What we got to eat?"

"Chicken," I said.

Dad smacked his lips. He pulled his gloves off and stuffed them into his hip pocket, then gave Mom a loud kiss on the cheek. "Hear we got sandwiches, today," he said.

"Who told you that?" she asked.

"Susie."

"She told you sandwiches?"

"Yep."

"No I didn't," I objected.

"You sure did," Dad said. "Sandwiches, an' fried worms, an' pickled slug legs."

"Huh uh."

"Maybe my ears're dirty," Dad said. "Isn't that what you heard her say, Percy?"

"An' chocolate-coated worm ears for dessert," Percy added.

"Don't listen to them, Susie," Mom told me. "If they don't behave, we'll just take the chicken back to the house and eat it all ourselves. Right?"

"Right!"

"Chicken?" Dad acted surprised. "You got chicken in there? Why didn't you tell me?" He scooped me up off the ground and gave me a noisy kiss all over my face. "Now I'm disappointed," he said. "I was lookin' forward to them pickled slug legs."

Dad dropped his hat to the ground and flopped down on the edge of the blanket. "I'm so filthy I get the ground dirty," he said. His hair was mashed from his hat, and he had on muddy striped bib overalls with holes in both knees. He leaned back on his elbows, looking off across the orchard. "Always get a little worried when I'm finished prunin'," he said.

"Why's that?" Mom asked.

"Just hard to believe them butchered-up stubs'd grow anything, much less fruit. Every year I look back at them fresh-pruned trees an' think to myself, 'I've killed 'em all.'" He looked over at me and gave my leg a light thump with his palm. "Few months them ol' stubby limbs'll be so heavy with fruit we'll have to prop 'em up to keep 'em from breakin' off."

"Dad," I said, "why do you prune the trees?"

"Prunin's like gettin' your hair cut, Susie. You get a haircut so's it'll be all even an' nice. Same thing with fruit trees. They get scraggly, too. Keeps trees young to prune 'em. You cut out the old limbs so's new ones'll grow." He began filling his plate with food, but kept right on talking. "Nature's big on prunin'. Winter comes an' things die back to their roots. Leaves fall off, seeds fall...you'd think there wasn't nothin' alive. Truth is it's really just Mother Nature cuttin' off all the old stuff. Then spring comes along an' we get new leaves, an' new flowers, an' new grass, an' baby birds, an' all the rest."

"What's wrong with lettin' the bears tear the limbs off, then?" I asked. "Seems like the same thing."

"Bears don't know much about prunin'," he laughed. "Be like Percy givin' you a haircut. I don't think you'd like how you looked. Bears just rip trees apart. Understand?"

I nodded.

"Pass the slug leg," he said. " I need another piece."

"Chicken," I corrected.

After eating, we sat back on the blanket to soak up the heat from the fire and watch the sparks float skyward like fireworks. The air was an orange glow and the flames leaped up as high as the trees. When the pile finally burned down to almost nothing, Dad took his pitchfork and went around the edges spearing unburned limbs into the center, where they blazed up. When he finished, he said, "Let's go home. Gettin' bedtime for you two." We picked up our things and all loaded onto the tractor, then headed up toward the house. Percy sat between Dad's legs, helping him work the levers. Mom and I stood on the hitch behind the seat, holding on. The tractor had one light that worked, but it shined fifty yards ahead and off to one side. The beam bounced along the hillside.

It was as we pulled up over the brim of the hill and came into view of the house that we realized something was wrong, but it took a few seconds for us to think what it was.

"There's a light in the window," Percy blurted.

Dad ground the tractor to a stop, and for a moment nobody said anything. Then Dad gasped, "Good God! It's on fire!"

The words shot through me like electricity. There was a flickering glow in the downstairs windows. Dad untangled himself from

Percy and shot off across the field toward the house. I'd never seen him run so fast. Percy started off after him.

"No, Percy!" Mom shouted, and he pulled up. "Take care of Susie! Don't you dare go in there! Understand?"

"Mom—"Percy pleaded.

"Mind me!" she screamed in a voice I'd never hard her use. Then she set off running, too.

It was pitch dark by now, and Dad and Mom were shadows against the glow from the house. Percy grabbed my hand and half dragged me forward. We stopped at the fence. About then, Dad disappeared into the darkness along the side of the house, and moments later Mom vanished behind him. Metallic clanking sounds came ringing out.

"What's that?" Percy's cried, and clutched the fencepost. We strained for clues to what was happening. Then the two of them came struggling out of the shadows into the glow from the window, dragging something heavy.

"The propane tank," Percy said. "They're gettin' it so it won't blow up."

They pulled the tank out into the trees and dropped it, then sprinted off in different directions—Dad back around the house again, and Mom toward the pickup.

"Mom's goin'!" I blurted. "She's goin'..."

"Gettin' help," Percy said.

She jumped in and tried to start the motor. It turned over and sounded pretty good, but nothing happened. It kept grinding slower and slower.

"Now the battery's dead," Percy moaned.

"Oh Percy, is it gonna burn down?" I started to cry.

"It'll be all right," he said. "We gotta stay calm."

But calm was more than I could muster by that time, and I began sobbing like a baby.

"Stop it," Percy ordered. He grabbed me by the shoulders and gave me a shake.

"All my stuff's in there," I blubbered. "I got a school book that ain't even mine. Oh Percy, it's all gonna burn down just like that limb pile."

About that time Mom jumped out of the pickup and ran over and climbed in the old flatbed. She slammed the door a couple of times before it would latch. We heard the motor spin over, then catch hold.

"Good ol' girl," Percy half whispered. He thumped the fence post with his fist.

The headlights popped on and we watched it rattle off down the driveway, the light beams jumping along the trees.

At the house Dad was now carrying buckets of water in through the front door to throw on the flames. He made several trips, but it was useless. He could have done as much good spitting on them. Finally he threw the buckets out across the lawn and disappeared inside empty-handed. But this time when he came out he had an armload of our belongings. He threw them on the ground then rushed back in.

"He's savin' stuff," I said.

"I'm gonna go help," Percy said.

"No, Percy," I objected. "Mom said don't."

"I ain't goin' in," he said. "That stuff Dad's haulin' out needs to be drug back. It'll burn up there." He ran toward the house and began pulling things back away. Dad was going out and in as fast as he could, now, with big armloads. At the edge of the porch he would give them a fling out into the grass, and Percy would drag them back.

By this time the orange glow was beginning to seep through the upstairs windows, too. I jumped the fence and ran toward Percy.

"It's burnin' upstairs now," I shouted. I was crying pretty hard again, but for the first time in a long time, I didn't care. I could feel tears running down my face, dripping off my chin, and it didn't matter to me in the least.

"It'll be all right," Percy consoled me. I clutched my arms around him with my head against his chest, which was something I had never done before, not even when I was real small. He seemed suddenly comforting. I felt his hand on my shoulder.

"Dad's been in there a long time," he suddenly said, and he stiffened. The realization struck me, too. I clutched Percy so tightly he winced. I could feel him shaking. We waited and waited, and a sick feeling gored into my stomach.

Then my bedroom window shattered. Something came flying out and landed down in the bushes.

"He's upstairs," Percy shouted. "It's your dresser! He's throwin' your stuff out!" Shoes and blankets and my toy box came flying out. He threw the mattress out.

Then there was a muffled noise from inside the house someplace, and flames curled out the front door and the side windows as if a bellows had fanned a huff of air on them. They lapped up the side of the house.

"Dad!" Percy shouted. He let go of me and ran forward a few steps. "Dad!" I heard him shout again.

Then Dad was at my window once more. He kicked away some broken glass, then climbed out and lowered himself until he was hanging from the sill by his fingers. He gave a little push away from the building and dropped, disappearing into the bushes.

A few minutes later, headlights came up the driveway. You could tell that they were driving fast by the way the light beams jumped along as they crashed through the puddles and ruts. It was Mom in the flatbed, and there was another car not far behind her...then a couple more. They spun up and stopped in a semicircle, facing the house with their lights shining on it. People were jumping out and running all over, but nobody seemed to know what to do. One guy ran up to the front door, but Dad waved him back.

"Let it burn!" I heard him yell. "Ain't worth gettin' hurt over." The guy came away and they all just stood back, watching.

It was quite a while before the fire rig from the Forest Service came bumping in. You could tell house fires weren't their thing. They reeled out their hose, but they didn't really understand how to attack the problem.

"Much water as they got in that piddly little tank won't do much good, anyway," Percy said.

Flames were coming through the roof by now. The Forest Service guys emptied their rig through the downstairs window, then they just stood back with the others to watch.

Jon's parents had come by this time. Mrs. Pindar was rushing around. Her hair was up in curlers and she had on one of Mr. Pindar's heavy trenchcoats over her robe, and she came flitting toward Percy and me. She always painted her lipstick out past her lips, making them look twice the size they really were, like those red wax lips you buy off the candy shelf. The light from the fire washed over her face, laying shadows around her eyes that made her look like the evil witch in one of my books.

"You poor things," she moaned. "You must be cold."

"We're OK," Percy said.

She told us how sorry she was a couple more times, then commenced to hug me. She was a big lady, and "well-endowed," as Dad always said, and when she pulled me up against her, I felt like a piece of food must feel when a big slug folds its body around it and sucks it in. I wasn't crying anymore, and I wasn't about to let Mrs. Pindar stand there pulling me into her like that. I wiggled my way free.

Then Mr. Pindar came over. He had a bald head and thick glasses with black frames. He asked if we wanted to come back with them to the lodge, but we told him no thanks.

The fire burned well into the night. All the people who had showed up to help had left, except the Forest Service guys, who wanted to make sure the flames didn't spread to the trees. When they were sure that wasn't going to happen, they left too.

Some time after midnight all that was left of the house was a glowing pile of embers. "There's no use in the three of you stayin' any longer," Dad said to us. Mom, Percy, and I left to spend the night with the Pindars at Russ Lake. Dad stayed on at the fire.

The next day we didn't go to school. Mom bought a few groceries from the lodge and made us some breakfast and a meal to take to Dad, and then we headed back to the ranch. We found Dad tossing junk and stray scraps of wood down into the smoking hole. His face was tired-looking and black with soot.

"Figure I might as well clean it up and get rid of the mess while she's still hot," he said. "I'll take the cat an' push her full in a day or two when it cools down. Wasn't much of a house, anyway."

"I only wish we would have insured it," Mom said.

"That's water under the bridge," Dad muttered. "Fire's like the weather up here. If it happens, it happens, We done our best, anyway."

Then Mom started laughing. She doubled over laughing. We all looked at her like she was crazy. "What's so funny?" Percy asked.

"I hated that old house," she said between fits. "It was the worst old house anybody could have had...but look...." She was pointing off to the side of the smoldering mess. "The worst part of it was that darned old outhouse...and it's still standing there without a mark on it."

Then we were all laughing uncontrollably, and the tension welled up out of us like springwater flowing from the ground. The fire and fear and all the loss that had been ours, flushed out like a fever breaking in a sweat, but this sweat was laughter and nothing could have felt better. It was the funniest thing any of us had ever seen—the black hole in the ground with smoke still drifting up, the chimney rising up from the ashes all seared, the strange empty place where our house had been. But perched beside it, unscarred and as good as ever, was Heaven.

"Well," Dad said, "we might not have a place to eat or sleep or keep warm, but we can still go to the bathroom."

"Sam," Mom said. "Promise me one thing. When you push that hole full, push that toilet in and bury it as deep as you can."

Chapter 6

With the tourist season still some time off, the Pindars offered us the use of one of their rental cabins at the Russ Lake Lodge. With no other options, we didn't have much choice but to accept, but the arrangement left my parents several miles by road from the farm and a herd of cattle that needed around-the-clock attention. For Percy and me, though, the setup was a bonanza. It planted us just yards from the Pindars' pop and candy machines, and smack in the center of prime bum-tracking territory. Along with Jon, Percy and I brushed trails like the best of Indians. The trouble was, we came up with nothing but blisters to show for our efforts. The bum had simply vanished into thin air. Since bums are a footloose lot that don't stay in one place long, this might have been understandable—except for the fact that we were still finding new things hidden under the board at the Rod and Gun Club cabin. It was a puzzle. It was also a puzzle why anybody, bum or not, would keep hiding stolen goods in the same spot week after week if three kids kept finding them and taking them away.

My parents had a puzzle of their own: how to build a house without money. They spent every evening talking at the table with long faces and scribbling figures on paper. It was a tense time. In the end they decided they had to do the one thing they swore they'd never do—sell a piece of the ranch.

What they decided to sell was some wooded acres along the driveway near the main road. It was rocky, thin-soiled land covered with scrubby lodgepole pine; there was a creek that hardly deserved the name, and a pretty little meadow. As farmland or timberland it was worthless, but giving it up was still painful. To our way of thinking, selling it deformed the ranch the way amputating an ear deformed a face.

The day we headed for town to list it with the real estate people, Dad was wearing clean pants and a bad attitude. Mom wasn't happy, either. "Well," she said, "when you have your rear up against a hot stove you've got some moving to do. Not much choice." Her reasoning made sense, but it was clear by the half-hearted way she said it that she wasn't fully convinced.

Dad didn't even nod.

As we drove along, Percy dozed against Mom's shoulder with his mouth hanging wide open. I was squashed up against the door.

"I wish we'd get enough money to buy a real car instead of this ol' truck," I said. "We're too big to stuff all of us onto this one seat."

"We'll just keep our fingers crossed, Susie," Mom said. "Maybe that will happen. Wouldn't that be nice?"

The real estate office was in a shopping mall between the all-night laundromat and the Upper Cut Beauty Salon. There was a lady at the front desk filing her fingernails when we came in. She had to go three doors down to a place called the Watering Hole to get one of the salesmen. He came in wearing a Watering Hole slow-pitch softball uniform and smelling like beer. He took us into a booth, found us chairs, and listened as Dad told him what we were up to.

From the start Dad made it clear that we wanted the piece sold strictly for recreational property—no motels or gas stations or anything like that.

The salesman popped a mint in his mouth, then offered each of us one. "That sounds fine," he said, "but you have to understand that you *are* selling it. If someone's going to buy it, it's going to be theirs, not yours, and you can't tell them what they can do with it."

"Be that as it may," Dad said. "This ain't your normal city lot. Sellin' it's like sellin' a leg. I don't have no intention of turnin' it over to somebody who's gonna mess it up."

The salesman suggested we lead him out to the property so he could take a look at it and snap a picture or two. While he loaded his camera and gathered up some papers, he pointed out some framed pictures of his own kids. He said they lived with their mother now, and that they had three-wheelers, snowmobiles, and their own TV sets.

The real estate man followed us back out in a big long car that bottomed out in every hole on our driveway. We parked by the little meadow and got out. Dad pointed out ridges and tall trees that he had figured as plot corners, and then led the way through the tall grass. The salesman was wearing shiny shoes and picked his way out through the trees like he was stepping through a barnyard full of cows on Ex-Lax. Dad pointed out things like the bear wallow, and a place where deer had been bedding down under a tree, and the pile of rotting logs that were all that was left of great-great-grandpa Simpson's original log cabin.

"Whoever buys the place will probably want to torch that," the man said.

Dad rolled his eyes.

"This is a nice spot," the man said. "But what do you do when you feel the urge for a pizza or movie? Long way from anything."

"Well," Dad answered, "seems to me we're right in the middle of it all, and you guys down there in town are the ones a long way from things."

"To each his own," the real estate man said. "I guess I don't have to live here. All I have to do is sell it."

At this point Dad made what was probably the mistake of his life. He asked the real estate man what this deal was going to cost him. The guy started listing commissions and fees, and Dad's jaw slowly dropped. "You're kiddin'."

"It's all standard," the salesman said. "It'll be the same anywhere you go. There's more to selling a piece of real estate than most people realize. It's money well spent."

But to Dad, there was no such thing as well-spent money. He began haggling, and the guy didn't appreciate it much. Finally Dad started throwing around words like "crook" and "swindler," and the salesman's vocabulary lit up with terms like "hick" and "hillbilly." It wasn't long before he stomped off to his car and left.

Dad walked back to Mom, who was waiting beside the truck and looking confused by the argument she'd seen but not heard. "The guy's a thief," Dad said. "You should've heard what he was gonna charge us. Wanted to fill out a few papers an' drive a couple of people out here in that big car of his an' charge us a mint for it. You or me go an' swipe that much money from somebody's fruit jar, and they'd throw us in the hoosegow. But some real estate shyster like him can swindle it outa somebody with a few swipes of the pen, and he's a big shot."

"Sam," Mom protested, "we don't know a thing about selling property."

"What's there to know?" he snorted.

Dad went and bought a "For Sale by Owner" sign at the hardware store and mailed it to a tree at the end of the driveway. He stapled a notice on the bulletin board at the Russ Lake Lodge and put an ad in the local paper.

A few days later when Percy and I came home from school, a car was parked off to the side of the driveway where the creek ran under it. Dad and a couple were standing out in the meadow up to their armpits in meadow grass. That couple didn't buy the property, but from then on there was a pretty steady dribble of people stopping by to look at the land. They came in all kinds of cars and wore all kinds of clothes. Finally we came home one afternoon to find Mom and Dad and the real estate man sitting around the picnic table with two people I'd never seen before.

"Meet your new neighbors, kids," Mom said to us. "These are the Turners, and they'll be buying the land we have for sale."

The man was wearing a shirt that was open almost to his bellybutton. He had a hairy chest and a gold chain around his neck. The lady was as tan as a walnut. She had on shiny gold sandals and even her toes were brown.

"Go play, now," Mom said to us. "This is grownup talk."

Percy pulled me around behind the barn. "Did you see the rings on that lady's fingers? She had one on almost every one—even her pinkie. Him, too."

"Think they have any kids?" I asked him.

"Are you kiddin'? They're the kind of people that have poodles instead of kids. They probably have two poodles with ribbons on their ears...an' a hot tub."

Dad was pleased as punch about his selling job. He got an old friend who had once done a little lawyering to draw up a fast deed for free. When the Turners' money came through, Dad gave them the deed, a receipt, and a handshake, and that was that. It was a done deal, and it hadn't cost us anything but the price of the want ad and the for sale sign.

"It all seems too easy," Mom said. "Are you sure there isn't more to it than this?"

"What more could there be?" Dad replied. "They've got their land, and we've got our money. No different than sellin' a cow or a ton of hay."

During the weeks while we were waiting for the money to come, our new house began taking shape on paper. Each night Mom and Dad sat at the table, leafing through pictures of houses in magazines, tearing out ideas, and making rough sketches on one of my school tablets. They were crude plans, to say the least, but Dad said they'd do fine for him. He said he built by eye and not by following lines on paper, anyway.

Then there was the matter of what Dad called "free building material." He believed that anything he found in the great outdoors that wasn't actually nailed down had been put there just for him to hammer or glue or cement into our new home, and he began gathering it in big heaps beside the house site. Mom and he didn't see eye to eye about this.

Dad was as honest as the day was long. He didn't lie or cheat, and if he said he'd do something, he'd do it. He always held Percy and me to the same standards. He just wouldn't tolerate dishonesty. But there was this one area where his behavior was questionable, to say the least. That area had to do with the laws covering the fruits of nature—things like fishing seasons, bag limits, hunting tags and the whole idea of having to pay a fee or get a permit to cut firewood or use a public campground or drift down a wild river. It wasn't that he was a crook. It was just that he never understood why those rules should apply to him. Mom said he'd never entered the twentieth century in those matters. She said it was his Daniel Boone gene. She called him a poachaholic, and he was. As far as he was concerned, the laws he was supposedly breaking were to keep city people in check. People like himself who were still living much like pioneers had the right to follow the old, ungoverned pioneer hunting and fishing ethic—meaning if you could shoot it or hook it or chop it down or pick it up, and if it wasn't too heavy to carry home, it was yours.

"You're going to get yourself thrown in jail," Mom would tell him.

But Dad would say, "Gotta have food to eat an' wood to burn. It's a right." He would pound his fist. "You don't need a permit to breathe air or drink water, so why in God's name is heat an' food an' the house you live in any different?"

"It just is," Mom would argue.

"No it ain't," he would say. "To us it's harvestin'. That's what it is. Them people down in town buy their food from stores. We hunt an' catch ours. Simple as that. They buy houses an' we build 'em."

The next few weeks, until the money from the land sale came through, Dad went on a harvesting binge. He began with rocks. He figured, "Why buy all that concrete for a foundation when central Oregon's one big rock heap?" So each day he would rush through his work and then head off in the flatbed for the sage lands down around Redbone to pick up rocks wherever he could find them. Around dark he would come back with the truck mashed down to the axles and the tires so ballooned they looked ready to blow their innards out. He'd throw the load out by the house site, and it wasn't long before we had a mountain of rocks.

"Where'd you get this load?" Mom would ask. And he would tell her he had found them in some farmer's field or a highway cut or stacked out beside a dirt road on BLM land.

Mom would just shake her head. "You know what's going to happen?" she would say. "About the time we get this place built, the police will show up and confiscate it as stolen property."

Of course, that didn't slow Dad down a bit. And when he finished with the rock, he began hauling cedar for splitting into a shake roof. We didn't have any cedar trees on the ranch. It was too dry for them, but he found some that had blown over along the edge of a clear cut a few miles to the west, where things were wetter. With a firewood permit you could take the cedar as long as you cut it in lengths eighteen inches or shorter.

"You follow the rules, Sam," Mom scolded him. "You get fined or put in jail and these could be expensive shakes."

"The trees're just layin' there gettin' rotten," Dad said. Then he grinned. "Anyway, if I cut 'em, let's say, twenty inches or so, the first eighteen inches are legal. It's just the last two that are against the law. What's two inches?"

Mom reached over and messed up his hair. "What logic!" she moaned. "Better wear clean underwear in case they pack you off to jail."

To set Mom's mind at ease, Dad finally agreed to get a wood-cutting permit down at the Forest Service office, but every hunk of cedar he hauled home was several inches longer than the legal length.

As the days went by, Dad's pile of cedar shake bolts grew up beside his mountain of rock. Finally, on what he figured was his last load, Dad talked Percy and me into going along.

"Don't worry, kids," he assured us as we rattled along the gravel road. "They don't throw honest people in jail. If we get caught with hunks a little long, we'll just tell 'em we thought it'd be OK. Now that's true, ain't it?" He reached over and flicked my knee. "Worst they'd do's tell us to cut the ends off. Anyway, that law's for the commercial guys...so they won't come up here an' take cedar for fence posts or sell it to shake mills. That's the reason for it."

He shifted down, then shifted down again. The truck chattered, then smoothed out. He glanced over at us to see if we were still listening, then went on. "Time was when you could cut all the firewood you wanted," he said. "Shake bolts, fenceposts, anything. No such thing as a permit. Weren't all these rules." The truck chugged up over the brink of the hill, and as the motor speeded up, he shifted back up through the gears again.

"Funny I should think of this," he said, "but if you look at it one way, we're a lot like that bear I threw a few shots at a while back. Bears an' us are just doin' what our kind's always done. Bears're gettin' a meal from our orchard, an' here we are cuttin' ourselves a shake roof from the Forest Service's little orchard. Rule-makers over in the capital tell me I can't take shake bolts over eighteen inches or they'll throw me in the hoosegow, an' we tell the bears they can't take fruit off our fruit trees or we'll shoot 'em." He gave a little grunt of satisfaction to himself as his thought sank in.

Finally, Dad pulled off down a rutty track and stopped by the cedar log he'd been working on. You could see sawdust where he'd already cut. He gassed up his saw and filed a little on his chain, then started it up and set to work.

We had the truck almost full of the illegal-length shake bolts when a pickup came creeping along the main road. It was painted government green, and by the way the driver was giving us the eye, we knew we had a problem.

"Now we've had it," Percy said.

A few minutes later the truck came back and turned up to where we were parked. It pulled up nose to nose with us and stopped. Percy's face had a pale look, and mine had a pale feel. I peeked over the top of the wood, fully expecting the guy to jump out and cuff Dad to a tree, or something. I looked over at Percy. "Do they put you in jail if it's more than eighteen inches?" I whispered.

"Course not," he whispered back. "But they take all your money."

"Oh Percy," I moaned, "I ain't got but some quarters an' a dollar bill. Do they take it all?"

"Sometimes," he said. "Depends on the jury."

But the guy climbed out of his truck and started up a conversation with Dad as though they'd been friends for fifty years. Dad picked up a pebble to roll around in his palm, then put his foot up on the bumper like he planned to stay a while. He was wearing his old red hunting hat with a floppy brim and coveralls that had black grease stains all down one leg. If anyone ever looked like a thief, he did. He dug his fingernail down between his teeth to pry something out, then asked the guy how much territory he covered in his rounds. The guy was headed around to the back side of our truck when Dad asked the question, but he stopped in his tracks and nodded to the truck he was driving. "Puttin' a thousand miles a week on that critter—dirt roads, gravel roads, some roads you shouldn't take a mule down. Drive 'em all a couple times a week."

"Catchin' any criminals?" Dad asked, grinning.

"Got the jails bulgin'," he laughed.

I looked over at Percy. "Did you hear that?" I whispered. "He's puttin' 'em in jail."

"He's just jokin'," Percy whispered back.

Now the Forest Service man pushed his hands down in his hip pockets and leaned back against a tree with his legs crossed, and he and Dad talked for a good five minutes without moving. They talked about how hard the roads were on a vehicle and how many people there were in the woods these days. Then they talked about the program the guy had playing on his radio.

Finally the man said he needed to be going, and he asked Dad to show him his permit—which he did. As the guy was leaving, he poked his head out his window and said, "There's a lot of cedar in these parts. Most people pass it up, but it'll make a half decent fire if you can stand the popping. Just keep it under eighteen inches."

Percy and I looked at each other, then began laughing. When Dad came back, he was grinning from ear to ear. "Guess we look honest," he said.

On the way back home with the heavy load of cedar, the truck kept overheating. We stopped at every creek we came to and carried water up in Coke bottles to pour down the steaming radiator hole. Several miles from the ranch we chugged up over a little rise, and there, standing with his back against a tree at the side of the road, was the bum. He had a partly filled garbage bag over his shoulder.

"Probably pickin' up beer bottles," Dad said. "And we think we got it hard."

Percy and I didn't say anything, but we looked at each other wide-eyed. I pressed my face up against the window, and Percy was leaning over my shoulder, both of us looking as hard as we could.

"Is it him?" Percy whispered.

"Yeah," I said. "That's him."

Chapter 7

Aside from Percy and my parents, the only person in the world I truly loved in those years was Grandpa Simpson, and I loved him as much as anybody could. I never knew Grandma Simpson. She passed away the year I was born, but from what I've heard about her, I would have loved her, too. Grandpa took it hard when she died. They say that for months after her death he moped through his days with no enthusiasm for anything at all, like he was dead himself. Then one day toward the end of fruit-picking season, he had what you'd call a transformation. They say he went out to the orchard that morning looking like a man ready to crawl into his grave, and came home at the end of the day acting like a teenager. They claim he even looked younger. Anyway, he came through the door that evening, threw his boots in the corner, and announced that he was going to Arizona for the winter. No one believed him, of course. He had never been outside Oregon and southern Washington in his life, and he swore up and down that airplanes had brought on the big snows of 1949 and 1950. But the next thing anyone knew, he had built himself a camper for his pickup, bought some sunglasses, a lawn chair, and a skimpy bathing suit, and was heading south.

Most of that first winter Grandpa lived in his camper at a campground outside Yuma, but when spring came and he returned to the ranch, the pickup and camper were long gone, and he was driving and living in a converted school bus. The outside of the bus looked exactly like the one we rode to school. It even had a metal "stop" sign that popped out by the driver's window. But he had the inside fixed up just like a little house, complete with a bathroom, a kitchen, and a wood stove with a stovepipe that stuck through the roof. Since that time, summer or winter, Arizona or Oregon, Grandpa had made his home in the bus.

The day Grandpa came home from Arizona each spring was the best day of the year to Percy and me—better than birthdays and Easter and the Fourth of July, and maybe even Christmas. Not only did he return to us, but he always bore gifts. He was the tooth fairy, Santa Claus, and the Easter Bunny all rolled into one.

Now that we'd seen the bum in the flesh, Jon, Percy and I had gone back to the old pine bough trick with real gusto. Even though it was Grandpa's homecoming day, we were out early checking for bum prints, figuring maybe we'd make a real killing by laying claim to the reward and Grandpa's gifts on the same day.

"Get the lead out," Percy yelled as he churned past on his bike. He was standing on his pedals with his head down and his fanny up and his elbows out. The coon's tail he'd tied to the old car antenna wired to his rear fender was flying straight out.

I had a playing card clothespinned to my front wheel to click against my spokes. It sounded like a machine gun, and I was pedaling fast, then slow, to make it change tune. Up ahead the boys were making big loops back and forth across the road. I finally caught up at the end of the lake at a little day beach called Sunrise Cove. Percy's handlebars were always twisting around sideways, especially when he did sharp swerves and flying mounts, and he had his bike down trying to wrestle them straight.

"If you guys don't get new bikes one of these days, these ones're gonna fall apart," Jon said.

"Don't worry about us," I said. "These ol' clunkers'll go any place yours will. Anyway, I'd lots rather have these big, fat tires on a gravel road than those skinny ones of yours. These'll go through anything."

"Floozie," Jon said, "if I had a bike like yours, I'd push it over a cliff." At that, he turned and went down to the lakeside to check for bum tracks around the garbage can. It wasn't long before he came running back, looking like he'd just found gold. "I've got some!" he shouted. He fumbled for his camera in the pouch that hung on the back of his bike seat, then led the charge to the can. In the brushed area around it there were some nice prints, all right, but heck, as far as I could see they could have been made by anybody, which is what I told them.

Jon tapped his finger against his temple. "Gotta use your head," he said. He was seeing something in the tracks that I was obviously missing. Rather than clear up the mystery, he drug it on by turning toward the lake, hawking up a goober and blasting it all the way to the water. He watched the rings expand out, then turned back and said, "Ever seen anybody with two left feet?"

I looked over at Percy, "What's he talkin' about?"

He just shrugged and stood looking down at the prints. Then, all at once, he threw his hands up and blurted, "Ahhh...now I see!" He bent over, pointing. "See, they're all the same. It's like he just has one leg."

"Maybe a one-legged guy put some garbage in the can," I suggested weakly.

"Not one leg, Susie-Doozie. Two left feet," Jon scorned.

"Nobody'd have two left feet," I said. "That's stupid."

"Not two real left feet," Jon said. "Two left shoes. These tracks were made by somebody with two left shoes."

"Why'd anybody wear two left shoes?" I objected. "That's stupid, too."

"Think," Percy said. "Bums do things like that. That's just how they are. That's probably what he wears."

"All this trackin' stuff's crazy," I said. "What if they are the bum's tracks? What good does it do? Just proves he's got legs an' knows how to walk. Heck, I know that already. I seen him. Anyway, what if they are his tracks? What we gonna do with 'em?"

"Evidence, dummy," Jon said. "Footprints're as good as fingerprints. We'll take a picture of 'em an' then the next time he breaks into a cabin or somethin', we'll look around for prints. An' if we find one…presto. We got him.''

Jon snapped a bunch of pictures, then we headed off around the lake to check more cans. At every one we found more of the same left-footed prints for Jon to film. Finally we rounded the south end of the lake and headed toward home, figuring it was about time for Grandpa to be pulling in. We were riding three abreast down the middle of the road, scattering like bowling pins each time a car came, with Jon and me debating whether or not he was going to poke my clacker card down my throat. He claimed it made his head hurt. Then Percy's bike chain flew off. He wobbled like a drunk, then disappeared down over the bank. The last thing I saw was his coon tail dropping from sight. I skidded to a stop and looked over the edge. He was wound up in bars and wheels like a pretzel.

"You all right?" I asked down.

He didn't answer, but set to work untangling himself. When he was free, he drug the bike up the bank and laid it out like a corpse. The three of us stood looking down at it like mourners. The chain was wrapped in the spokes and the old car antenna was bent over with the coon tail hanging limply.

"I think it's broke," I said.

"You've got a problem," Jon said, soberly. "That's one bent wheel." Spokes were sticking out every which way, like it had had a run-in with a metal porcupine.

Percy gave the scrapes down his leg and arm a quick inspection, then set out making his bike rideable again. It was a tall order. Jon and I pitched in on the twisting and heaving, but even when we were finished, it was still a sick-looking machine.

"You ain't gonna try to ride that thing, are you?" I asked.

Percy didn't give me an answer but just swung his leg over and pushed off. The wheel wobbled like a top that had just about spun its last spin, and there was a scraping noise almost as loud as my clicker card, but it was holding him up and moving.

"I guess he's goin'," I said to Jon, so the two of us jumped on our own bikes and headed after him.

We were as far as the gravel road that led down to Viewpoint Beach when a big pop split the air and Percy went out of control again. He stayed on the road this time, but his back tire was as flat as a dollar bill. He gave it a kick and, without saying anything, rolled his bike out into the trees and laid it behind a log.

"I'll get it later," he mumbled. "We're gonna be late for Grandpa."

"What you gonna do, walk?" I asked.

"I'll ride your bike," he said, "an' you can ride in the basket."

I gave him a disgusted look. "You ever ride in the basket on a gravel road?"

"Don't argue," he said.

"I'd rather walk," I said.

"Don't act like a girl," he scorned. "An' don't pout. We're gonna be late gettin' home. Grandpa's probably there right now."

I shoved my bike his way. He took it and held the bars while I squirmed my heinie down in the basket. I could feel the wire mesh through the seat of my pants.

"Don't you dare hit the bumps, dummy," I warned.

Chapter 8

om said Grandpa had a clock in his head. He could wake up in a pitch-dark morning any time he wanted, or come in for dinner right on the dot and never even peek at his watch. Along with being able to play the spoons and whittle, this sense of time was one of the few things he liked to brag about. Grandpa had instilled this same trait into my dad, and Dad had done his best to pass it on to Percy and me. The trouble was, every sign pointed to the likelihood that it was coming to a dead end with us. This bothered Dad. He had taught us how to tell time even before we were in school, and we both wore watches before our arms were big enough to fill the smallest bands. But know-how and equipment weren't enough, and when our watches weren't lost or broken or dead from lack of winding, they might just as well have been, because we could just never remember to look at them. It wasn't that we didn't try, but looking at a wristwatch wasn't in our nature. In the end, Dad laid the blame on bad genes from Mom's side of the family, and just started telling us to do things or be places a half hour before we actually needed to be. Crazy as it sounds, this worked pretty well, because we were almost always exactly a half-hour late.

So that spring day, the usual thirty minutes behind schedule, Percy had just pedaled us onto the driveway when Grandpa came bumping past in his bus. With his old floppy-brimmed gray felt hat pushed back on his head, he slowed to a crawl and leaned out the window to yell down to us. "Nice buns you got in that basket!" he blasted.

"Grandpa!" I hollered back. Percy tried to wave but almost put us in the ditch.

Grandpa flapped his stop sign out and in a few times, gave his horn a long blast, and went on ahead with his red lights flashing.

The rest of the way in, Percy seemed a lot more concerned about getting home fast than giving me a smooth ride. He crashed through every bump and hole. When we pulled up beside the bus, Percy was rubber-legged and out of breath from the hard pedaling, and my bottom felt like a waffle.

There was one odd thing about Grandpa—he never changed. I suspect that if he'd gone away for fifty or a hundred years, he would have come back looking exactly as he had when he left. I asked him about this once, and he explained that it was because of his face. He said that when he was younger, he'd been almost good-looking. Then, about age six, he figured, the aging process had set in, and slowly (or maybe not so slowly) he'd started getting uglier by the day. Finally he'd gotten about as ugly as a guy could get, and then he just stayed stuck forever in that exact condition. He said as long as he stayed away from mirrors, it wasn't so bad.

I had another theory about his eternal sameness. I thought it was because of his clothes. He always dressed the same. Always. When some item of clothing wore out, he'd just buy a new one exactly like it. If you could have stood his clothes up elbow to elbow with any number of other outfits in one of those police lineups, I could have picked his out with my eyes tied behind my back—baggy bib overalls, a stretched-out gray sweat-shirt, and scuffed-up black work shoes that hadn't been greased or polished from the day he'd bought them. That was what he was wearing as he stood waiting for us beside his bus with Mom and Dad. As Percy and I rushed up to him, he spread his feet and stretched his arms out to wrap around us. His leathery face wrinkled into a grin that nearly wiped out everything from his nose to his chin.

"Nuts from the crazy house!" he bellowed. "Get me a couple o' straitjackets." He grabbed me in one arm and Percy in the other and lifted us both up off the ground. "Wait! Wait!" he said, with his arms still clamped around us. "These ain't crazy people. They're aliens from outer space." Then he smacked a kiss on each of our foreheads and set us down. "Where'd you find these two creatures?"

"They just showed up one day," Dad said. "Found 'em out eatin' with the hogs."

"The hogs?"

"Snortin' 'round in the mud."

"Too bad," Grandpa said. "I kinda liked them two kids that used to live here. What was their names?"

"Percy an' Susie," Dad said. "Naw...we got rid of them a long time ago. Sold 'em to the zoo."

About then I cut in and asked where the presents were.

"Presents?" Grandpa acted surprised.

"You know..." I said.

Grandpa rubbed the end of his nose and looked over at Mom. "I hope they ain't waitin' for presents," he said. "I spent all my money on them good-lookin' Arizona women this year. Didn't have a penny left for any runty little kids." He turned his eyes back to us. "You don't expect nothin', I hope."

"Go get 'em, Grandpa," I said. I took hold of his baggy pants and turned him around in the direction of the bus door and nudged him inside. He disappeared, and when he came out he was carrying an armload of gifts. He had new fly rods and fly reels filled with double-tapered fly line, and insulated hip boots with loops on the tops to hook your belt through to hold them up.

"I like 'em," I said. I put the boots on but they came halfway to my neck.

"We're gonna have to cut arm holes in 'em, Susie," Grandpa said. "Them's as small as I could find."

But I was happy with them the way they were, and I wore them the rest of the day with the tops rolled down and a piece of rope cinched around each thigh to hold them up.

After we'd paid all the presents due respect and thanked Grandpa more times than we could count, we took him over to where the old house had burned down. That was a sad moment, because Grandpa had not just lived in it and raised his family in it—he'd also built it.

"Musta made a nice fire," he said. "Hope you had some wienies."

"Just marshmallows," Dad said. We all laughed, but then we stood around a while, not saying much and doing a lot of poking at the dirt with the toes of our shoes.

"Cryin' shame," Grandpa said. "Sometimes there ain't no justice in this ol' world."

"Things always work out for the best," Mom said. "I wish it hadn't happened like this, but that old house had seen better days."

Then we took Grandpa to where the new house would soon stand. We showed him the plans and the piles of lava rock and shake bolts.

"I'm a shake splitter from way back," Grandpa said. "Where's your froe an' mallet?"

Dad gave him the tools, and Grandpa pulled up a hunk of wood to sit on, then ran his eyes over the shake bolts. He pulled one over to him and lodged it between his knees, then began splitting. He pounded the froe blade into the cedar, then pulled back on the handle. The wood gave a hard pop and a shake jumped off. "All the stuff this straight?" he asked, wiping his forearm across his nose.

"Some of it's a little knotty," Dad said, "but most of it's pretty decent."

"You get me pullin' shakes and it's like chasin' them old Arizona widows," he said. "Can't stop. Give me some shake bolts an shakin' tools an' a shady spot where I can see me a mountain, and I'm happy as a clam." He split off another shake, then looked over at Mom. "I'm like to starved," he said. "You can bring my lunch right down here, an' I'll have you a roof split in no time."

Mom went and fixed lunch, and we all sat around for the next hour or so listening to Grandpa tell stories about Arizona and watching him split shakes. By the time he had run out of things to say, he had a pile of shakes that would have filled the back of a pickup.

Our barn was a big old weatherbeaten thing that looked like a barn should look. It wasn't like those newfangled aluminum monstrosities you see these days. It was made of rough-cut lumber with honest-to-goodness slivers in it—beams, siding, floors, roof, all of it. It had real character. Grandpa built it one winter in the forties when there was three feet of snow on the ground. He'd notched all the joists and beams into the posts so perfectly you'd have a hard time sliding a playing card between them. When asked how he'd managed to get those big timbers thirty feet off the ground with nothing but his bare hands, he looked up, pondering a moment, then said, "That's a good question." When he had it up, he brushed some kind of oil on it to keep it from rotting, and over the years it had faded to a natural gray that fit its surroundings as though it might have rooted and grown there on the spot from some sort of barn seed.

Early on, Dad decided that we needed someplace closer than the Pindars' rental cabin to live while he and Grandpa put up the house, so he took some boards from the lumber pile he always kept around and built us a nice three-room apartment in the downstairs of the barn, right next to the cow stalls. Rooms in a barn don't sound like much, but they were actually quite nice. Except for the faint smell of cow poop that filtered through the walls now and then, you couldn't tell you weren't in a real house. Mom named it the Taj Mahal. There was straw between the studs for insulation and plaster on the walls. Dad found some old pieces of carpet to spread on the floors and dug up an old rusty wood stove for heat. The only thing we lacked was good furniture. We had a homemade table and some shaky chairs in what Mom called "the parlor," and in the two bedrooms we laid mattresses out on the floor to sleep on. We had moved in the day before Grandpa came home.

Late that afternoon, when Grandpa's shake-pulling arm quit functioning, he and Dad pulled his bus up between the barn and the hog house, where they jacked it up and blocked it level.

"Can't say much for the neighborhood," Grandpa said, "but this'll do fine."

"Just keep your windows up and a clothespin for your nose, an' you'll be OK," Dad laughed.

Following dinner that evening, Grandpa took Percy and me to troll for trout over at Big Slide Lake. After a winter in Arizona where the only water he saw was in a glass and the only fish were in magazines, Grandpa always came home with the fishing fever. Percy and I wore our hip boots and life jackets. Dad had tried to talk us out of the boots, telling us morbid stories about people who had drowned falling out of boats with hip boots on, but we assured him that we were better swimmers than those guys and that Grandpa was probably a lot better boatman, too.

Big Slide Lake was four miles down the road from Russ Lake and about half its size. It wasn't as picturesque as some of the others around, but it put out fish like nobody's business. If you wanted to fish in a lake, and if you wanted to catch fish, it's where you went. There was a little log cabin that sat on the south shore facing out across the water, where an old guy and his wife lived, rented boats, and sold gasoline and a few groceries for about four times the price you could get them anywhere else.

We unloaded the boat and tied it to a tree, then parked the truck up above. As we walked back down to the boat, the sun glinted off the water. The surface was as flat as a windowpane, with the reflection of South Peak sitting so sharp on it that if it weren't upside down, you'd have sworn it was the real thing. Grandpa was whistling quietly. You could tell he was feeling good about going fishing again. He took a big sniff of air. "Smell them pine trees," he said. "Just hope them fish're hungry."

We piled our gear in, and Percy and I waded out in our new boots to push it into the lake. Grandpa hooked up the gas line, squeezed the bulb to prime the motor, and started it on the second pull.

"How's that for not bein' started for six months?" he said. "Just two tugs." He goosed it a time or two until it ran smoothly, then put it in gear and took us to deeper water, where he slowed to trolling speed and set us on a straight heading across the lake. We baited up and dropped our lures over the side.

Fishing is a funny thing. Some days the fish are in the mood to bite, and some days they aren't. Then there are other days that are even harder to explain, when the fish seem in the mood to bite one person's hook and nobody else's. That's what happened that day. Grandpa and Percy couldn't buy a bite, but by the time we had reached the end of the lake, I had already caught two fish and lost another. As we turned, I hooked one more. I began taking a ribbing.

Grandpa looked over the Percy and said, "Does it seem to you that a certain person's hoggin' all the fish?"

Percy nodded. He always hated getting outfished, especially by me. "Put the net over her head an' push her in," he said.

As we trolled along the west shore I hooked another one, and the ribbing got brutal. They questioned whether I'd gone over their heads and made some sort of deal with God, what I'd eaten for dinner, whether I was spitting on my line, if I was wearing some sort of special underwear. Then Grandpa yelped, "Wait! Check the bait, Percy. I bet that's it. Check an' make sure she ain't givin' you an' me the bad ends of them worms. Could be she's nippin' the heads off for herself an' givin' you an' me the patooties!"

"Does it matter?" Percy asked.

Grandpa slapped his leg and laughed. "Heavens, no! You know better'n to believe an ol' liar like me. I doubt an ol' trout could tell the difference between a worm's head an' patootie, anyway."

It was about then that I happened to look out across the end of the lake toward the road. I don't know why I looked just then, but I did, and there, plain as the nose on your face, was the bum, and he was pushing Percy's bike. I gasped and pulled on Percy's line to get his attention, but I pulled too hard and made him drop his pole.

"Watch it," he snapped.

I glanced to make sure Grandpa wasn't looking, then, without making a sound, I mouthed, "BUM...YOUR BIKE," and I pointed emphatically in the direction of the road.

"What?"

I mouthed the words again and pointed once more, but it was too late. The bum had disappeared behind the trees. I gave my thigh a whack with my fist.

"What you sayin'?" Percy asked.

I leaned close to his ear, and whispering a bit louder, said, "I seen the bum over on the road, pushin' your bike."

"You're kiddin'," he whispered back. He peered that direction. "You must be seein' things."

"I seen him," I whispered, gritting my teeth.

Just then Grandpa let out a whoop and cut the motor. His pole was bent double, and out on the end of his line a trout was doing everything but cartwheels.

"Got one!" he cheered. "Look at that booger jump."

"Get him, Grandpa," Percy shouted. Then he glanced back at me, and by the look on his face I could tell he was taking seriously what I'd just told him.

Grandpa's fish was going wild out in the lake. Even with a bunch of trolling gear to drag around, it was dancing all over the top of the water.

"It's a dandy!" Grandpa whooped. His pole jumped in his hands.

Percy and I reeled our outfits in to keep from getting tangled.

Grandpa's fish fought like a champ for a minute or two, then started wilting. Grandpa slid me the net, and when he had it worked close enough to the boat I scooped it out.

"I think you beat me, Grandpa," I said. "Yours could eat all of mine an' still have room for dessert."

"Well, you got a nice batch, too," he said. "Anyway, I'd be happy if I didn't catch nothin', an' that's the gospel truth. They got good weather down there in Arizona, but gol-dang it, there ain't nothin' down there like fishin' in an Oregon mountain lake."

The water was clear as a bell where we were, and not too deep. You could see basalt ridges on the bottom below, and now and then you'd catch the glint of a lure some troller had lost. Up in the top of a snag there was an osprey's nest with mama osprey perched on a limb beside it.

We made another pass around the lake and caught several more fish, but both Percy and I had our minds elsewhere now. Grandpa kept teasing and telling stories, but the two of us spent most of our time looking back toward the open end of the lake at the road. We finally quit fishing a bit before dark.

On the way back to the ranch we had Grandpa drive us around to the back side of Russ Lake to where Percy had left his bike in the woods. We looked out through the trees and up and down the road, but we couldn't find hide nor hair of it.

Then Percy waved me over to him. "Don't say nothin', Susie," he whispered to me. "Look here." He pointed to the snake-like track in the dust heading back toward Mallard Lake.

"He stole it, all right," I said.

"Yeah," he said. "But look at this." He led me off a little ways and pointed down to a clump of left shoe prints in the dirt, as clear as you please.

"Shoot," I said.

"Ol' coot," Percy muttered.

Chapter 9

J on Pindar was a runt, but nobody said it to his face. He claimed he was little because he was putting his energy into growing good looks and brains instead of size. He said he couldn't see any future in being big if he was dumb and ugly. Some of the girls at school thought he was cute. I didn't, and I didn't mind telling him so. He was smart, though. The trouble was, he was smart in a negative way. If he had put his mind to achieving something constructive, like doing his studies, he would have been a genius. The wheels in his head turned some direction other than forward. His mind cranked out ideas that normal people (people who didn't especially relish living their lives in hot water) wouldn't even have considered. When we played Indians, he always wanted to be the bad guy. That was how he liked it. He said he could think like a crook, which was something to be proud of, as far as he was concerned. But most people would have taken it further than that and said he was on his way to becoming a crook, which was probably about as close to the truth as you could get. The crazy thing about him, though, was that bad as he was, he didn't do really bad things. He was more of an irritant, like the itch in the middle of your back you can't quite reach to scratch. And the really crazy thing was that, much as I hated his guts, I was drawn to him like a magnet. Being with him was like jumping off a roof, or diving off a high rock into a lake, or walking across a river on a narrow log. He tipped ordinary days on edge and made them memorable.

Three days after Percy's bike disappeared, school ended for the year. During those three days, Jon's mind was in high gear with its accelerator to the floor. He was bound and determined to start summer vacation by getting the bike back and sending the bum to the electric chair, all in one fell swoop. He studied his Indian book on the bus, in class, after school, at recess, and even at the end-of-the-year picnic. By the day the school year ended, he had drawn up the worst bunch of harebrained schemes ever to hit a sheet of paper.

"This stuff's dumb," I told him. "This guy ain't Superman. We don't need poison arrows an' invisible ink an' all that stuff. Why don't we just use our eyes? That's what they're for, you know."

Jon didn't take my judgment gracefully, but to his credit, he did realize there'd be no help from either Percy or me if he didn't tone things down. So he did. He finally came up with a plan we all half-liked that had the three of us splitting up in special camouflaged hideouts so we could spy on nearly the whole lakefront at the same time. He made a map and a schedule of assignments. He even worked out signals so we could communicate between our various hiding places. By day we would flash signals with mirrors. By night we would use flashlights (provided free of charge, he said, compliments of the Russ Lake Lodge). One flash meant the signaler had spotted the bum and that the other two should come as fast as they could around the north end of the lake. Two flashes meant to come around the south end. And three flashes meant the signaler was being attacked by the bum and that the others should come by whatever way they could get there fastest, and be ready to fight. According to the plan, we'd start building the camouflaged hideouts the first morning of summer vacation.

When we came home after the last day of school, Percy and I found Dad and Grandpa digging the footing for the new house. They had the corners staked off and nice straight-sided trenches finished nearly the whole way around. Grandpa leaned on his shovel with his hat pushed back on his head, and as we came up he said, "I ain't decided what it is, yet." (Meaning the trench.) "Either a gold mine or a hot tub." There was a wet crescent of sweat around the neck of his sweatshirt, and you could see where it had begun soaking through his felt hat, too.

"I thought we'd decided it was a dungeon," Dad said. "Remember? We agreed we needed a place to keep the kids." He had his shirt off, and his winter-white skin almost shone.

"Well, I know this," Grandpa said. "The way my ol' bod feels right now, we might just wanta make a grave of it an' roll me in. I'm a hard ol' coot. I'd hold up the side of a house—even dead."

Mom fixed an early dinner that day and brought it to the house site, where we ate in the shade. Grandpa stretched out and lay looking up into the branches with his plate balanced on his chest. "I ain't use to this diggin'," he said. "Got outa shape chasin' them old Arizona gals 'round the trailer park. They don't move very fast in them wheelchairs an' walker contraptions. Guess I should go after some of them young fillies now an' then—just for the trainin'." He rolled his head to the side and looked at Mom. "I think I'm gonna need some medicine." He was smiling, so you could tell he wasn't serious.

"Medicine?" Mom asked.

"Yeah."

"Like what?"

He rolled his head back so he was gazing up again. He felt around on his plate till he found a pickle, then took a bite off it. While he chewed it he said, "Fishin'."

"I thought you said medicine."

"I did," he said. "For what I got, fishin's the only medicine."

"I suppose you're going to tell us it's terminal," Mom said.

He took another lazy bite of pickle and rolled his head toward Mom again. "Worse'n cancer," he grinned. "Don't reckon you'd wanta see me kick off till this house's up, now, would you?"

"Couldn't have that," Mom laughed.

"Worse part is that it's contagious. I think Susie an' Percy's got it too," he said.

"That true?" Mom asked.

We both said we had it, too.

When we'd finished eating, we agreed our health was more important than any house, so Dad, Grandpa, Percy, and I headed off to try out our new fly rods and have some medicine. The four of us crossed the pasture with grasshoppers clicking up in front of us. A batch of cattle stood off by the trees where they'd been grazing. They watched us as we passed—heads up, ears out like ping-pong paddles, chewing dully with grass hanging from the corners of their mouths.

"I'll be darned if I can look a cow in the eye without thinkin' of beef steak anymore," Grandpa said. "Know what I mean? Been around 'em too long, I guess, or maybe it's all this fancy breedin' they're doin' these days. But the darned things have lost their personality. They ain't nothin' but walkin' hamburgers. One o' these days I reckon they'll breed 'em with buns an' relish right on 'em."

Dad chuckled. "I see dollar bills is what I see," he said. "Dollar bills with horns on 'em."

We followed the trail through the pine groves and meadows beside the creek. The air was warm from the day, but the sun was low in the sky and filtered through the trees in patches. The air smelled like pine and dust. At Mallard Lake we crossed the bridge and filed along beside the shore. New reeds were sprouting up above the surface in the shallows, and there were circles on the water where trout were rising for bugs.

At the far end of the lake, where the river flowed out, we divided up, with Grandpa and Percy heading down one bank and Dad and me crossing to the other.

"We've gotta have one understandin'," Dad said as he showed me how to rig up my new fly pole. I don't mind teachin' you how to fly fish, but if you catch more'n me, girl, you're apt to find yourself throwed in." He handed me a little box full of flies and a container the size of a watch with some stuff in it he called "fly dope" that I was supposed to rub on the flies to make them float. "You're tryin' to make ol' mister trout think this little wad of feathers is a bug that's floatin' to his dinner table," he said.

The river flowed out of Mallard Lake in a big sweeping curve, split around a grassy island, and then dropped off toward lower country in earnest. It was about as wide as a good cast, and strewn with boulders and fallen trees to form better trout water than you could expect to find anywhere else outside heaven, and maybe not even there.

Dad and I walked to a stretch of river where he claimed the trout would be lined up and waiting their turn to bite my hook. He showed me how to read the water so I'd know where they'd be laying. Then he stood behind me and guided me through a few casts by moving my arms for me. When he thought I had it he stepped back.

"Now you're on your own, Whiplash. You can hook your own limbs." Which is what I did. For the next half hour or so, as we worked our way downstream, I hung dry flies in trees and brush like Christmas-tree ornaments, and when I did manage to hit the river my fly splashed down so hard all the fly dope in the world couldn't have kept it afloat. To make matters worse, every time I looked up, one of the others was landing a fish. Even Percy.

I was ready to call it quits, when a miracle happened. The fishing god took my fly and laid it soft as a feather atop what must have been the nicest trout in the whole darned river. The trout shot up from the bottom with such a rush that when it broke the surface for a bite of my hook, you'd have sworn a small bomb was going off. I pulled back on the rod, and it felt as though I had struck into a log, it was so solid. Dad gave a cheer. I cranked on my reel and a fish the size of my arm went wild on the end of my line. My rod was bent in half. Dad was giving advice, and Grandpa was shouting more from across the river. Even Percy was rooting me on. It was a knock-down-drag-out, and why I didn't lose it I'll never know, but little by little I felt it slowly grow weaker.

"It's a whopper," Dad said. " Be patient, now."

The trout made another short run, but it had lost its zip. Finally I coaxed it into the shallows where it lay gasping on its side with my fly hooked in the corner of its jaw.

Dad waded out and slid his hand carefully in behind its gills and lifted it out. "Not bad for the first try," he grinned. He lifted it high so Percy and Grandpa could admire it too, and we had a nice little celebration on the two sides of the river.

We fished our way downstream a while longer, but as was usually the case that year, my attention span was on the short side.

It wasn't long before I was throwing more rocks and catching more water skippers than I was making casts. Finally Dad suggested that maybe I and my fish might want to head back to the farm. I said I would if Percy would, too, so we negotiated across the river at the top of our voices, while Dad and Grandpa stayed on to fish what was left of the daylight.

Percy and I had just come in sight of the footbridge when we spotted the bum. Percy was the first to see him. He started flapping his arms and pointing emphatically upstream at a figure crossing the bridge from my side to his. From the distance I couldn't make out his features, but by his hunched shape and the way he plodded along without really lifting his feet, there was no question who it was. My fish and I dived down behind a bush, and Percy plastered himself to the back side of a tree. We didn't move, except to crane our necks for quick peeps, until the bum was back on solid ground again and heading up the trail away from us. At that, we sprinted for the bridge.

"What we gonna do, Percy?" I panted when we met.

"Follow him, of course," he said.

"What if he sees us?"

"We won't let him," he said.

The bum was up to the little cove at the east end of the lake by now. Percy and I ripped our rods apart and took off after him.

Chasing a bum with your finger shoved up the gill of a fish darn near as long as your arm isn't easy. And this bum, for someone who moved about the way you'd expect someone with two left shoes to move, was out-and-out fast. Percy was doing fine, but it was all I could manage to keep up. We ducked from bush to bush and tree to tree, hunching along close to the ground. As rigor mortis set in on one arm, I'd switch my fish to the other.

Finally the bum came to where the trail forked and turned up the eastern branch that led over the ridge to some beaver ponds.

"I bet a jillion dollars I know where he's headin'," Percy puffed.

"Me too," I said.

As the bum disappeared into the trees up the hillside, Percy and I sprinted to make up ground. When we came to the fork, we turned uphill after him. We hadn't gone but a dozen yards when the bum appeared against the sky on the ridge above us, and Percy blurted, "Dive!" We hit the ground like we'd been shot. The trouble was, I hit the ground smack on my fish. And to make matters worse, a divot of dirt thrown up by Percy's boot flew into my eyes.

"I think he seen us," Percy gasped. "Be ready to run!"

"Shoot," I said. "You kicked dirt in my eyes. I can't seen nothin'."

"Oh-oh...I think he's comin' this way," Percy whispered with sudden desperation. "No...wait. He ain't. Hold still, now."

My eyes hurt like fire. I was pulling on my lids and blinking, but it wasn't doing much good.

"Did he see us?" I whispered.

"I don't know," Percy said. "I think he might've."

"Let's don't go further," I pleaded. "If he's seen us he might be waitin' up there for us."

"No," Percy said. "You go home if you want to, but I'm gonna stay with him."

I had one eye semi-cleared, now, but the other one still had enough dirt in it to plow and plant.

Still trying to clear it, I grabbed my pole and tried to poke my finger through my fish's gill to carry it again, but it had been dived on and flung down one too many times. Its head was nearly off, so I grabbed it by the mouth and followed Percy up toward the ridge.

This branch of the trail wasn't used much. It led over the hill to a series of meadows and beaver ponds and ended there. Staying low, we edged forward. We crept in wide arcs around anything that could conceivably hide an angry bum. At the top of the hill the trail turned left, and we sped to a jog along the open ridge. Mount Thompson was so close we could almost reach out and touch it, and it was taking on a dusky orange color. For the first time, I realized it wouldn't be long before night. There was no way I wanted to be out there with the bum in anything but broad daylight. "It's gettin' dark, Percy," I whispered.

"I know," he answered. "But we're too close to stop now."

"I don't wanta go back in the dark," I said. "What if he's hidin' for us?"

"Go back if you're scared," Percy said. "He's gotta be camped up here at the beaver ponds." He moved off, again, and I kept following.

The trail crossed some open scree, then dropped down through a close stand of lodge pole pine where the trees grew like a wall beside the path. It was like going through a tunnel. We were sneaking along, stepping over sticks that might crack underfoot and being careful not to kick rocks or cough or let any bodily functions fire off on their own. When the trail opened up into the meadow, we slipped in where we could scan the scene in front of us.

"I don't see him," Percy whispered.

The main beaver pond and the dam lay out in front of us with drowned, whitened trees standing in the shallows. The trail swung down to the edge of the water then disappeared around the corner.

"He must be a little further up," Percy whispered. He bit thoughtfully on his lip. "Well, I guess he could have crossed the dam, but I don't think so. Let's sneak back along the edge of the woods and see if he's on up there."

We slipped back into the cover of the trees and paralleled the trail and pond until we came out on a little basalt outcropping that had a huge spring running from it. It gushed a full-blown stream that bubbled across the meadow into the beaver pond forty yards away.

"I still don't see him," I whispered.

"Shh." Percy pulled me down with his finger up to his lips. "He's a little further up. You can see smoke from his fire above those trees." He pointed.

Sure enough, even from where we were crouched, you could see a blue smudge of smoke hanging in the air. Percy motioned for me to follow. Moving more carefully than we had ever moved, putting our feet down like we were walking on eggs, we crept back through the trees again, then out onto another outcropping of basalt much like the first one. But this time there was no good place we could spy from. A low cliff hid us from sight but was too tall to see over.

"Get down on your hands an' knees so I can stand on your back," Percy whispered.

I laid my pole down behind me with my fish, or what was left of it, then got down on my hands and knees while Percy climbed on my back. I held him there until my arms began shaking, which wasn't very long. "I'm gettin' weak," I whispered.

Finally he climbed down, and holding his face right up close to mine, he said, "I seen him. My bike, too."

"Did you see a gun or anything?"

He shook his head, "No."

"Let me up," I whispered.

Percy got down on his knees the way I had, and I climbed up, but I wasn't quite tall enough. I raised up on my toes but still came up just a little short.

"Nuts," I whispered. "I'm too short." So I reached up and caught hold of something solid with my fingers, then walked my toes up the rock until I had my eyes over the top. There below me was the bum's crude tent pitched in the grass beside the upper beaver pond, with an old campfire smoldering beside it. He was sitting cross-legged with Percy's bike laying on its side nearby.

Just then the rock I had my fingers locked to decided to move. I grabbed for another hold and got nothing but air. The next thing I knew, Percy and I were tangled in a pile on the ground and a small avalanche of rocks was clattering down off the other side of the cliff into the stream. We leaped up and sprinted for the trees, hurdling logs and brush. Halfway up the hill we hit the trail, and we didn't slow down until we were back to the main trail around Mallard Lake. From there we jogged the rest of the way back to the ranch.

It wasn't until we were coming up the path to the barn that I noticed Percy still carrying his pole. "Oh shoot!" I said.

Percy looked over at me.

"My pole...an' fish."

"You didn't...."

"I did," I answered.

"Where at?"

"Back where we seen the bum."

"Dang."

Chapter 10

Explaining to Mom how Percy and I had gotten so dirty and scratched up on a little fly-fishing outing, without letting her know her two children had been spying on a dangerous bum, wasn't easy. And when Grandpa and Dad came in right behind us, clean and unmarked and ready to brag on the big trout I had caught, we did the unthinkable. We lied! All kids twist the truth now and then. You have to, or you wouldn't be a kid. But we didn't just twist the truth, we tied it in knots.

And where Percy got the inspiration to explain away the mess we'd come back in by blaming it on a bear was beyond me. And now he was looking over to me for help in carrying his story forward.

"A bear?" Mom gasped.

I gave a half-hearted nod.

"You tell 'em about it," Percy said to me.

"You tell," I said, realizing that so far Percy had told all the lies and that I was still only guilty by association.

"Where'd you see this bear?" Dad asked.

Percy looked to me again, but seeing my lips sealed, stammered, "Comin' round the lake.... down by that big meadow.... where that creek comes in."

"Along the trail?" Dad asked.

Percy shook his head, stood silent for a moment, then said, "Back up off the trail a ways."

"You guys sure it was a bear? You sure it wasn't a log or rock or somethin' that just looked like a bear? Starts gettin' dusky out an' a guy's eyes'll play tricks on him," Grandpa advised.

"No, it was a bear," I said, then stood stunned as I realized I was now as guilty of lying as Percy was. "It came out of the woods behind us," I said, getting warmed up. "And we couldn't get back to the trail."

"What were you doing up there, anyway?" Mom asked. "You were supposed to be coming home."

"Pickin' flowers," Percy said.

"For you, Mom," I said. "We were pickin' 'em for you."

"Let me get this straight," Dad said. "The two of you were out in the meadow pickin' flowers an' a bear came out behind you so you couldn't get back to the trail?"

"Uh huh," Percy mumbled.

"And then..."

"And then...he started pawin' an' snortin' an' actin' real mean," I blurted. I demonstrated.

Mom looked horrified.

"That's when we started runnin'," Percy said. "An' the bear started comin' after us. But Susie accidentally dropped her fish, an' when the bear saw it he stopped an' ate it an' forgot about us."

Dad and Grandpa were looking at each other with blank expressions on their faces. "You mean this bear chased you?" Grandpa asked.

"Yeah, he did," Percy said. "Till he got to the fish."

"That's odd," Grandpa said. "I don't reckon I've ever seen a bear 'round here that wouldn't show his heels to a person. Maybe a wounded one or somethin'...you sure it wasn't a she-bear with cubs?"

"I don't think so," Percy said.

"How'd you get all scratched up?" Dad asked.

"Runnin'," I said. "Runnin' through the woods." I felt a little better about saying this, because it was true. We had gotten scratched up running through the woods. It was just that we'd been running from a bum instead of a bear.

Then I remembered about my new pole. I looked at Grandpa. "Grandpa," I said, "I think I lost my new fishin' pole when I was runnin'."

Grandpa just shrugged. "New poles're a dime a dozen, but granddaughters're hard to replace."

We finished off our story while Mom washed our scratches and painted them with medicine that burned. But down inside, I had a rotten feeling that burned even worse, and I could tell by the way Percy turned his eyes away each time I looked at him that he was feeling the same way.

Later that night the consequences of our fib began hitting home when Mom banned us from going anywhere out of sight of the house until the matter of the bear was taken care of. "A bear that would do what that one did is dangerous," she said.

We assured her that such drastic measures weren't called for and that the bear had probably reformed its ways by now, but she wouldn't budge.

Then Grandpa told a story about some people who had been eaten alive in their sleeping bags by bears in Glacier Park. "Worst thing you can do when a bear's got its dander up's to run," Grandpa said. "Remember that...even if he's chawin' on you. You gotta just lay still so's he'll think you're dead."

The color was draining from Mom's face, and much as I liked Grandpa's story, I was wishing he'd bring it to a speedy end before she locked us in our room and barred the door.

"Percy and me're fast runners," I said.

"Not as fast as a bear," Mom said. "If that bear had kept chasing you, it wouldn't have been a contest. You're just lucky you dropped that fish."

The next morning at breakfast Grandpa stood his rifle by the door and laid his hunting knife and box of shells on the table beside his plate, and announced he was going out to see if he couldn't locate this bear with the bad temper. As he ate, he quizzed us again. He wanted to know exactly where it had been, how big it was, what color it was, and anything else we remembered about it. I let Percy do all the answering, because I was feeling a bad case of guilt that was all but terminal.

"I won't be too long," Grandpa said as he got ready to leave. He threaded his knife scabbard onto his belt and stuffed a box of shells into his pocket. "If I'm not back by winter, just come a-lookin' for a bear with a bellyache," he grinned.

"Any bear that'd eat a tough old man like you would likely die from lockjaw," Mom said. Then she said, "Why don't you take Sam along? It'd sure make me feel better. If something goes wrong, two are better than one."

Grandpa gave me wink and said, "Nothin's gonna be eatin' me, anyway. Them bears hear I'm out with my gun, they'll likely all just up an' leave the country." He headed down the Mallard Lake trail with his gun across the crook of his arm, singing at the top of his lungs.

After we'd finished helping with the breakfast cleanup, Percy and I fully expected to head straight for Russ Lake to let Jon Pindar know he could scrap his camouflaged hideout plan, because we'd found the bum's camp without it. Trouble was, Mom was still holding firmly to her vow not to let us out of sight of the house until the matter of the bear was taken care of. Instead, she gave us the privilege, as she put it, of weeding the garden. Under normal conditions, this would have roused a major squawk from us, but this time we didn't utter a word. We knew we'd gotten ourselves into this pickle with no help from anyone else, and that the least we could do was to take our medicine with some semblance of dignity. While we ripped crabgrass and dandelions out of the vegetables, neither of us uttered so much as a word about what we'd done, but our silence spoke loud and clear. We were both ashamed. And to top it off, I was feeling rotten to the core that poor Grandpa was now off putting all this effort into finding something that didn't even exist.

Around midmorning Mom came out and asked us if we'd seen any sign of Grandpa, and we told her we hadn't. A little later she was back asking the same question again. About eleven or so, when Dad pulled up with a load of hay to unload, Mom met him and said she'd like for him to go check on him.

"You heard him at breakfast," Dad said. "He don't wanta be babysat. Anyway, he knows more 'bout bear huntin' than I ever will. He's probably just takin' a nap under a tree someplace."

But Mom was clearly worried. Finally, Dad shrugged and said, "What the heck....you kids wanta take a little hike?"

"Oh, Sam, don't take them," she said.

"Don't be a worry-wart," he said. "They can show me where they saw this bear. Right, kids?" He looked over at us.

We both said we'd like to go along, and Mom knew she was outnumbered, so Dad got his gun and a pocketful of shells and the three of us headed off in the direction Grandpa had gone. When we were almost to the meadow where we said we'd had our bear encounter, we stopped and listened for any sign of Grandpa. We heard the creek running and crows cawing and some jays chattering up in the trees, but there wasn't a man-made sound.

"Bet he's snoozin'," Dad said.

The meadows thereabouts were nearly always the remnants of old lakes that had either filled with sediment or sprung leaks and lost their water, but the one at the north end of Mallard Lake was a mystery. It wandered up the mouth of the little stream that flowed from the bum's beaver ponds, then swept up a gentle hillside almost to its top. It was a hundred acres or so of grasses and wildflowers with a few spotty groves of trees. We headed off across it, hollering as we went, but still didn't see a sign of Grandpa anywhere.

Finally, Dad said, "Hold your ears." He worked a shell into the chamber of his gun, pointed the barrel at the sky, and pulled the trigger. The blast echoed back to us.

We stood listening, again hearing nothing but forest sounds.

Then, from up the hill somewhere, the crack of Grandpa's return shot broke the silence. We made our way in that direction, shouting now and then as we went. We finally found Grandpa in the top of a pine tree about halfway up the hillside. He was sitting on a limb with one arm around the trunk and his rifle resting across his lap. He was so high that the treetop was listing over from his weight. "Mornin'," he said down to us. He had a sheepish look on his face, and his feet were dangling over the limb he was sitting on like a little kid's.

"What in tarnation happened?" Dad asked. "How'd you get up there? An' how in the dickens do you ever plan on gettin' down?"

"Flyin'." Grandpa's voice sounded thin.

"You OK?"

"Yeah, I'm OK." Grandpa unwrapped his arm from the tree and began working his way down from limb to limb. When he came to the last limb he dropped the gun to Dad, then wrapped his arms and legs around the trunk and slid down. He wiped his pitchy hands on his pants, then turned toward us with an odd look on his face. "Wanta hear another bear story?" he said. He shook his head like he couldn't believe what he was about to tell us. "This new bear friend the two of you found don't like old men," he said. "You almost had to find yourselves a new grandpa." Then he looked at Dad and said, "I guess my huntin' reputation ain't what it used to be, either." At that, he paused and leaned over to take a peek at his pants. "Got a draft," he said. The whole crotch was ripped wide open. "Oh, well," he said. "Warm day, anyway. Gotta quit the tree climbin', I guess."

Then he jerked his thumb in the direction of the hillside. "See where that stump is? That's where I was when I seen the bear. Wasn't but five or ten minutes ago—just before you guys got here. Just an ordinary lookin' bear—probably the same one you kids saw. Hard to tell, though. One bear looks a lot like another. Anyway, it come down outa the trees. Didn't even know I was here—just pokin' 'round up there by where them bushes are, mindin' its own business." He nodded in the direction he meant. Then he took a big breath and said, "Well...I decided to move up for a closer look. I don't know why I done it, but I did. I kept gettin' closer an' closer—just like I told you kids not to do. Never wanta surprise a bear, but it's just what I done. Anyway, when it finally caught wind o' me, I was so close I coulda hit it with a rock. Honest. If I'da had a good rock I coulda winged it up an' nailed him. Well, instead of runnin' off, the ol' boy raised up on his hind legs like King Kong. Now, I won't say I'm any braver'n the next guy, but I don't scare easy. When he raised up like that, though, my ol' spine just melted like solder. Now that it's over I reckon he was probably just standin' up to get a peek at me—wantin' to see what was down there. But let me tell you, when he stood up like that, he looked twenty feet tall, an' the next thing I knew I had my gun pulled up a-shootin'. I'm sure I hit him. Had to. But he didn't even flinch. Just dropped on all fours an' headed down the hill right at me."

Grandpa raised his arms up like he had the gun in his hands and the bear was coming down the hill at him. "I just started blastin' away," he said, and he worked his imaginary lever again and again as he spoke, just like it was happening again. Then he dropped his arms and looked at Dad. "An' then, just when I was thinkin' I was ready to find out what the inside of a bear's belly looked like, the ol' guy flipped an' done a big roll, head over teakettle, right on past me."

"Jesus," Dad muttered.

"Was it dead?" Percy asked.

Grandpa shook his head. "Dang thing jumped right up an' ran off down in that draw over there—down toward the creek." He paused a moment and looked off in the direction where the bear had gone. There was a smudge of pitch on the side of his face. He looked over at us again, sniffed, then spit. "I figured I had me a wounded bear on my hands," he said, "but it took me a while to get up the nerve to go after it. The longer I waited, the further away it was gonna get, though, so I loaded up again an' snuck off after him. My knees was knockin' together so hard I wonder you didn't hear 'em clear back at the ranch. Anyhow, I was almost over there to the edge of the draw where the creek is when I heard the most god-awful noise you've ever heard...an' that done it."

"You ran?" Dad asked.

"Like a bat outa hell," he said. "A bullet couldn'ta caught me. Thought the ol' boy was comin' up outa that draw after me again. Next thing I knew I was up the tree—rifle an' all. God knows how I done it."

"What about the bear?" Dad asked.

Grandpa shrugged. "Never saw hide nor hair of him. Heard a few more sounds, but that's all. Could be dead, or could be he's off in the woods someplace."

"You think you hit him?"

"Oh yeah. Then again, maybe I didn't. The way he flipped comin' down the hill makes me think I did, though. The noises, too. Them was hurtin' sounds."

"I'd better go have a look," Dad said.

"I'll go, too," Grandpa said.

"No... I think you've had enough for one day. Why don't you stay here and keep an eye on the kids?" Then Dad smiled. "Maybe while I'm gone you could show 'em how you climbed that tree with a gun in your hands."

Grandpa gave a little laugh. "Motivation's gone," he said. "Can't do it without the right motivation." He ruffled my hair. "Anyway, it's a trade secret."

Dad pulled a handful of shells from his pocket and put them in his rifle. "You might give me your knife," he said to Grandpa, "Just in case I find him dead an' need to stick him."

We followed Dad to the edge of the draw. The flat, marshy end of Mallard Lake lay off to our right. Below us and to our left, the meadow wound out of the trees along the creek. Dad angled down the slope, jumped the creek, then turned upstream. If he went far enough, he'd eventually hit the bum's camp, but that didn't seem likely. He was moving slowly, squatting down now and then to check for drops of blood or tracks or some other sign. Finally, he turned off into the trees and disappeared.

Now, Grandpa, Percy, and I climbed onto a lava outcropping and sat in the sunshine, watching for Dad to return and straining for any sounds that might signal he had found the bear. From time to time, we'd turn to scan the other directions.

"I shoulda gone with him," Grandpa muttered.

It made me feel bad knowing that I had been the cause of these troubles, and I shuddered to think what might have happened if the bear had hurt or killed Grandpa. A lump grew in my throat then, as I realized that the ordeal was still going on, even at that moment, and that if Dad came on the wounded bear the new ending might not be so happy. I leaned over against Grandpa and he put his arm around me. My eyes grew hot and blurry.

I watched the trees where Dad had disappeared until my eyes crossed, and Grandpa kept checking his watch. "If he ain't back in another couple minutes, I'm goin' after him," Grandpa said. He stood up on the rock and slowly turned like a beacon in all directions. I looked over at Percy. He had a worried look on his face too.

Finally Dad came back out of the woods at about the same spot he'd gone in, and time started moving again. He jumped back across the creek and climbed up in our direction. As he drew close, he said, "I think that ol' bear's gonna live to see another day."

"Lose the trail?" Grandpa asked.

"No," Dad said, "but the blood he's losin' I could put in a thimble. He ain't hurt bad."

As we walked back through the meadow alongside the little creek, Grandpa said, "You know, I can't say I'm sad I didn't kill that ol' booger. I just hope he keeps a-goin' an' don't come back."

"I'd rather it was dead," Dad said, "but I know what you mean."

"Seems to me, bears're gettin' stuck with the short straw these days," Grandpa said. "Just ain't a place for a bear no more. We turn forests into parks, then get all riled up when they raid a garbage can. Someplace else we cut the trees down to dirt an' burn the stumps so's we can put in a farm, an' then we get upset when they eat our prunes. Goes on an' on like that." He looked over at Dad and raised his eyebrows. "If I had to do it to keep these two kids safe, I'd shoot every last bear there was, but down inside I hope they'll come out on top sooner or later. Know what I mean? Gotta happen sometimes, or there ain't gonna be none left. Ain't gonna be nothin' wild—bears, fish, trees, rivers, Indians. I mean, where's it stop?"

We were all quiet for a moment, letting what he had said sink in.

"Amen," Dad finally said.

As we made our way back to the trail, I looked behind me more than once, imagining the bear standing at the edge of the trees with a bloody patch on its fur, watching us leave, and having Grandpa's hopes, but in reverse—hoping that it had shaken us up just enough that we would never come back.

Chapter 11

Jon Pindar announced he was going to grow a moustache. He fished around in the underwear in his drawer and pulled up a baby-food jar half full of a smoky liquid. He sloshed it for us to see. "Makes hair grow," he said. "Rub it on the soles of your feet or anyplace, an' the first thing you know, they'll be hairy as a dog's back. Swear to God."

"Who'd want hair on the soles of their feet?" I said.

"Nobody, dummy. It was just an example."

"Where'd it come from?" Percy asked.

"My dad. He uses it on his head," he said. He opened the bottle and poked a Q-tip in, then held his face close to the mirror and drew it back and forth over his upper lip. "Gotta be careful not to get it on your fingers," he advised. "Get sloppy an' you'll have hairy fingers." He jutted his face close to the mirror again and sucked in on his lip to make the skin stretch while he made another swipe with the Q-tip.

"What kinda moustache you growin'?" Percy asked.

"Fu Manchu—a big, droopy one like the bad Chinamen wear in the movies. Comes down like this," and he slid his thumb and forefinger down around the sides of his mouth.

"I think it's stupid," I said. "Why's a kid want a moustache?"

"A girl wouldn't understand," he said. "Wanta feel?"

I told him I wouldn't touch his face with a ten-foot pole, but Percy did, and he said he couldn't feel anything.

"Feel harder," Jon said.

"This is dumb," I sneered. "If you show up at school next fall with a moustache, the kids'll laugh so hard they won't be able to stand up. Anyway, the stuff don't seem to be doin' much for your dad. He's as bald as a watermelon."

"It works better on kids, stupid," Jon said. "Old people's skin's wore out." He thrust the Q-tip up in my face and sneered, "You start actin' nice to me, puke head, or I'll take you down an' rub this stuff on your eyeballs."

I pushed him back. "Just try. I'll pour the whole thing down your throat and you'll choke on hair."

Jon twisted the lid back on the jar and stuffed it back beneath the underwear. Then he grabbed his big black cowboy hat and mashed it down on his head, saying, "We better get goin' if we're gonna spy on the bum." He dug the pistol he'd found out from under his mattress and slipped it inside his shirt.

"Do you have any bullets for that thing yet?" Percy asked.

"No. Have 'em for the rifle, though, but it's over at the cave with the other stuff. Anyway, we've got more weapons'n the Marines." He rubbed his lip one more time to check for new growth, then led us out the back door.

We circled the north end of the lake. It was summer now, and there were people staying in most of the cabins, with camping gear on the porches and wet clothes hanging from the railings to dry. A cluster of fishermen were anchored off the rock slide, and a sailboat was becalmed up by the dock with its sails hanging like rags. When we came to the Rod and Gun Club cabin, Percy suggested we drop by and see if there was anything new hidden there, but Jon said it wasn't any use. He hadn't found anything there for several days.

"He's probably just stashin' it at his camp now," Percy said.

We followed the trail over the ridge, then cut off through the woods to the cave. At the back of the cave, where we had the stuff stashed, we each dug out what we wanted. Percy got himself the rifle and a handful of shells, and poked one in. "You sure it works?" he asked.

"Shot it myself," Jon said. "Kicks like a mule."

Percy leaned his elbow on the rock at the cave mouth and sighted across the lake. "Pow!" He looked over at me and grinned. "I oughta go shoot that bear that charged Grandpa," he said. "Wouldn't Dad an' Grandpa be surprised?"

"Just keep a bullet for the bum," Jon said. "He's what we gotta worry about now."

Percy raised the rifle again and followed a crow across the sky. "Pow," he whispered.

By the time we left the cave, the three of us were so loaded down with weapons and gadgets we looked like bums ourselves, with all our worldly possessions hoisted on our backs. We skirted the north end of the lake, trying to stay out of sight as much as possible, then turned up the trail to the beaver ponds where the bum was camped. From here on, our progress slowed to a snail's pace as we unfurled our arsenal. Jon was clutching a Swiss army knife opened to the longest blade in one hand and his bulletless pistol in the other. Percy had the rifle, and I had a ballpeen hammer and a hunk of fishnet to throw. When we reached the spot on the trail where it turned down from the ridge toward the ponds, we angled off through the woods and came out above the bum's camp behind the same little cliff where Percy and I had spied on him the first time. I hunted around for my fishing pole and the remains of my fish. They were both gone, but in their place were a lot of left-footed shoeprints pressed in the dust. "He's been here," I whispered.

Percy nodded. "We gotta find another place to spy."

So, we slipped back into the trees, again, and worked our way in a wide semicircle around the bum's camp until we came on a big, blown-down ponderosa pine with its mushroom of roots turned up like a wall.

"Perfect," Percy whispered, and we both nodded.

The spot wasn't more than a hundred yards from the bum's tent, and where the roots had pulled up out of the ground they'd left a crater that made a natural hiding place.

"Looks like a foxhole," Jon whispered.

I gave a thumbs-up.

Peeking around the edges of the roots, we could see the camp, the whole upper end of the beaver pond, the spring where the stream gushed out of the rocks, and a big part of the meadow. There was nothing between us and the bum's tent but a stretch of meadow grass and a couple of old logs.

"I'm gonna make a peephole," I said as quietly as I could. I figured that if I was going to spend time spying, I might as well be comfortable doing it. So I prodded a stick into the soil that clung to the roots until blue sky showed through, then took a peek. It worked like a charm. Seeing my success, the boys dug their own holes.

"Bike's still there," I whispered. It was laying in the grass in the same spot we'd seen it on the first visit.

"The old thief," Percy muttered. "I bet he has your pole down there, too."

Jon pulled a camera from his pocket. "This is evidence," he whispered. He held the camera up to his peep-hole and clicked it, never mind that the evidence he was filming would be nothing more than a dot on the picture at this distance. "Great," he grinned.

"I bet he's got all kinds of stuff down there," Percy whispered. "I bet he's got that whole tent full of stuff he's stole."

"It ain't much of a tent," I said. "Couldn't be too much stuff inside."

The tent was made from a rope strung between a rock and a little tree, with a sheet of black plastic draped over it. The edges seemed to be held down with rocks, or maybe some sticks driven into the ground. The back of the tent was up against a boulder which blocked our view of the inside. The front faced away from us toward the beaver ponds. Near the opening of the tent, but off to the side, was a circle of rocks for a campfire.

Now Jon was using his binoculars. He had one lens up to the hole, peering through the eyepiece the way you'd look through a telescope. "Cripe!" he muttered. "A dog...look...off by the tree."

We all pressed our eyes to our peepholes.

"Looks like a big rat," I whispered.

"I think it's a Chihuahua," Jon whispered. "I bet he stole that too." He had his cowboy hat turned around sideways so he could get his face up to his hole. "Shall I get a picture of the dog?" he whispered to Percy.

"Too far," he answered. "We'll have to get closer."

We spied through our holes for a long time and speculated as to whether or not the bum was in his camp. Jon dug his hole bigger so he could fit both lenses of his binoculars through. Finally he said, "I'm sure he ain't there. We'da seen him if he was. I think we should go down an' look around."

"Don't be silly," I said. "He could be sleepin' in there right now. You don't know."

"It'll be noon in not too long," he whispered. "Who'd sleep this late? I bet he's off stealin' stuff."

"I don't think he's there, either," Percy whispered. "I'll go down with you." He turned to me and said, "You be the lookout. Anyway, Jon an' me can run an' fight better'n you."

"Well, I ain't dumb enough to go down there, anyway," I whispered.

Percy checked to make sure he still had a bullet in his rifle, then told me, "Whistle like a bird if you see him comin'."

"I can't—I can caw like a crow, though."

"Then do that," he whispered.

With his hat still on sideways, Jon Pindar led the way out from behind the roots. The two boys dragged themselves on their bellies with their elbows, like World War II leathernecks closing in on any enemy emplacement. Each time they came to one of the logs, they rolled up against it with their heads together, planning their next move. The nearer they got to the camp, the slower they crawled.

The Chihuahua must have spotted them then, because it let loose barking, and bore at them like it was going to tear them limb from limb. When it hit the end of its rope, it did a nice back-flip.

The boys flattened against the ground.

At almost the same instant, a movement on the trail caught my eye. I jumped over to Jon's peephole and screwed on the binoculars until the blur through the eyepieces crystallized into the image of the bum.

He was already halfway around the beaver pond and moving at a good clip. The boys were hunkered down, but out in plain sight, and the dog was still yapping up a storm.

As planned, I let loose with the best crow caws I had in me. The boys' heads raised together. I could see them looking this way and that, and then I could tell they'd spotted the bum, because in unison they began clawing like gophers across open ground to some bushes. Jon grabbed his hat off his head and squashed it down under him.

By now the bum was across the little stream and circling the last pond. When he reached his camp, he dropped his garbage bag down beside his tent, then went straight to his dog, which was now bouncing around like a rat on a pogo stick at the prospect of some attention from its master. It had forgotten all about Percy and Jon. The bum untied the rope and picked up the dog and held it tight against him, petting it lovingly, while it gave his face a bath with its tongue. He held it there petting it for the longest time, and it occurred to me that the Chihuahua was probably the only friend he had in the world. By the way he cradled it and stroked it, you'd have thought he was holding his own child. I suddenly felt a little sorry for him, and almost ashamed that we were there with guns and knives, spying on him.

Finally the bum carried the dog back to where he'd left his garbage bag beside the tent. Sitting down cross-legged in the grass with the dog curled up in his lap, he dumped the contents of the bag out on the ground. Looking through the binoculars, I watched him examine each item then lay it out beside him. There was a half-eaten candy bar, part of a watermelon, a wiener, a jar of something, a broken fishing reel, a ball of tangled fishing line, and some other scraps of food I couldn't identify. He set the dog down and gave it the wiener and the better part of the food, then took what was left over to a board beside the campfire that served as his table. He then disappeared into the tent.

This was the moment the boys had been waiting for, and they launched themselves up out of the grass toward me. Jon's hat, which he had been carrying, flew out of his hand. He hesitated a split second, as if to go back and get it, but about then the

Chihuahua let loose yipping again, and the bum's feet and legs were reappearing as he backed out of the tent. Jon left the hat lying and lit out sprinting. Just as the bum's head popped up, the boys dived down into the hole beside me.

"Did he see us?" Percy puffed. His eyes were as big as hubcaps.

I pressed to my peephole, ready to turn and run if I didn't like what I saw. But everything looked normal. "I don't think he seen you," I whispered.

"That was close," Percy sighed. "Let's get outa here."

"Can't," Jon said.

"Can't?"

"My hat! It fell off." Jon looked at each of us as though expecting support, but he didn't get any.

"You ain't goin' out there after that stupid hat, are you?" I sneered.

"Course," he said.

"I ain't helpin'," I said.

"Me either," Percy whispered. "I ain't goin' back out there for nothin'. Period. All you're gonna do is get us all in a mess."

Jon didn't answer, but you could tell nothing was going to keep him from getting his cowboy hat back. He crawled back to his peephole and began watching the bum through the binoculars. From time to time he'd look away to rest his eyes, but you could almost see the wheels turning in his head.

The bum had gone over to his board table now. He twisted the lid off the jar he'd brought in his garbage bag and dug his finger in to get the contents out. I couldn't tell what was in it, but it looked like maybe a pickle or some kind of fruit. There wasn't much, whatever it was. Then he ate the piece of candy bar and a bit of watermelon.

"I wonder if that's all he has to eat?" I whispered. "He gave the dog more'n he got."

"He probably eats dogs," Jon whispered back.

When the bum had finished eating, he leaned back against a log with the dog curled in his lap. Little by little his head sagged forward, until his chin rested against his chest and stayed there.

"He's asleep. Now's my chance," Jon whispered. He took his knife in hand again, then looked over to Percy. "If he comes after me, shoot, okay?"

Percy nodded and put the barrel of the gun up to his peep-hole.

"You shoot him and they're apt to throw you in jail," I said. "That ain't a toy gun." I was feeling uneasy about what we were doing. Pretending was one thing, but this was getting too real.

"He's probably a killer," Percy said. "I'd probably get a reward."

"Let's just go home," I whispered to him. "He don't need that hat."

But as I spoke, Jon slipped from behind the roots into the open. He wriggled along the ground with one eye on the hat and the other on the sleeping bum. Coming to a log, he rolled up against it, then looked back at us, with his arms up in the shooting position to remind Percy what was expected of him. Percy stiffened and pressed the rifle tighter to his shoulder. He squinted his eye.

Then Jon rolled over the top of the log and began inching forward again. He moved one arm and one leg at a time, and very slowly. When he finally reached his hat, he lifted it overhead in a signal of conquest, then cast one more glance at the bum and started back.

Then, disaster!

Out of the blue, the little dog we'd thought was asleep on the bum's lap sprang to the ground, yipping stiff-legged like a windup toy. The bum's head jerked up.

All heck broke loose. Jon was up and running like a bat, with his hat flailing in his hand.

Then, from beside me a shot burst out!

Percy rolled back on the ground with the rifle on top of him. As Jon came streaking past, he screamed, "Run!"

And did we ever!

It was like another rerun of the same old movie. We were crashing through brush, stumbling in holes, leaping logs, and getting bludgeoned with limbs, all over again. The rifle was slowing Percy down, so I wasn't getting left in the dust this time, but Jon was up ahead, covering ground like he'd never done before or since. When we finally came to the trail, we kept right on running, down to Mallard Lake, around past the bear meadows, on across Mallard Creek, and we didn't stop until the three of us flopped down behind the rocks at the mouth of our cave hideout. We sounded like locomotives puffing, and nobody said anything or even looked at anybody else until Jon said to Percy, "Did you shoot him?"

Percy didn't answer at first. You could have cut the silence with a dull knife. Then he said,"I don't know...I just shot."

That was all that was said about it, but there was a pall hanging over us so thick you could almost see it. Jon beat his hat back into shape and pulled it down on his head. We put the stuff back in its hiding place, and without making any plans or even saying goodbye, we split up and headed home.

That night, Percy was quiet at the supper table and hardly touched his food. Mom tried to take his temperature, but he said he was just tired. After the meal he said he was going up to the barn loft to read, and didn't want to be bothered. I said I was going down by the creek to play. But when I was out of sight of the house I set off at a slow jog toward the bum's camp. I had no idea what I'd find there, but I had to know. I cut off the trail at the top of the ridge, again, and came out of the woods at the spying place behind the upturned tree roots. For a moment I stood there, feeling my pulse pound in my temples. Then I put my eye to the hole.

The bum was in the same spot he'd been when Percy had fired his shot, and he was as still as a rock.

"He's dead," I thought.

My head swam. I felt like throwing up.

But then, as I watched, he moved. He stood and stretched and looked up into the sky to gaze at a heron as it flapped over the meadow. I felt my eyes grow hot, and I realized I was crying.

Then I was aware of somebody else with me. It was Percy. He looked at me expressionlessly.

"He's alive," I whispered.

He wilted. We hugged and cried.

For the first time, we made our way home from the bum's camp without running.

Chapter 12

As the days passed, I found myself drawn to our hiding place behind the tree roots to spy on the bum. Sometimes I went with Percy and Jon, but more often than not I trumped up some excuse and sneaked off by myself. I was always filled with fear on these visits, especially when I went alone, but I was pulled there as if by a magnet. As I spent more time watching him through my peephole, I lost some of my fear. And seeing the way he lived— his poverty, his simple wants, and the way he skimped along at the edge of survival—strong feelings grew in me, the kind you might have for a runt pig or chicken that is useless and defective and yet blessed with some sort of redeeming quality.

Some days when the bum emptied his garbage sack into the grass beside his tent, nothing to eat fell out. On those days, as far as I could tell, he went without food. On other days, even the best of them, his meals were smaller than anyone should have had to survive on, and he always shared them with his dog before he took a bite himself. When I could get out of the house with a bit of food in my pocket or wrapped up in a napkin, I'd bring it and leave it on a rock beside the trail at the edge of the meadow where he would see it. The first few times I did this, he passed it by. But then one day I returned after leaving food, and it was gone. After that, everything I left was taken. As time passed, I left other things for him. I left an old blanket one day, a fishing net another, an old pan I had used for playing house. I often saw him using these things. One night I told Percy.

"He's an old thief," he said. "Course he'd take stuff if you left it by the trail. He'd take it outa our house, too. And what's more, he'd probably knock us in the head to do it."

"You just think that," I argued. "All I've ever seen him with is stuff from garbage cans. That ain't stealin'. It's just usin' what other people don't want."

"Don't be dumb," he said. "What about them things we've been findin' at the Rod an' Gun Club cabin? He didn't find them in garbage cans."

"We don't know he stole that stuff," I argued. "We don't know nothin' for sure. Maybe he's just a hungry ol' guy, an' maybe that stuff we been findin's been hid there by somebody else?"

The next week, Dad came back from a trip to the Russ Lake Lodge with news that a couple of cabins along the north shore had been robbed, and that in one of them a weapon had been taken. Then, sure enough, a day or so after that, Jon Pindar met us at the cave with a gun he said he'd watched the bum hide under a log over by Mallard Lake.

"I bet he's got weapons hid all over," Jon said. "I bet we ain't found half of 'em."

Jon seemed fascinated by weapons. Both he and Percy were certain they were dealing with a dangerous criminal, and Jon continued to bring weapons with him when we spied. Percy was as engrossed in the detective part of it as Jon, and he talked incessantly about getting evidence and earning rewards, but he never again took a weapon. I was glad of that, and I told him so. Playing Indians, dropping down out of trees on one another, slinking through the woods on make-believe chases, even spying on the bum from our hiding place were all pretty innocent fun. But almost putting a bullet through someone was a whole different matter.

For days after Percy's shot, I was troubled by the thought of dying. For the first time in my life, I understood that what had almost happened to the bum would sooner or later happen to all of us—that we would all die. One night, with a weak light shining through the window from Grandpa's bus outside, I lay, unable to sleep. I could make out Percy's shape in his bed across the room, and I felt the need to talk. I said his name in a loud whisper, but he didn't answer. I lay quiet for a while, trying to decide if he was awake or not, then said his name again.

"Be quiet." His voice didn't sound friendly.

"What do you think about when you're tryin' to go to sleep?" I asked.

"Geeze, Susie."

"Percy. What would you have done if you'd shot the bum?"

He pulled his arms under the covers and rolled over away from me.

"I'm glad you missed," I said, talking as much to myself as to him.

We lay there, silent for a while. I could hear the faint sound of my parents' and Grandpa's voices out in the motor home, but they sounded like night sounds, like the croaking of frogs or hooting of owls, and I couldn't make out the words they were saying.

"Do you ever think about dyin'?" I asked. "I don't mean dyin' like in stories and stuff. The real kind."

Percy was lying on his back again, and his shape was silhouetted against the wall. Staring at the ceiling and speaking in a voice that was suddenly friendlier, he said, "You gettin' afraid of dyin'? I swear, Susie, that ain't somethin' for a kid to worry about. You get to be a hundred or so, then you start worryin' 'bout that. Anyway, dyin's nothin'. When you die you go to heaven an' just go on livin' there...an' it's even better'n livin' here."

"Jon Pindar says heaven's just a trick grownups play on kids to make 'em be good—like the Easter Bunny an' the Tooth Fairy an' stuff," I countered.

"Jon Pindar don't know half as much as he thinks he does," Percy said. "Grownups might of made up the Tooth Fairy an' those things, but everybody knows God's real."

"Jon Pindar says grownups made up God too," I replied.

"Who you gonna believe, me or Jon Pindar? Anyway, don't be afraid," he said.

"I been tryin'," I said. "But it's gettin' harder—especially in bed. It was easy before I got big. I used to just lay here, an' think about all sorts of fun things...and then the first thing I'd know, I'd be asleep. When I was real little, I'd think about my dolls—like they was real, you know? They'd do stuff with me...like real people. After that, when I was just a little bigger, I started thinkin' about brave stuff—fightin' an' stuff like that. I'd think about stories that'd go on night after night, and I could hardly wait to go to bed. But gosh, Percy, now I can't make it happen no more. I try to think about those good things like I used to, but the first thing I know, I'm thinkin' about dyin'."

"Just don't do it. Make yourself," he said.

"I can't. That's what I mean."

"Sure you can," he muttered. "Just make your mind do what you want. Close your eyes an' see it."

"I just can't any more," I said. "Percy..."

"Yeah."

"You know—some day we're all gonna die...Dad an' Grandpa an' Mom...even you an' me. We won't be here no more."

"Yeah...I know," he said. He rolled back over on his other side again.

"You afraid?" I asked.

He didn't answer.

We didn't talk any more. I lay there a long time, even after the lights had gone out in the bus and Mom and Dad had come into their own beds. I couldn't see Percy any more, but I could hear his breathing get regular and long as he fell asleep.

From time to time, though, the sound of his breathing would fade away and I could not hear it, and the silence would be as loud as the loudest sound. I'd strain as hard as I could and wait and wait until I was sure he would never breathe again. I'd raise up on my elbows, groping for the sound. Then I'd hear him, and with my heart pounding so hard in my ears it seemed it would make me deaf, I'd drop back down on my mattress, wondering what death would feel like and if it would hurt. I felt hollow right down to my toes.

One day not long after that, Grandpa and I went down to the mouth of Mallard Creek to fish. Salmon were moving up the creek to spawn, and as usual they were drawing a lot of big trout in behind them. The trout were feeding on the salmon eggs. The salmon were too old and beat up by the time they'd come this far inland from the Pacific to be worth catching, but the trout were good sport and made good eating.

We walked along the trail beside the creek, looking down at the fish. The stream flowed over clean, gray gravel and the salmon, spawning in the gravel, lay in pairs in the places where the current was right. The water made slow swirls behind windfalls and rocks. Off in the pines along the ridge to our right we could hear our dog Rocky barking.

"We shoulda tied him up at home like we usually do. All he does is cause trouble," I said.

"Hope he ain't found a porcupine," Grandpa said.

"He's always findin' porcupines," I said. "He thinks he's a pincushion."

The trail led off into the woods for a short ways and the stream dropped down out of the meadow through a little canyon. The sun shone through the trees in patches. In some of the patches columns of insects buzzed. Rocky's barks continued, high-pitched and coming in volleys.

"It's no porcupine," Grandpa said, "less'n it's wearin' track shoes."

We stopped and listened to try to figure out what was going on. "Maybe he's got a bear," I said.

"Let's hope not," Grandpa smiled. "I don't feel like doin' no tree climbin' today."

The trail angled down toward the creek again and crossed it on a log bridge near the head of the lake. The upper end of the lake was marshy and more a jumble of shallow ponds and channels than an actual lake. The last stretch of the stream between the bridge and the lake was where we always had our best luck fishing. We had a log raft hidden along the shore to fish from.

We walked out onto the bridge. Rocky's barking was coming from nearer now, from upstream.

"We'll soon know," Grandpa said. "Whatever he's got's comin' this way."

Around the corner, stumbling through the shallow sections of water and swimming in the deeper parts, came a deer. It was a small doe moving desperately, with Rocky yipping at her heels.

"I'll be," Grandpa muttered.

The doe fell, staggered back to her feet and turned back upstream. The two disappeared around the bend.

Grandpa laid his pole against the bridge railing. "Let's go up there," he said.

I laid my pole beside his and followed. When we rounded the bend we found the doe down on her side in the shallows with Rocky holding her by the rear leg, pulling hard. The doe was flopping like a beached fish. Her head thrashed flat against the water. Her mouth gaped open and her eyes were round with fright.

"Good lord," Grandpa said. He stopped for a moment as if not knowing what to do.

I could feel my heart thumping in my chest. I whistled then shouted for Rocky to come, but he held on like his life depended on it.

Grandpa tried to call him off too, but with the same result.

I was used to seeing animals die on the ranch. I had killed fish and gored salamanders with sticks. I had even helped kill chickens and rabbits for the dinner table. It was a normal part of life as I had known it, but this new scene was different. It was morbid and unexpected, and it shocked me.

"Stay back," Grandpa said. He waded out through the shallows and grabbed Rocky by the collar and pulled him off. He strained against Grandpa's grip.

In the water the deer struggled to regain her feet, but she couldn't make it.

"Do we have anything to tie him with?" Grandpa asked, holding Rocky with his two hands.

"I don't know of anything," I said.

He thought for a moment. "Well," he said. "I can't let him loose. I'll tell you what—I'll take him back to the barn an' tie him up. Will you be OK here, or do you wanta go with me?"

"You'll be right back?"

"Yeah. Fast as I can."

"I'll stay here," I said.

"Stay away from that deer, now," he warned. "If she catches you with them hooves it'll be the end of you."

Half dragging him, Grandpa pulled Rocky up through the trees to the trail, then back toward the ranch. I sat down on a log. The deer lay in a half foot of water and her eyes were the most frightened things I had ever seen. Her white tongue lolled in her open mouth, and I could see her sharp bones through her wet hair. Twice she tried to get to her feet, but both times she fell again. On the third attempt she made it up and stood spraddle-legged with her muscles quivering. She stood that way until Grandpa returned.

"It's hurt, isn't it," I said.

"I don't think so," he answered. "She looks sick to me. At least I don't see no blood. Do you?"

"No."

"Skinny as a rail," he said. "Looks like she ain't been eatin' for a while."

"Poor thing," I said.

The doe stood hunched. Grandpa walked to the bank and waved his arms, but she didn't move. He waved his arms again. The deer's head nodded on her neck like a ripe head of grass on a thin stalk, heavy with rain. She tried to shake it but lost her balance, falling down again.

I looked away. "Can't we do somethin'?" I asked.

Grandpa shook his head. "Hard to tell what's wrong, Susie. Rocky wouldn't've had a chance to catch her if she was all right. I could shoot her an' put her out of her misery, but we don't know that she won't be OK. It's a tough ol' world here in the woods. Mother Nature's got a hard heart."

"Couldn't we tie her up an' carry her back to the barn an' call a vet the way we do for our animals?" I asked.

Grandpa shook his head again. "We've done 'bout all we can. At least Rocky won't bother her now."

"She won't die, will she?" I asked.

"Hard to tell," he said.

We stood there for a while. Several times we tried to scare the doe to her feet again, but she couldn't make it. Finally, Grandpa suggested that if we went away she might do better, so we left.

At the log bridge we got our rods and stood looking down into the water. Salmon were moving up—old, dark-skinned spawners that slid from the cover of one rock to another, avoiding the current. When they crossed the shallow places, their dorsal fins broke the surface.

"Tough lookin' ol' critters, ain't they," Grandpa said.

"They remind me of that deer," I said. "They look like they've been in a fight."

Grandpa spit down into the water. "Don't know that they ain't," he said. "They've probably fought more fights in the last month than you or me have all our lives. All the way from the ocean to here's a long way to swim on an empty stomach."

The sound of the water coming over the rocks filled the air. I looked up toward the bend, thinking how good it would be to see the deer standing there, well and strong, and maybe with a fawn beside her. There was nothing there, though. I looked over at Grandpa and saw the wear of his own life on his face and on his hands and in his bent stance. I looked back at the water.

"These salmon're sure somethin'," Grandpa said, leaning his elbows on the rail. "They don't do nothin' we don't do, I guess, but they do it in such an impressive way. You know? Kind of inspiring. I've seen a lotta salmon runs in seventy years. Seen some runs so big you'd wonder how the water'd hold 'em all, but it still chokes me up just like the first time. Maybe a little more. When you get as old as I am, you start seeing yourself in the darn things."

"I wish nothin' ever died," I said.

"That'd be nice," he said. "But I'm afraid it wouldn't work. Dyin's one of Mother Nature's miracles, Susie. It's like the days. One day ends so's another one can start. Last thing this world needs is a mess of sick, ol' critters hangin' 'round forever—sick deer, spawned-out salmon, worn out ol' men...dyin's Nature's way of makin' room for her younguns."

I was holding on to the railing. He reached over and hooked his arm around my shoulders and gave me a hug.

"You ever thought what'd happen if fish an' deer an' birds an' people an' all the rest kept havin' kids like they do, but nothin' ever died?"

"Be crowded," I said.

"Be more'n crowded. We'd be standin' on each other's heads, an' I'll tell you somethin' else. We'd have one heck of a time findin' a bite to eat." He rubbed his stubble beard and ran his tongue around his lips. "Wanta know what dyin' really is?" he asked.

I nodded.

"Dyin's love, Susie."

"No it ain't," I objected.

"Sure is," he argued. "Take these salmon. What ol' mom an' dad salmon're doin' when they die's this: they're steppin' aside and givin' all their babies a place here on earth so's they'll have room to swim 'round an' food to eat. Oh, they don't know they're doin' it, but they are, because when it comes right down to it, love's somethin' you just can't help. They're sayin', 'Babies, I love you so much I'm gonna give you everything I got—the air I breathe, the water I swim in, the food I eat...everything'."

I looked up at him but didn't know what to say.

"This dyin' business's kinda hard on the ol' noggin when you're just a girl, ain't it?" he said.

A brown leaf turned on the current and floated across the pool below the cascade. It drifted over an old, nearly spent salmon that lay in quiet water near the shore. A puff of current shifted the fish over onto its side. It righted itself again, but its fins were unmoving. It opened and closed its gills ever so slightly.

"Does it hurt to die?" I asked.

"Oh...I don't think so," he said. "Livin's the hard part, Susie. Oh, it might hurt a little for a moment, but I can't really say. Never died before." He chuckled. "Remember when you got your tonsils out?" He looked at me to see me nod. "I figure that's how dyin' is. The doctor pokes that needle in your arm an' it stings for a moment, but the next thing you know it's all over with an' it didn't hurt at all. You see, when you're dead there ain't no more toothaches or cut fingers or nothin'."

"Do dead things go to heaven?" I asked.

"Some people think so, an' some of 'em don't. Lotta people'll tell you they just don't know. You can make up your mind about that when you get older. I'll tell you one thing, though. As I see it, it's like with these salmon. They don't really die, not as long as they make it up here to spawn.

"You know how plants keep comin' up year after year from the same roots? Strawberries're like that. You see a strawberry plant in the winter an' you'd swear it was deader'n a doornail—all brown an' wilted an' all. But then spring comes around an' these green shoots come up outa the ground an' you realize it wasn't dead at all, but just down there in its roots takin' a little snooze.

"In a few days if you come down here you might see that ol' salmon over there floatin' belly-up, an' you'd swear it was dead. Then you come back a while later an' you see a swarm of little baby salmon comin' up outa the gravel where they hatched, an' then you realize the ol' salmon ain't dead, either. It's just pulled back down into its eggs to take a snooze—same way's the strawberry plant did, an' it's still alive. Ol' dead fish carcass ain't no different than dead leaves. That's true. It's still alive all the time—down there in the gravel in its eggs. An' when the eggs hatch, ol' mama salmon pops right back to life again, but now she's all young an' new."

He was silent a moment. "That make sense to you?" he asked.

"Kind of," I said.

"Well, just remember...when I go belly-up some day, I won't be dead, either, Susie. I'll still be alive in your dad. An' when he's gone some day, we'll both be alive in you. An' some day you'll have kids, and we'll all be alive in them. We're just like that straw-berry plant pushin' up new green leaves, or the salmon gettin' born all over again out of its own eggs. We're all just different chutes growin' out of the same roots. So dyin' ain't really dyin'. Life don't end. It just keeps passin' on an' on. It's how Mother Nature makes old things new and young again. The Indians use to have a nice way of sayin' it. They said everything was round. Sun's round, moon's round, earth, stars—everything's round...even life. So nothin' has a start or finish. Things just keep goin' round an' round, an' when somethin' gets to what looks like the end, it's really the beginnin' all over again."

He patted me on the leg. His big old hand was scarred and wrinkled. He had a black and blue fingernail. "It's somethin' to think about," he said. "Anyway, we got fish to catch."

We took our rods and walked on to the lake, where we found the log raft beached. We pushed and heaved at it until it floated free. We poled up the northern lobe into the slow current where Mallard Creek flowed in. Behind us we left patches of mud torn from the bottom and bleeding brown from our poles. When we came to where we wanted to fish we threw a rope with a rock tied to it over the side to anchor us on the spot.

We fished for a while and caught several trout and lost some more. But my mind was elsewhere. I could see the bridge in the distance, and I could see the falls. I wondered if the deer had gone. And looking behind me in the other direction I could see the open lead of water at the northern end of the lake with the reeds hemming it in. And behind that was the low hill that separated the lake from the meadow and beaver ponds where the bum was probably sorting through the contents of his garbage bag for a meal. I wondered if bums ever had children.

"Can you let me off on shore?" I asked.

"Tired of fishin' already?"

I nodded. Grandpa hoisted up the rock and poled me over to the bank. The grass overhung the water, and I had to stretch to make solid ground.

"Don't go too far away," Grandpa said. "I don't think I'll fish much longer, either."

"I'll be up by the bridge," I answered. I watched him as he poled back out onto the lake and dropped his rock again. His sweat-shirt blossomed out from his pants under his dirty suspenders. I could see the stains under his arms and down his back where he had sweated in his work.

When I came to the bridge, I crossed, then followed the stream up past the little falls and around the bend. I found the doe where we had left her, but now she was standing. Coming up, I startled her. She staggered out into the center of the stream and lost her footing. The current pulled her along. But she swam better than she stood, and she swam toward the other shore. Touching bottom, she struggled up into the shallow water and hunched there with her legs spraddled and wobbling.

I was encouraged by this.

Moving one leg at a time the doe climbed out onto a gravel bar. She fell again...then stood again and fell again. Each time it took her longer to stand. Her head drooped on her neck, heavier than her muscles could support. Then she fell again, but this time, back into the water and on her side. She flailed her legs in the air like a turtle on its back. Then as her energy ran out, her head sank below the surface and her thrashing weakened to pathetic twitches. Once she lifted her head almost out of the water, but she could only hold it there for a moment. It slowly sagged back down until it was submerged again.

My stomach turned over. I splashed out a few steps into the water then stopped.

Bubbles oozed up from the doe's nostrils and mouth to the surface of the water. She struggled weakly, but she was running down, and she no longer tried to lift her head free. Only one tall ear stood above the surface. It slapped against the water the way a referee's hand slaps against the canvas, counting a wrestler out.

I looked away, then back again.

The little doe's legs were straight and twitching ever so lightly now, and her round belly bulged up above the surface with its hair plastered tight against her skin. The ear still flapped limply at the surface, but there were no more bubbles. Then the head sank deeper and the ear, which had been the last symbolic sign of struggle, wilted down into the water, also.

I sat beside the trail until Grandpa came, and we walked back to the ranch together.

Chapter 13

If you'd tried to set your watch by the bum's routine, you'd have had a problem. It was about as predictable as the weather. Most days he took two separate turns through the garbage cans and dumpsters around Russ Lake, but some days just one, and now and then he'd hike on to Big Slide Lake and poke around there too. Even the rounds were hit-and-miss. Many days he'd stop at every can, but on others he'd just visit the ones where he'd been making his best finds. Besides that, evidently depending on his mood and how empty his belly was, he'd sometimes take the time to dig to the bottom of every can, while at others he'd do little more than lift the lids. So spying on the bum as he made his rounds was something you couldn't just do in your spare time. It was a full-time job.

But Jon and Percy were convinced it was worth the effort. They were certain they were on the trail of a thief. It was just a matter of time, and if they followed him around long enough, sooner or later they'd catch him at some terrible act. The trouble was, the theory didn't seen to be panning out. The only thing they'd caught him at so far was digging through garbage, which was sick and vulgar, to our way of thinking, but a long way from being against the law. They finally came to the conclusion that he must be committing his serious thievery and mayhem after dark, when we and the rest of the god-fearing world were asleep. Working on that theory, the two of them spent two whole nights huddled behind the tree roots, ready to follow him off to an evening of crime, but they witnessed nothing more than a lot of pitch blackness and bum snores rolling up to them from dusk to dawn.

I had begun to lose interest in this detective work, in part because it seemed to be going nowhere, but mostly because I was beginning to think the bum was innocent. The more I watched him, the more he looked to be nothing more than a harmless old man scraping along on the rest of the world's throwaways. I felt sorry for him.

Finally the boys decided that the only way they were ever going to get the evidence they wanted was to make a return visit down to the bum's camp. They were sure it was chuck full of stolen goods. Since the fiasco of the first visit, when Percy had nearly committed murder, neither of them was especially eager to try it again. But now, they figured, they didn't have any other choice.

So late one afternoon the three of us hid behind the tree roots and waited for the bum to leave on his rounds. Needless to say, I was in a negative mood. As we watched him shuffle out of sight, I whispered, "This is the stupidest thing in the world. What if he comes back too soon an' catches us down there? Anyway, that dog's gonna yap the whole time."

"You ain't goin' down, anyway," Jon said, letting his voice raise now that the bum was out of hearing range. "Me an' Percy'll do that. You're the lookout. You just take the rifle up on top of the hill an' watch the trail."

"I ain't takin' no gun," I objected.

"You're gonna have to unless you have a better way," Jon said. "It's the plan." He lifted up two fingers in front of his face, as though he was putting a cigarette to his lips, then turned his fingers aside and blew out like he was blowing a big puff of smoke in my face.

"I ain't takin' no gun," I said. "An' that's that. You shouldn't be bringin' the dumb thing along, anyway. Somebody's gonna get hurt. We ain't real police. We're just kids."

I was putting up a pretty good stink, but stinks were something Jon was an expert at. The next thing I knew he'd shoved the rifle into my hands and told me to either get up there and use it the way I was supposed to, or get it used on me, and that was that. I went.

The top of a hill in the middle of the prettiest place on earth is a good place to burn off a pout. The weather was perfect, the view was spectacular, and gun or no gun, it wasn't long before I'd pouted myself out and started almost enjoying being lookout. Trouble was, a half hour or so into it, I was still there, and boredom was setting in. It was then that the hole in Jon's plan came clear. He'd told me where to go and what to do, but not how long to stay. And he'd said nothing at all about how or where I was supposed to rejoin them. I loaded a shell into the rifle in case I needed to signal, then sang "Ninety-nine Bottles of Beer on the Wall" through twice from start to finish—once the right way and again, substituting "glue" for "beer" and changing the words to "drank one down and stuck to the ground."

About then, I decided that bum or no bum, I'd been on lookout long enough. So I hoisted the gun up and headed down the trail toward the bum's camp.

I hadn't gone but partway down the hill when I met the boys coming up toward me. Percy was pushing his bicycle, flat tire and all, and puffing up a storm.

"Why ain't you up there lookin' out?" Jon demanded.

I didn't like the way he said it. "I stayed as long as I thought I was supposed to," I gritted.

Jon kicked the dirt.

"Great," Percy said. "What if we meet him on the trail, now. If he catches me with this bike it's hard to tell what he'll do."

"Yeah, I know," Jon said. "Some people can't do nothin' right...Susie-losie."

"Nobody told me how long to stay, Jon-Bon-Ton-Brain-Gone. Your dumb plans are always messed up, anyway, so don't blame me."

We traded a few more rounds of insults, then Percy said, "Let's get outa here before he comes," and we did.

Percy immediately began dropping behind with his bike.

"You oughta just push that thing in the bushes an' forget it," I said. "It's no good anyhow."

At that moment, a flash of color that was Jon Pindar in full flight came streaking back around the curve toward us. As he shot past us, he puffed out, "The bum's comin'!" The two of us spun in behind him like two dogs on a leash—me a step behind, and Percy with his bike in the rear. At the meadow we kept going, right on past the ponds and bum's camp and yapping dog and our spying place, and on down into a ravine where the stream poured over the main beaver dam. Jon and I dived down behind cover to catch our breath as Percy came into sight. He splashed through the feeder stream where it gushed out of the rocks, then did a flying mount and pedaled like a madman out across the grass on the bare rim to where we were. He threw the bike down and flopped in beside us. "Where's he at?" he wheezed.

"Comin'," Jon puffed. "He was after me."

"Chasin' you?" My voice was two pitches higher than normal.

"I think so."

At that we were off again, not following the trail any more but sprinting along beside the stream. The going was good at first. The ground was solid, and it was downhill. Percy coasted on his bike when he could.

But then the pitch flattened out and the solid ground turned to muck with skunk cabbage growing in it. In no time flat we were halfway up to our knees in mud, and our feet slurped with every step. It took the three of us pushing and pulling to move Percy's bike along.

"Look at the trail we're leavin'," Jon moaned. "A blind guy could follow us."

"Maybe he won't follow us here," Percy huffed.

"Wanta bet?" Jon said. "Can't we ditch the bike?"

"No way. I pushed it too far to leave it now," Percy said.

To get to firmer ground we waded across the stream. We circled a tongue of trees and brush, then came to another beaver pond. Percy was lagging behind again.

"Geeze!" I said. "We ain't ever gonna get outa here."

"Let's wade across this one," Jon urged. "It don't look deep."

Percy came huffing up again. "I think I seen him," he said. "Back kinda by the beaver dam."

"Close?"

"Pretty."

"Here, you carry the gun so I can help Percy," Jon said. He thrust it over to me. I held it up to keep it dry and pushed out across the beaver pool. I hadn't gone but a few steps, though, before I'd sunk up to my waist, and in a couple more I was up to my armpits.

"It's too deep," I groaned. "It's quicksand."

The boys muttered and slogged back to firm ground with the bike hoisted over their heads.

"It's too slow with the bike," I said. "It's way too slow. We gotta run!"

Percy was just opening his mouth to tell me to mind my own business again, when sounds up in the brush whipped our heads around. We froze like statues in freeze tag.

Jon hissed, "Watch out! He might have a gun!"

We dropped like the grass had been pulled out from under us, expecting a bullet to come screaming over our heads. But nothing happened—no bullet, no more sounds, nothing.

Percy finally whispered, "Might just've been a deer or somethin'."

"Yeah," Jon agreed. "Probably wasn't nothin'." But you could tell he didn't believe what he was saying. He leaned over close to Percy and asked, "How far's it on down to Mallard Lake if we keep followin' this creek?"

Percy shook his head.

"It's gettin' dark," I whispered.

"I think we're probably just hearin' things," Percy said.

Jon gave an uneasy nod. "Yeah...probably ain't nothin' but an ol' deer or somethin'. Here, give me the gun back." I slid it over to him, and we crept off around the pond.

We hadn't gone but a short distance when there was movement in the brush where, moments earlier, we had heard the sounds. We dropped, again. From beside me, there was a faint metallic snap as Jon clicked the safety off the rifle. "Got any more shells?" he whispered.

I looked over at him, horrified.

"Don't shoot him. Let's just run."

"Come on. Give 'em to me," he demanded. He held out his palm and jerked his fingers impatiently. I dug down in my pocket and worked the shells out and dropped them in his hand.

Then the bushes started moving like they were alive.

"He's comin' out!" Percy whispered, urgently.

"Run," I said.

"No, wait!" Percy wobbled his hand to keep us where we were. The bushes looked like someone was beating them.

"It's a bear!" I blurted, and a big, brown, scruffy shape came lumbering out into the open.

Jon rolled over onto his back and thumped his hand over his heart. "I was sure it was him."

"We ain't outa this yet," Percy whispered. "Keep real still."

The bear nosed around the edge of the woods, then wandered down the slope toward the creek, stopping now and then to sniff or paw at something.

"It's gettin' too close," Jon breathed.

In the dusky light it waded into a bog full of skunk cabbage, poked around there for a while like it was bored with the whole affair, then plowed across the creek right toward us.

I glanced over at Percy. He looked calm enough, but I knew he was remembering what had happened to Grandpa, and figuring, like me, that being in the same area, it was probably the same bear.

All at once the bear seemed to sense us, and out of the blue it reared up on its hind feet, just the way Grandpa had said. I suppose it was an average-sized bear, but to us it looked straight out of a Paul Bunyan story.

Then I heard Percy blurt, "Wait!" And the next instant a blast tore the air apart and Jon Pindar went flipping over backwards like a pinwheel. He sat up, shaking his head and clutching the rifle.

Percy was on his feet shaking his fist in the air, yelling, "You got him! You got him!"

The shot had knocked the bear over on its back and for a moment it did look dead, but not for long. It struggled back to all fours and stood there wobbling.

"Good lord," Jon gasped. "I just shot his ear off!" He began fumbling with the rifle to eject the spent cartridge. Sure enough, there was a bright blotch of red covering the bear's fur where its ear had been. It shook its head and moaned the most awful sounds I'd ever heard.

Jon groped in his pocket for another shell, but he was having trouble getting one out. All at once the bear rose up on its hind feet again and it let out a pained bellow. That did it for Jon: he turned, vaulted a log, and sprinted off down the creek, trying his best to poke the shell into the gun as he went. I started out after him, but Percy grabbed me by the arm. "Don't run, Susie. Remember what Grandpa said."

The bear dropped to all fours again, then took a short, wobbly sprint toward where we were. That was enough for me. I tore loose from Percy's hold and ran as fast as my legs would move. Percy came too. Up ahead, Jon had finally gotten another shell into the chamber and as he threw the bolt shut he screamed, "He's comin'!"

I spun around as Percy sprinted on past, and coming up the slope behind me, madder than a hornet, was the bear, its one good ear laid back and its other just an ugly smear of blood.

"Run, Susie!" Percy's voice seemed far away.

I tried to move, but my legs wouldn't budge.

Varoom!

I heard Jon's shot, but it was just a sound and it didn't register in my mind. And the bear didn't even flinch.

Then it was like a big dark cloud coming over me. I could hear Jon shouting and Percy shouting, and I could hear myself screaming...but nothing made an impression in my brain.

All at once it was on me, the dark cloud, smothering me, and the world went all out of kilter, spinning so crazily I couldn't tell up from down. It was like I was inside a washing machine. It didn't hurt and I didn't feel scared so much as it was just happening. Then I could hear this crunching sound, and though it still didn't hurt, I knew it was the sound of my own bones breaking. There was a funny tightness in my arm and I knew that must be what was breaking—my arm. But it was as if it was all happening to someone else.

Then I felt the grip loosen on me and there was a dull "thwunk," and another and another. I was vaguely aware that something new was happening. There were new sounds mixed in with the others, but they were cloudy and far away.

"Susie! Susie!" I could hear Percy's voice coming from somewhere.

Then I sensed that something was different. I couldn't hear my bones breaking any longer or feel the weight of the cloud down on me.

"Thwunk!" I heard again.

Then there was a muffled groan somewhere nearby.

"Susie!" Far away....

Again the groaning sound...

Then nothing at all.

Chapter 14

Fuzzy words came to me as if I was dreaming. Voices drifted around me, slipping into and out of focus, but nothing was connected. I thought I might be asleep. I tried to open my eyes and could feel my eyebrows straining against my skin, but my lids were drawn down tight. Then there was a fuzzy light in front of me, without shape, but suspended over me like a star, and the thought occurred to me that I might be dead and about to learn if it was Jon Pindar or Jesus Christ who'd gotten the true word on heaven. I strained harder than before to open my eyes, and I felt my lids flutter.

"She's wakin' up." It was Dad's voice, and it was more a whisper than speaking. I felt someone's face down close to mine.

"Doctor, come over here! She's got her eyes open!" It was Mom's voice.

Now I knew I wasn't dead, and a blurry circle of lamplit faces peered down at me, with a Coleman lantern hissing out white light overhead. The faces were distorted, like reflections on lake water that's being played over by a light breeze, but I recognized them. There was Dad's face and Mom's and Percy's, and some others I couldn't place.

"Gonna be all right," Mom whispered. She kissed me. I could feel her rubbing my arm.

I closed my eyes hard, then opened them again to clear my head. Dad was bent over me, holding something against my scalp.

"What happened?" I asked.

In a gentle voice he said, "You been in a rasslin' match with a bear, sweetie. Gonna be all right."

It was then that the recollection of what had happened began returning to me, and I understood that I'd not only been in a tussle with a bear, I'd lost it. I tried to lift my right arm. Hot pain flushed through it. I closed my eyes again, hard, and clenched my teeth. I cried out for Mom.

"It's OK, sweetie." Mom stroked her hand over my face and down across my cheek. I started to cry. But then I got hold of myself and gritted my teeth again. "My arm hurts, Mom."

"It's busted, honey," Dad said.

Then other hurts came out of hiding from all over my body. For a moment they came together in my stomach and I thought I was going to get sick. I kept my eyes shut until the feeling went away. Reaching up with my good hand, I touched my hair. It was wet and sticky. Mom caught my hand and eased it down. "Just a little scratch, sweetie," she said.

"How you doin', Susie?" Percy's face appeared against the light above me. His voice was so tender that at first I thought it belonged to someone else. I looked at him but couldn't rouse a response. Then he moved back, and Doctor Brown's face took the place of Percy's. He had a kindly, impartial look, and without saying anything he reached down into his bag. He pulled out a tiny light and held it in front of me, saying, "Follow this with your eyes, Susie."

I followed it from side to side as he moved it. He nodded then put the light away. "Can you feel this?" He was doing something to my toes then, and I told him I could feel it. He smoothed the blanket back over me again, then asked how I felt. I told him I was kind of hungry.

He laughed at that and said I must be getting well already. Then he said, "You're going to need to get yourself a left-handed fork to eat with for a few weeks. Do you have one? Or a left-handed spoon?"

I turned my eyes toward Mom for help with an answer, still not thinking straight or understanding that it was just a joke and that he didn't expect one.

"Tell him you can just turn one of our right-handed ones upside down," she said. She was laughing, but her lips were quivering and she had tears coming down her cheeks.

I looked back at Doctor Brown and he was smiling, too, and he rubbed the bridge of his nose between his thumb and finger. "I don't know why I never thought of that," he said. "Here all these years I've been havin' all these people buy left or right-handed spoons and forks and pencils and things when they didn't need to." He winked at me. "Anyway, some people have all the luck. I'm almost sixty years old and I've never had a cast yet, and here you are, just eight, and you're already gonna get one."

"I'm nine," I corrected him. I looked down at my arm. It was hurting a lot more now as my head cleared, with the pain coming in pulses each time my heart beat. It was splinted with some sticks and tied up like a birthday present. The bandages were soaked red in one place.

"You just lay real still now, Susie," Doctor Brown said.

"How's the guy?" Mom asked the doctor.

"Real beat up," he answered. His face left the circle of light above me, then returned. Looking down at me he asked, "Who's your friend?"

I didn't know what he meant and didn't feel much like talking.

"He's just an old bum who's been around," Mom said.

As if a veil had been pulled back by her words, my mind suddenly cleared and I knew what had happened. "The bum...." I struggled up to a sitting position. It hurt so much tears came to my eyes again, but this time I didn't fight them back.

"No, Susie." Dad made a weak attempt to lay me down again, then supported me.

"Better stay laying down," Doctor Brown said. But I stayed upright.

Not far away, out across the meadow grass, another lantern lit the darkness. Several shapes were bent down over a covered form laying on the ground.

"It was the bum, Dad," I said, looking at him. "He saved me."

Dad nodded and smiled weakly. I tried to stand up but couldn't make it by myself.

"Don't get up. It'll be better if you stay down," Dad said. But I tried to get to my feet again, and this time I felt him lifting. I was wobbly, but with Dad holding me around the waist, I was standing. I supported my bad arm with my good one. The blanket I had been covered with fell in a heap at my feet. Mom put it over my shoulders. One leg of my pants was ripped from the thigh down and hung open. With Dad's help I slowly made my way to where the bum was lying. The men who were working over him moved back to let me in.

The only part of the bum's body not covered by the blanket was his head. His face was as pale as milk under the light. His mouth was a tight-pressed line on his face as he fought the pain. He had swollen eyes, but they were open, and a long cut down his cheek that had been cleaned but left unbandaged was seeping a thin line of blood that disappeared in his tangled hair. He was looking straight up into the night sky, but as I stood there his eyes moved slowly to me. A weak light came into them. The corners of his mouth bent up ever so slightly, and his lips parted just enough to let out a sound that resembled a groan, but that I knew was his greeting to me.

Grandpa was standing opposite me in the full light of the lantern. "I guess you two know each other," he said. "Been doin' a little tag-team bear rasslin' together, I understand."

The bum let out a weak, high-pitched squeak that was supposed to be a laugh. He winced, then coughed and fell back expressionless.

A dizzy wave came over me and my legs turned rubbery. I felt Dad's arm tighten around me. "I think that's enough standin'," he said.

A man I didn't recognize moved in and took my other arm and he and Dad lowered me gently to the ground. They adjusted the blanket over me.

"Did you know it was him?" Percy asked.

"I don't think she feels much like talkin' right now, son," Dad said.

Percy looked over at Grandpa and said, "Grandpa, I've never seen nothin' like what he done—never in my whole life. He come runnin' an' jumped on the ol' bear's back an' just started hittin' him with a stick."

Grandpa shook his head admiringly. "You're a pretty brave guy," he said to the bum. "Can't say's I got much admiration for your choice of weapons, but we're all mighty glad you was around." Once more I heard the screechy laugh followed by a bout of coughing.

"A stick's a mighty puny weapon for fightin' a bear," Dad said, looking over at Percy. "What happened after that?"

Percy pulled at his mouth, glanced at the bum again, then said, "Well, I ain't sure of all that happened after that, cause it happened so fast—at first the bear had Susie down. That's when he come runnin' outa the woods from behind us someplace. I didn't see him at first, but he had this big stick an' he jumped right on the bear's back an' started beatin' on him. It looked like he was ridin' a buckin' horse. He had his legs straddlin' its back an' just whippin' an' poundin' to beat the band."

Jon Pindar slipped into the circle of people around me. I could see he had been crying. His face was dirty and there were tear streaks down his cheeks and smeared places around his eyes where he had rubbed them. He smiled at me. I remember thinking to myself how odd it was to see him smile at me, because he had never done that before.

"What'd the bear do when he started beatin' on him with the stick?" Dad asked.

Percy said, "Well, it was kinda like when you see a dog fight. There was a lotta rollin' around an' scufflin', but everything happened so fast I'm not sure what I seen. But I know this—the bear forgot all about Susie. That's for sure. After the bum came an' started ridin' him an' beatin' on him, that was all it cared about. The two of 'em kinda rolled off over here where we are now, but the bum never lost his stick—just kept hittin' at him the whole time. But then the bear swiped him with his paw. Just pulled back an' whomp!—like that." Percy made a long sweep with his arm. "He must've flew twenty feet through the air. When he came down he was like a rag doll. Never moved after that."

Percy looked down at the bum for a moment, then ran his tongue around his lips and turned his head to Grandpa. "Remember when you told us about layin' still when a bear was chewin' on you?"

Grandpa nodded.

"I think that's what happened," Percy said. "Funny how it was, but after the bear swatted him an' he was just layin' there, it seemed to lose interest in him. It really did. Susie was layin' in the grass over there where she was, an' the bum was layin' right here where he is now, an' Jon an' me was still up there by the trees...an' the ol' bear just didn't seem to know what to do anymore. It'd bat the bum around with its paw for a little while—kinda hard, but not real hard. Then it'd walk off a little ways."

"I think its head was hurtin'," Jon Pindar said.

"Yeah," Percy said, "it kept shakin' its head an' pawin' at where Jon'd shot its ear off, an' it was makin' some funny sounds too—really mad ones. Then it came back down to where the bum was an' kinda pawed him around again—just kinda like a cat playin' with a ball of yarn or somethin'. It did that several times— go off a ways an' make these noises, then come back an' poke him around a bit...then go off, then come back. Then it finally just left."

"You're all lucky to be alive," Grandpa said.

The trip back to the ranch and then on to the hospital was the slowest and most painful of my life. They put both the bum and me on stretchers, then carried us back up through the meadow and out past the bum's camp. The first part, where they didn't have a trail to follow, was the toughest. I could hear the guys cussing and the bum moaning behind me on the other stretcher. Finally they hit the trail and things got better, but even then, the guys carrying the stretchers would trade off every little while as they got tired. And each time they did this, the new guys would bounce me around a while until they got themselves in step. When they were rough they made my arm and head hurt so bad I'd cry, and no matter how hard I would try, I couldn't stop. Mom walked close behind me, and each time they paused for even a moment, she would come up and take my hand to comfort me. Several times they held up for longer stops and set us both down, and with their lanterns held low, they would work over the bum, talking quietly among themselves and shaking their heads a lot.

"I don't know," I heard someone say. "It doesn't look good."

And someone else spoke quietly, saying, "It might be for the best, anyway. Ain't much to look forward to, living like he was."

Then there was a raspy old cough.

Chapter 15

Dad inched the old truck down the rutty driveway the way you'd make your way through a minefield. I had my swollen arm cushioned on a pillow in my lap, and there was a red splotch on the side of my cast where blood had soaked through the plaster. Dad kept looking over to me, reading my face to make sure he wasn't bouncing me too much.

"Danged ol' road," he muttered.

"Hurt?" Grandpa asked.

"Not too much," I said.

The windows were open, and I sucked in the scent of pine trees and dust and thought to myself how good it smelled after the sterile hospital odors. We were packed in the seat elbow to elbow, and as the truck bumped along we bobbed like weeds in a wind. We wove our way out of the woods and across the pasture with cattle grazing on both sides of us. Some of them lifted their heads as we passed.

Dad parked beside the new house. I had only been gone to the hospital a few days, but in that time he and Grandpa had gotten a good part of the foundation done. The mortar between the rocks was a wet-looking dark gray color, and the rock pile had melted to half its size.

"Starting to look like something now, isn't it?" Mom said.

"We'll be movin' in tomorrow," Grandpa grinned.

Mom rolled her eyes and shook her head. "Dreamer," she said.

"We're gonna call it Susie's General Hospital," Grandpa said. "Got a wing for people with liver problems an' one for ladies havin' babies an' one for girls with broken arms. The broken arm wing won't be done for a couple o' days, but you can just stay with the ladies havin' babies till then."

Dad leaned forward as he twisted the door handle. "The broken arm wing takes a little longer to build," he said. "Takes an extra day just to put in the swimmin' pool an' skatin' rink."

"An' ice cream shop," Grandpa added.

Dad and Grandpa climbed out the driver's door. I sat for a moment letting my eyes gaze over the scene. It seemed like I had been away for a hundred years. The cement mixer sat beside what was left of the sand and gravel piles with its drum tipped down to drain. The hole where the septic tank would be buried was dug and walled in by big mounds of dirt they'd thrown out as they shoveled. Not far away, the guys who were milling our lumber were setting up their portable sawmill next to a small mountain of logs Dad and Grandpa had drug up. The pile was twice as tall as a man, and there were more logs waiting back in the woods to be brought down.

Dad had hardly touched the ground when one of the mill guys hailed him over. By the way they kept shaking their heads, it looked like he was telling Dad some bad news. They were looking at a piece of red paper that was tacked to one of the trees.

Mom gave me a hand down out of the truck. "What do you suppose it is?" she asked Grandpa.

He shook his head. "Hard to tell, but I think I smell red tape," he said. "Only guys'd be out here nailin' notes to trees'd be them bureaucrats from the state or someplace."

"What're bureaucrats?" Percy asked. He was peering down between the rail slats in the back of the truck where he'd been riding.

"You don't wanta know," Grandpa groused. "They're guys that sit around shufflin' papers all day makin' life miserable for hard-workin' people like us."

"Don't be an old grouch, now," Mom said. She shut the truck door. When it didn't latch, she drew it back and banged it twice as hard. "Your grandpa's just in a negative mood, Susie. He gets this way when he wears his itchy underwear." She wrinkled her nose at him.

Grandpa poked his hand down in the side of his bib overalls to tuck in his shirt that had worked its way out, but when he withdrew his hand there was more tail hanging out than when he'd started. "Hasn't got nothin' to do with itchy underwear or bad moods," he said. "It's just the truth. I don't like bureaucrats. An' I don't know nobody that does."

Mom had me sit down on the running board and gently slipped a sling under my cast. She passed it around behind my neck and tied it.

"I don't like bureaucrats, either, Grandpa," I said.

"Good girl, Susie," Grandpa said. He twisted his arm around behind his head to scratch his back up above his shoulder blades. "Them guys is worse'n snakes. Fact I'd rather get bit by a rattlesnake. Leastwise a rattler'll give you a buzz afore he lays his fangs in you. An' a rattler ain't gonna bother nothin' less'n it's botherin' him. But them guys that work down there in them government offices make a livin' goin' around bitin' people. Don't matter who you are." He swung his other arm around and dug at the other side of his back. "When they start nailin' stuff to your trees, trouble's a-comin'."

It was bad news. The red notice on the tree was from the building inspector telling us to stop working on the house until we had a building permit. Dad was fit to be tied. He didn't lose his temper often, but this time he was so mad his face turned the color of a ripe apple. "There's been three houses built on this place in the last hundred years," he fumed, "and they ain't one of 'em's had a permit. Guy'll need a permit to blow his nose next thing you know." He swatted at a fly buzzing his head but missed. It landed on his arm and he took another swing but missed again.

"They just want your money, son," Grandpa said. "That's all they're after. One of 'em says, 'Hey, I need me money for a new TV!' So they get their heads together an' come up with some new rule so's they can charge you or me a hundred bucks to make sure we don't break it. Trouble is, people're afraid of 'em. Ol' mister bureaucrat holds up a hoop an' everybody jumps through. That's the problem. Everybody jumpin' an' nobody sayin', 'Hey, wait a minute, here.'"

"Long as they've got people bluffed, they'll get away with it," Dad said. "Thing is, there ain't nothin' to be afraid of. What can they do to us? So I go ahead an' build my house... What're they gonna do—make me tear it down? Can't. They can send their guys out here and staple notes to every tree I got, but they can't stop me, now, can they? How'd they do it—hide my hammer?" A grin spread across his face, and you could tell he was upset but starting to enjoy this.

"What's a guy got land for if he can't use it?" he said. "Anyway, this is private property. I don't recall givin' 'em permission to come out here an' snoop around. You remember anything like that?" He gave a quick look around at us. "Criminently, these're my trees an' my land, an' it's my sweat. Who do they think they are tellin' me I can't build me a house to keep my head dry without one o' their gol-danged permits?"

Then Dad took the inspector's notice and ripped it into pieces and tossed it down. "I'll get a permit when they come out here an' hold a gun to my head," he said. "An' I'll tell you another thing— they'd better be ready to use that gun."

"Amen," Grandpa said.

Dad ignored the "stop building" notice and went right ahead pounding boards like nothing had happened. There was still some talk about bureaucrats and building inspectors, but not much. As far as they could see, it was the old war of right against wrong, and they, of course, were right. There was more than a house involved. There was a matter of principle, and they were happy as clams to be bucking what looked to them like unfair rules.

With Mom, though, it was different. She didn't say much about the matter (mainly because she knew it wouldn't do any good), but you could tell by the way she acted and the questions she asked that she thought the two of them had "right" and "wrong" turned upside down. She was all for getting a permit.

Dad and Grandpa worked on the house the better part of every day, and Percy and Mom helped where they could. The two millers had their mill going full blast, and the board pile began to look imposing. I was still feeling pretty punk, though, so they found me a shady place close by where I'd be out of the way. I made me a nest on one of Grandpa's lawn chairs. I had to keep my arm elevated or it'd hurt like the devil, and the stitches in my head and leg were still giving me trouble, but on the whole, I was on the mend. I read and dozed and looked at the mountains, and there wouldn't be more than a few minutes pass without somebody coming over to give me a good word. And as the days passed and my wounds started healing, my outlook perked up even more. I can't say I would have chosen being hurt over being well, but it wasn't bad.

When I finally got up and around and began leading some semblance of a normal life, it didn't take me long to figure out that my hard luck had a good side to it. As a starter, I'd become a celebrity. Each time I went over to Russ Lake, Jon and Percy led me around, showing me off to campers or anybody who could be impressed by a little overstated gore. I was like a circus freak. One day we draped some sheets over a wire in front of the lodge to make a booth and charged a fifty-cent admission for people to come in and view me. I was an attraction like the five-legged horse or the one-thousand-pound fat lady at the fair. Percy took the money, Jon related the details to the customers and did the sound effects, while I exposed my scars and injuries. Business was good, but Jon's parents made us quit because the bear story was scaring campers and driving off lodge customers.

Besides fame, another benefit of my condition was sympathy. It was a wonderful situation! Jon and Percy turned almost nice to me. They began by welcoming me home with gifts. Percy gave me the coon tail off his bike and a leather belt he'd outgrown with emeralds and rubies on it. Jon gave me some Indian pictures to keep until I got my cast off, which for Jon was a lot.

The presents were a one-time affair, but the thoughtfulness and sympathy they heaped on me went on for days. It was revolutionary! When we played Indians, they actually let me choose what I wanted to be. If I wanted to be Sitting Bull, they'd say "Sure thing." Whether I wanted to be the good guy or the bad guy, all I had to do was ask. And best of all, when we went off someplace, they stayed right with me instead of running off ahead. I don't know if they were under orders from above or what, but I loved it. They escorted me like suitors, walking my speed, going where I wanted, smelling flowers or chasing butterflies or picking up pine cones or whatever I wanted to dawdle along doing.

My attitude through all this probably wasn't the best. I had a habit of milking a good thing, and this was definitely a good thing. But like they say, you're only queen for a day. I didn't do anything too flagrant, but it wasn't beneath my dignity to give a little whimper or moan now and then when it seemed called for. If it looked like the boys were beginning to forget my condition, I'd just make my voice a little fainter or cradle my cast up against my body and rub it a bit—nothing too dramatic, just subtle little hints of pain and suffering. I couldn't see any harm in it, and it worked.

Chapter 16

That first day in the hospital, the word was that the bum might die. They figured the bear must have given him a karate chop right in the belly, because his insides looked like they'd been crushed. But the next day he was still alive, and the day after that, too. And by the end of a week or so he was not only alive but eating like an elephant.

I was overjoyed.

News of the bum's feat spread fast and he became an instant celebrity. Flowers and cards came in by the dozens, and reporters from as far away as Portland showed up to do stories on him. One TV crew even drove over to do what they called a "human interest" piece. The trouble was, interviewing him in his condition was like talking with a stump. I'm afraid he wasn't a very good subject.

Then there was the oddness about his name. It seems he didn't have one—at least not that anyone could find. He didn't have any I.D. on him, his fingerprints led them nowhere, and all they could get out of him was "Rooster" (or "Wooster," as he said it). So that was the handle they hung on him—what they put on his hospital charts and in the newspaper stories, and what we all called him— Rooster. At first they figured the bear had probably hit him on the head during the fight and given him amnesia. They said it was a common event and not to worry, because his memory would come back. But as time passed, they realized it was less a case of him forgetting, and more one of his never knowing. In short, it became clear as day that he wasn't very smart (to put it mildly), and that "Rooster" was the only name he knew for himself.

During my own stay in the hospital I asked a number of times to see him, but I kept getting the answer, "He's too sick." Finally, on the day I went home, they took me to his room. He was lying flat on his back with tubes stuck in his arm and down his nose. The tubes made gurgling noises, and as he lay there with his eyes closed, pale as a ghost, I could have sworn he was dead. The only signs of life were the small movements of his chest as he breathed and the beeps coming from the contraption beside his bed each time his heart beat. They only let me stay a moment, then led me away.

"He needs rest," Mom said.

As we drove back to the ranch that morning, I remember asking what would happen to him. Mom and Dad shook their heads. They didn't know. I asked who would pay for his doctor bills. They didn't know that either. Then I asked if we could bring him to the ranch and let him live with us. I knew it was a dumb idea, and the two of them shrugged off my question. A week or so later, though, they brought it up at dinnertime.

It wasn't hard to see that Rooster was going to need some time to get back on his feet, and in his condition he sure as heck couldn't live the way he had been. Digging through garbage cans and sleeping under a makeshift tent just wouldn't cut it. What's more, Grandpa had taken a special liking to him. He'd been in to visit him in the hospital a number of times and had gone back to his camp and moved Rooster's few belongings—including his beloved Chihuahua—back to our place. "We owe the guy somethin'," he said. "If it hadn't been for him, Susie here'd most likely be livin' in a bear's belly now."

You could tell Mom agreed, but she was cautious. "We don't know anything about him," she said. "For all we know he could be a murderer hiding from the police."

"There's some things you just know," Grandpa said. "He's harmless. He's got a heart as big as the barn, an' he's about as down an' out as they come."

Mom didn't debate that statement, and by the end of the meal it was decided that when Rooster got out of the hospital we would take him in to stay with us.

By the time they released Rooster from the hospital, I was nearly back to normal. My bruises had faded from deep blue to yellow, my stitches were out, and I had already ruined one cast and was well on my way to destroying a second. Dad had this one held together with duct tape.

We had a little one-room building off to the side of the barn that Grandpa had originally built as a workshop. Since then it had done stints as a toolshed, a sick calf barn, and finally a hideout for Percy and me. We decided it would make a good cabin for Rooster, so we cleared it out, scrubbed it from top to bottom, painted the walls, and hung the windows with curtains. Grandpa even made a few sticks of furniture for it.

"I think it looks nice," Mom said. "I do wish it was bigger, though."

"Don't worry about how big it is," Grandpa said. "Remember, he's probably spent his life sleeping under bridges. This'll be a mansion to him."

Mom smiled and said, "Can you imagine what people would think if they came in and saw how we're living? Here we've got one whole family living in a barn, a grandfather living in a school bus, and now we're putting a bum in a toolshed."

They released Rooster from the hospital on a Monday morning. Grandpa took the truck to town to get him, while the rest of us put the final touches on the cabin. We set flowers on the table, hung a wreath from the door, and on a piece of white cardboard we'd found at the bottom of a grocery box we made him a sign that said, "Welcome home, hero." Percy had found a TV antenna along the highway that had evidently fallen off someone's Winnebago, so he nailed it to the roof, and he laid a red saddle blanket in front of the door for a red carpet.

In the summer you could spot a car coming in the driveway by the plume of dust it sent up. We waited like expectant parents as the plume lifted above the trees, moving steadily toward us.

I was holding a picture I had drawn of Rooster fighting the bear. I'd folded it into an envelope, and on the front I'd written the words "To my FRIEND Rooster." I had "friend" printed in big letters with hearts all around. As the truck ground toward us across the pasture, Grandpa laid on the horn, and he kept it up until he squealed to a stop in front of us. He shut off the engine and climbed out onto the running board, hooking one elbow over the door to hold himself in place, and bellowed, "Hear ye, hear ye! Presenting his royal excellency, King Rooster."

Through the dusty window you could see Rooster's head snapping right and left to take everything in. Grandpa lowered himself to the ground and walked around to open Rooster's door. "Shoulda had a marchin' band," he said.

If I hadn't known that the guy who came out of that cab was the bum, I doubt I would have recognized him. His face was shaved and his hair was combed and cut, and he was wearing new, clean overalls and a red plaid flannel shirt. He reminded me of a kid whose mom had spiffed him up for the first day of school.

It took Rooster a while to climb out. He swung his legs around to the running board one at a time, and Grandpa gave him a hand down to the ground. He stood clutching a paper bag, while everybody circled round like he was a new pet. I stayed close to Mom.

"Welcome," Dad said. "You're lookin' a lot better."

Rooster flapped a nervous hand aside his nose, covering his mouth, and you could tell he was grinning by the wrinkle lines that fanned out across his face. Sounds came out of him that were evidently meant to be words but weren't much more than noises. He looked over at Grandpa, like maybe he needed some help on what to do next.

Grandpa gave his nose a pull and sniffed, and said, "Tells me he wants to go dancin'. Says he's heard there's some good lookin' women out here that kinda like doin' the jig with ol' men." He rubbed his whiskery face and gave me a wink.

Rooster's head whipped back and forth in denial of Grandpa's jibe and again his hand flapped like a broken wing in front of him.

"There'll be plenty of time for dancing with the girls later," Mom said. "Anyway, the only good lookin' women around here are

Susie and me, and we don't dance with anybody unless he drives a Cadillac and has rings on his fingers."

Then Dad said, "Rooster—Susie here's got somethin' for you∆." And he motioned me forward.

Rooster shied away when I gave him my envelope. He didn't open it, he just shoved his hand down to the bottom of his pocket and thrashed it around like there was something alive in there. His fingers finally latched on to what they were after, and he pulled out a little wad of paper swathed in Scotch tape. He curled his hand around it, clutching it up against his body for a moment, then, about as cautiously as a kid reaching to pet a biting dog, he gave it to me. As he did, he mumbled the first honest-to-goodness recognizable words I'd heard him say, "She give me lots," he slurred. His words ran together and sounded a whole lot like what you'd hear from a baby, except in a man's voice.

I worked the paper loose from Rooster's gift. Inside was an old chain necklace I recognized as one I'd left for him on the rock alongside the trail to his camp weeks earlier. Then a light went on in my head. Rooster must have known that all the things he'd been finding beside the trail were from me. That's why he'd fought the bear! Whether he'd forgotten that the necklace had come from me in the first place, I had no idea, but giving it to me was certainly bringing him pleasure.

"I like it," I said. I held it up to my neck.

He slapped his thighs as hard as his injuries allowed, and he screeched the laugh we'd heard before. "Like? Huh? Huh?"

"Yeah, I really like it," I said.

He squirmed like a happy puppy whose master had come home after a long absence. His joy was getting the best of his body. His head wagged like a tail. In fact, his whole body wagged.

Mom took the necklace and fastened it around my neck. I stroked it as though it was made of diamonds.

Rooster was no normal person and likely not even a normal bum. This may be hard-hearted to say, but when brains were passed out he must have been somewhere else. In the history of the world, I doubt there's ever been a kinder, gentler, more faithful and yet duller person. As time passed, the place he filled in our family was more that of a pet than a person. In fact, he became almost like a good dog to us. He ate with us, played with us, relaxed with us and was a part of everything we did, but at our heels rather than our sides.

As Rooster's health perked up, he began to help with some of the easier chores around the place. We were up to our eyes in work as we tried to run the ranch and build the new house at the same time, so Dad especially appreciated another set of hands. The secret of getting work from Rooster lay in knowing what jobs he could understand. There was no such thing as a simple job to him. He had a hard time wrapping his mind around the easiest instructions. But once he did, he'd slave away with so much gusto you'd finally have to call him off, the way you'd have to call your dog off a treed coon. We once had an Irish setter that thought his calling in life was fetching sticks. We named him "Beast." You'd step out the door and Beast would be at your feet with a stick he wanted you to fling, and his tail whipping like a dropped fire hose. And dog heaven was fetching sticks from water. He'd romp after anything you'd throw into a lake or river. Trouble was, his attention span for retrieving was a good sight longer than any human's for throwing. He'd chase sticks till your arm ached, and still sit on his haunches belly-deep in the middle of the stream for you to throw just one more. Rooster was so much like Beast it was scary.

One chore tied to putting up a new house is keeping the place cleaned up. As Dad said, building was half a matter of nailing up and half a matter of carting off. Every board you cut leaves a scrap of wood and a pile of sawdust underfoot. One day early on, Dad figured he'd show Rooster how to pick up these board ends and stack them for use as firewood. This sounds simple enough, but he'd just as well have been trying to teach him quantum physics, because instructions just whistled right through his head.

At first Rooster carried everything away—not just the ends, but whole boards, sheets of plywood, even tools. So Dad showed him again...and again, and again, patiently carrying boards and saws and hammers back from the woodpile to where they'd been in the first place. Finally, though, something struck a spark in

Rooster's head. You could see it in his face and posture and everything about him. He understood! From that moment on, we had the
cleanest building site anywhere. Rooster would stand like old
Beast, waiting for a saw to stop and a chunk of wood to come flying
out, and it'd no more hit the ground than he'd have it run off and
stacked away.

But the most doglike thing about Rooster was his inability to
change old behaviors. Once he learned something, it was chiseled
into his brain. One day Percy pulled me aside. "I got somethin' to
show you," he said, and he towed me around to the back side of the
barn.

Rooster was sitting on an apple box out in front of his door,
holding his little Chihuahua in his lap and trying to stay awake. His
head would slowly settle down toward his chest and his body would
lean to the side until he'd tip so out of balance he'd begin to topple.
Then he'd jerk himself back upright and pry his eyelids half open,
and he'd go through the whole pattern again.

"He's gonna fall off that box," I whispered.

We squatted down and duck-walked until we came up behind
his back window.

"Look in," Percy whispered.

I rose up on my toes, then laughed out loud.

Percy shushed me, and I whispered, "He's got his tent set up
in there."

"That's what I mean," he whispered back. "An' did you see
where he's sleeping' an' where he's got his stuff?"

I peeked in again and, sure enough, there, stretched out under
the black plastic tent, I could see his blanket laid out and his
belongings stacked. The rest of the room was bare. "What'd he do
that for?" I whispered.

"Beats me," Percy answered.

"Suppose he's cold?" I suggested.

"Don't be silly. It's July."

"Let's go get Dad," I said. So we went and got Dad and had
him look through the window. He broke into a silent laugh and
turned back to us with a shrug. "Guess he's afraid the roof'll leak,"
he whispered.

We brought Mom and Grandpa, too, to take a look. Mom just shook her head. Grandpa took a peek, smiled, then turned and whispered, "Reckon he's slept out under the stars so long, an' just ain't used to havin' a real roof over his head. If it pleases him, I guess he might as well pitch his tent anywhere he wants."

The tent never came down the entire time Rooster was with us. When we asked him about it, he gave us his usual empty-eyed, head-bobbing, ratchety laugh, like it was a good joke, but you could tell he didn't understand what we were asking about, and it certainly didn't click in his head that there was anything out of the ordinary about setting your tent up in the middle of your floor. It was as if some primitive part of his mind wouldn't let him do things any other way than the way he always had. He was like a moth that spins its cocoon out of instinct and could no more alter that instinct than spin a hot pad or camel's-hair sweater—except Rooster's cocoon was made of black plastic.

Not long after Rooster put the tent up in his cabin, Percy and I met Jon Pindar down at Mallard Lake. He had an old log raft beached below our cave hideout, and was trying to nail a limb to it to make a mast for a sail, so we could play Huckleberry Finn.

"Huck Finn's raft didn't have a sail," Percy said. "They just pushed it with long poles."

Jon fished down in his pocket for another nail. "I seen a picture," he said. "He did too have a sail—an' a rudder thing on the back they swished back an' forth."

"That ol' stick you're nailin' on won't hold nothin' up," I said. "It'd fall over if you spit on it. Anyway, this ol' raft's half sunk."

Jon went right ahead nailing. When he finally got the stick fastened upright, he wired another one crosswise and hung one of his dad's old white shirts from it. "Looks like a real sail," he said.

"Looks like a clothesline to me," I said.

We beat around in the woods for a while until we each found a long pole, then we took our shoes off, rolled our pants up like Huck and Tom, and started poling down the lake. The raft was so waterlogged it floated like a submarine with the three of us piled on, and Jon's sail didn't help a bit. Percy was Jim, Jon was Huck, and I was still reaping enough benefits from my pain and suffering to be Tom Sawyer. We poled and drifted down through the reedy channels, fighting battles with thieves the whole way. At the deep end of the lake we let the "bad guys" off the hook and took a swim. I was still sporting the remnants of a cast on my arm, so I swam like the Statue of Liberty with her torch aloft.

We were floating with our elbows over the side of the raft, seeing who could spit water geysers highest, when Percy blurted, "Hey, there's Rooster."

Rooster was limping along the trail around the end of the lake. And to our horror, when he came to a garbage can by the boat ramp, he stopped, opened the lid, and spent the next minute or so with his head down in the hole rummaging around.

"I'll be..." Percy muttered.

"Don't you feed him over there?" Jon asked. He laughed out loud.

Rooster made his way from can to can through the whole campground, dropping his finds in his plastic bag. We watched in silence.

Finally Jon said, "Let's follow him and see where he goes."

So we poled ourselves ashore and ducked along behind.

"This is crazy," Percy muttered.

"I think he just has stealin' in his blood," Jon said.

"This ain't stealin'," I objected. "Stealin's when you take stuff that ain't been throwed away."

"Well, it ain't normal. That's for sure," Jon said.

When we came to the main road, we ducked down beside the road bank and watched Rooster turn off onto the trail that led to the boat launch at Russ Lake. He obviously intended to hit the cans there, too.

About then Jon said, "My feet feel like raw meat." He had his leg bent up like a pretzel, picking at his foot. "I ain't goin' no further," he moaned. "Goin' bare-footed mighta been all right for Huck Finn, but my feet're used to shoes."

"Mine too," I said.

We hobbled back through the gravel and pine needles to the raft. When we got there the wind had picked up from the wrong direction. We poled like crazy, but we couldn't make any headway. Finally we beached the raft and walked. By the time we got back to the cave where our shoes were, we were limping badly.

From that time on, we saw Rooster leave his cabin almost every day to make his rounds of the garbage cans at Mallard and Russ lakes. Dad, Mom, and Grandpa all sat him down and talked to him about it, but they didn't make an inch of headway, and he kept right on doing it.

"He's like one o' them bears they got over there raidin' the campgrounds at Yellowstone Park," Dad said. He looked over at Grandpa.

Grandpa nodded.

"Gets in their blood, an' it's next to impossible to get 'em stopped," he said.

"Well, it don't make sense," Grandpa said, "but I guess it's harmless."

The trouble was, it wasn't as harmless as we thought. Not long after we saw Rooster going through those first garbage cans at Mallard Lake, Jon met us at the cave with another .22 pistol and two boxes of shells. He told us he'd seen Rooster hide them under the floor at the Rod and Gun Club cabin that very day.

Percy and I looked at each other like we had just had the wind punched out of us.

"If anybody finds out about this, they'll put him in jail," Jon said.

"We won't tell," Percy said.

As the weeks passed, more stuff began showing up. We just stashed it away in the cave and never said a word about it to anyone.

Chapter 17

O ld Dolly was probably the world's slowest horse. You could kick her or whip her or probably do worse than that to her, but she wouldn't run. If you got her to break into a slow trot for a few steps you were accomplishing a major miracle. I thought it was just because she was so old, but Dad said she was born that way. She was a kind of musty gray-white color, the color of stove ashes, and besides being slow, she was the hardest thing to get your legs around I've ever seen. Her back was so wide and flat that riding her was like doing the splits, especially when your legs were as short as mine.

The morning the Turners started putting up their vacation home on the land we had sold them, Percy and I rode Dolly out to put some letters in the mailbox. We were riding double, with him in front holding the reins and me on the back with my one good arm around his waist. Not far from the meadow at the second gate, Percy reined her to a stop.

"What's that noise?" I asked.

Dolly snorted and slobbered and bobbed her head a time or two, then stood quiet. We listened.

"Sounded like a train," Percy said, "'cept there ain't no trains out here."

There was a sort of rumble with metallic screeches now and then. "Sounds like a tank," I said. "Sounds like a tank in one of them war movies when they're comin' through the fog."

Percy jiggled the reins and I sank my heels into Dolly's ribs. She inched forward again. When we came out of the trees into the meadow, the gate was standing wide open and a big truck was pulled off to the side with a gigantic bulldozer parked out behind it with its engine idling. It was the biggest machine I had ever seen. Its blade was as tall as I was.

"So that's what it was," Percy muttered. He pulled Dolly up again and we sat looking.

"What're they gonna do with that, I wonder?" I said.

The operator stood and unbuckled his belt, hitching his pants. He poured a bit of coffee from his thermos and sipped it down as he surveyed the land with his eyes. Finally he slid the thermos down under his seat, sank down in front of the controls, and revved up the engine. A wave of sound rolled out across the meadow. A flock of crows and a heron squawked up out of the grass and flapped away. Old Dolly, who normally had the temperament of a rock, didn't appreciate the racket either. She reared up, pawing the air like a wild stallion and Percy and I slid straight off her back. By the time we'd untangled ourselves, she was racing off in the direction of the ranch. We found Dolly almost back at the barn. As if nothing had happened, she was chewing grass along the fence-row, switching her tail, with her reins hanging down to the ground.

Later that morning we went back to the meadow, this time on foot, and we watched what was going on. The giant bulldozer rumbled out across the meadow, pushing over everything in its path. It pushed over trees and the old homestead cabin and the cattle pen, and it filled in the low, swampy places by moving the hill. In two days' time the better part of the meadow at the second gate had been dozed so flat you could have skated on it. The grass was gone. The birds and frogs were gone. And the little stream was buried in a culvert.

Then the guy loaded the dozer back on the truck and left, but that afternoon another guy with a backhoe pulled in and dug the drainfield. Then the first guy, the one with the big dozer, came back again, but this time in a big candy-apple-red dump truck with a chrome grill and mud flaps. He spread a load of gravel and went for another. He came and went and came and went, and by the time he was finished he had covered the better part of two acres so smoothly it looked almost like the parking lot at the Safeway store in town. The day after that, with the grading done and the gravel spread and the drain field in and the power company setting power poles along the driveway, the Turners came and tacked their permits to the only tree left standing on the site, then watched a crew from A-1 Affordable Housing tow in a new double-wide mobile home. They jacked it up right in the middle of the graveled area, midway between the drain field and the place where the creek had once run. They propped it up with concrete blocks and fastened imitation wood-grained aluminum skirting to it to cover up the wheels. Finally the power company had the last pole set and the wire strung, and they hooked it up to the electricity...and that was that. The Turners moved in.

Over the next few days a stream of carpenters and installers came. They built decks, put in a hot tub, and threw together a prefab aluminum garage and toolshed. Some guys who looked like college kids came and strung a nice chain-link fence to keep the dogs in. They topped it all off by setting a birdbath, two concrete miniature deer, a flagpole, and a half-dozen rhododendron bushes in the middle of a kidney-shaped expanse of bark dust.

The next Saturday the Turners had the biggest housewarming party you've ever seen. Every person they knew must have been there, and by the noise they made they must all have had a good time. When the wind was right we could hear their music clear over at our place. The next day, Sunday, when the party was over, we listened to them again, this time riding their motorcycles from sunup till sundown—nonstop.

"Gosh dang!" Grandpa groaned. "Don't they ever stop to eat?"

Dad, who hadn't slept all night, told him, "Dad, I have a suspicion we'd better get used to that noise." He gave him a long, tired look. "You ever thought about what they done over there? Makes me depressed. While we were puttin' up two or three stinkin' little stud walls and the upstairs floor, they got a whole house done an' moved in. Criminy."

Grandpa shrugged and said, "We'll just see which one's here fifty years from now. Takes a little longer to do it right, but I wouldn't trade this house for that tin can for nothin'. Be like livin' in a lunch pail."

"Yeah...tortoise and the hare, an' we're the tortoise," Dad muttered. He looked down at Rooster who was sitting cross-legged on a mound of dirt, waiting for the next scrap of wood to drop so he could fetch it to the barn. "Right, Rooster? Tortoise and the hare?"

Rooster nodded eagerly, even though he had no idea what Dad meant.

Then Dad turned back to Grandpa and said, "A house ain't done till it's up an' paid for. When we're finished with this one, at least it'll be ours. But I'll bet ya' a bundle the bank owns that thing o' theirs."

We knew when we sold the Turners their property that the day would come when they'd build something on it, but somehow when that day arrived, we weren't quite ready for it. Part of the problem was the speed at which it had all happened. According to the rhythm we lived by, changes were supposed to take place a little at a time. Grass should start short and grow steadily long. Seasons should come and go at a pace measured over weeks and months. The same with young things growing up and old things getting older. And houses should go up nail by nail. That way your mind has a chance to swallow change by taking it down in smaller doses. But this had been like a snowstorm hitting in July. Bang, out of the blue. One day there was nothing there, and the next there was.

But when it came right down to it, the real problem had less to do with how long the project took than what the result was. To our way of thinking, the Turners' double-wide mobile home didn't fit. It was wrong for the place. In the backs of our minds we'd assumed that when the time came, they'd build some nice little cabin and tuck it back out of sight in the trees at the edge of the meadow. Well, the double-wide was about as far from a cabin as you could get, and there weren't many trees left to tuck anything behind. And the meadow was plain gone.

There was one good thing that came from all this, though. With the power line brought a half-mile closer to our house, electricity was now in our price range.

"Let's get it," Mom urged.

"It's still gonna cost a bundle," Dad said. "It'll mean we'll have to skimp on some other things. Does electricity mean more to you than bay windows and tile on your floors?"

She pinched his cheek. "I'll pretend I didn't hear that question," she said. "I need me two things to be happy in this world." She held up two fingers in front of his face. "I need an inside toilet that flushes when you push the handle, and a light bulb. That's all. Now, you get me those and I'd be happy in a tepee."

So it was settled. We sent the power company the biggest check we'd ever sent anyone, and a few weeks later there was a string of power poles that stretched right up to the barn. It was a big day, and Dad carried Mom over to the temporary service the way a husband would carry his bride over the threshold. And while he held her there, he let her plug in the new electric drill he'd just bought. She squeezed the trigger and it buzzed to life. We all cheered.

"Just think what this means," Mom said. "Radio and television and electric toasters and washing machines and lights you can turn on and off whenever you want."

"And electric bills," Dad said.

Percy said he wanted an electric train, and I said I'd like an electric blanket. Dad said the only thing he was going to need was some sort of electric money-making machine to make the money to buy all those gadgets.

Dad and Grandpa went to town that same day and came back with a big roll of wire and a cardboard box full of receptacles and fixtures. They rigged the barn for electricity. It wasn't code, they said, but who'd ever know?

The next evening, when they finished the wiring, they plugged it in and the first electric lights ever to shine at our ranch popped on. Mom and Dad hugged and all the rest of us (even Rooster) let out a cheer. We ran an extension cord to Grandpa's bus and another to the new house site. Dad bought himself an electric Skil saw and a string of lights so he could work before sunrise and after dark. We ran another extension cord to Rooster's cabin and hung a single bulb down in front of his tent. He liked it so much he never turned it off. He even slept with it on, and any night after that you could look out to Rooster's cabin and see the muted glow of that bulb seeping out through the windows.

Chapter 18

Rooster came to us looking like he'd just stepped out of a soap ad. He was spotless. But he didn't stay spotless long. The clothes he'd fought the bear in were ruined, of course, and since he couldn't be sent out of the hospital naked, the doctors or charity or someone had pitched in and decked him out in a whole new outfit. The trouble was, they didn't give him a second outfit to wear, the result being that for the next month or so his clothes and the skin under them never once came in contact with soap or water. Rooster gradually took on the hue of a plowed field. Mom finally had enough, and she gave the order to either get the dirty clothes off him so she could wash them or she'd wash them with him inside. Grandpa said he didn't want to see that, so shortly afterwards he and Rooster disappeared into Grandpa's bus, and when they came back out, Rooster was wearing a lavender, flowered Hawaiian shirt and a pair of suntan pants.

"No holes or nothin'," Grandpa said.

"I didn't know you owned any clothes without holes," Mom chuckled.

"Well, I do," Grandpa said. "Right, Rooster?"

Rooster's head bounced and his hand flapped up over his mouth like it always did when he laughed. A squealy cackle slipped out between his fingers. Grandpa handed Mom Rooster's dirty wad of clothes and said, "Better boil these."

About then, Percy announced, "Barn door's open, Rooster."

We all laughed, but Rooster didn't know what a "barn door" was. He jerked his head around trying to figure out what was going on, understanding the joke was on him but not knowing why.

"Didn't think you'd notice," Grandpa said. He looked over at Rooster and, pointing down to the front of his pants, said, "Zipper...kaput."

Rooster looked down at his pants, then back up, then down again. Then he fumbled to zip them up.

"Don't waste your time, Rooster," Grandpa said. "They're broke." He looked over at Mom. "Got a safety pin?"

Mom went and got a pin and Grandpa helped him pin it shut. That solved the problem for then, but remembering a little thing like a safety pin was a big job for Rooster, and he usually forgot. From then on, he wore clean clothes, but if he had on the pants Grandpa had given him, they were usually unzipped. After a while, nobody even noticed, and when we took him places, it was the group's responsibility to make sure Rooster either wore the pants he'd gotten from the hospital—or had his pin.

The rooms Dad finished for us in the barn were nice. We had bedrooms and a living room with a table where we ate our meals. Mom used Grandpa's bus as her kitchen. One room we still didn't have, though, was a bathroom, and this made baths awkward. For a while we used the round metal tub Mom washed clothes in, but it was on the small side. I had to roll up in a ball to pack myself in, and the grownups could only fit by hanging their legs out. We finally gave up on the washtub altogether and started taking our baths in the cattle watering trough. The trough was an old skinned-up cast-iron bathtub. I don't know how long it had been there or where it came from, but as tubs go, it was a monstrous thing. Dad built a low wooden wall around it to keep the cattle out and sightseers from looking in, and it worked like a charm. We didn't have a single complaint from the cattle, because they still had the creek to drink from, and for us it was actually a nice private place to wash the dirt off. Mom scoured the scum and slime off as best she could, and when we wanted to bathe, all we had to do was carry a couple of buckets of hot water from the stove and mix it with the cold stuff from the pump. As long as the sun was shining and the air was warm, it was quite pleasant. As Grandpa said, "Where else could you wash between your toes and get a suntan at the same time?"

Rooster had a problem with baths. I don't know if all bums get pleasure from being dirty, or if it was just him, but he wouldn't go near the tub. Dad led him out to it several times and filled it with hot water, then left him with a wash rag, a towel, and soap, but all Rooster would do was slop a little water on his face and hands then call it quits. As the weeks passed, clean clothes or no, he started to take on the smell of something you don't talk about in mixed company. Nobody ventured close to him, and when we ate, we jammed together elbow to bellybutton at one end of the table while Rooster sat all alone at the other. It was a bad situation. Finally Mom laid down the law. She told Grandpa to either make Rooster take a bath or find him someplace else to eat.

"Why's it my job?" Grandpa objected.

"He's your buddy," she said.

The next day Dad quit work on the house an hour or two before supper and headed into town to get some nails. Grandpa and Rooster disappeared into the bus and came out wearing only their undershorts and hats and untied boots, and carrying towels and soap and two buckets of hot water. Their bodies were so white they almost glowed. Percy and I were playing in the hayloft when we spotted them through the loft door.

"Let's watch," Percy said. "This oughta be funny."

"But they'll be naked!" I objected.

"Grandpa wears his shorts when he takes a bath out here," Percy said. "He don't trust the fence."

"Nobody does that," I said.

"Grandpa does. Anyway, nobody'll know. Mom's out workin' in the garden. Besides, if they were here they'd spy, too. That's too good to miss."

We eased the door almost shut, leaving a gap to see through. I squatted down low and looked out the bottom while Percy leaned over my shoulder.

Grandpa and Rooster were at the tub now. The loft door was high enough that we could see over the fence Dad had built. Grandpa sat the buckets down and as he flexed his fingers he said something to Rooster they both thought was funny.

They looked like two scarecrows laughing in the sunshine in their underwear. Grandpa hoisted the buckets of hot water into the tub then pumped in cold. He'd stop now and then to test the temperature, then pump some more, talking the whole time, waving his hands and laughing, and Rooster was bobbing his head with his palm cupped in its usual place. He was a good audience.

Then you could tell Grandpa was telling a really big story, because he went on and on and Rooster's eyes were glued to him like he was hypnotized. When Grandpa came to the end he doubled up laughing, slapping his knees and wiping his eyes, and when Rooster saw that Grandpa was laughing, he laughed, too...but you could tell he didn't understand what he was laughing at.

Finally the water was the right temperature and Grandpa stepped in. He gave Rooster a grin then reached down and flipped a little water in his direction.

"He does wear his shorts in the tub," I marveled.

"Told you," Percy said. "Now I wonder if Rooster'll get in."

"If he starts takin' them underwear off, I ain't lookin'!" I said.

Grandpa sat down and settled back with his hands laced behind his head and a look on his face like he'd died and gone to heaven in a bathtub. He slopped water up on his face then gulped a mouthful and spurted it out, geyser style. Rooster was enjoying the fun and showing signs he was thinking about climbing in.

Grandpa motioned for him to join him, then splashed some more water his way and motioned again, but Rooster didn't budge.

"He's thinkin' about it," I hushed.

In slow motion, Rooster swung one leg over, then the other. You'd thought he was climbing into a tank of alligators. He stood there in the water rubbing the gray, frizzy hair on his chest with the heel of his hand, then lowered himself down. Grandpa slid back to make room.

All we could see was their heads and shoulders above the tub rim.

Grandpa lathered the washrag to a froth and scrubbed it around on Rooster's back. Rooster held as still as a dog getting its ears scratched. When Grandpa was done, he splashed the suds off, then gave Rooster the soap and rag. Rooster smeared a fleck of soap on the rag and dabbed it around here and there without much enthusiasm. You could almost see the dirt give a sigh of relief. Grandpa was shaking his head in a disapproving way and had Rooster turn around so they were facing each other. Then, without a rag but pretending he had one, he showed him the right way to wash— under his arms, behind his ears, and about every other bodily place you could think of. He rubbed and scrubbed and laughed and sang, and Rooster started getting inspired. He began whipping the soapy rag around his body just the way Grandpa was. When Grandpa scrubbed his face, Rooster did, too. When Grandpa washed his elbow or his toes or leg, Rooster followed along. He made the rag fly. Water was going every which way, and Grandpa was cheering him on. Finally Grandpa plucked Rooster's stocking cap off his head and frothed up a good lather in his hair, then dumped a bucket of water over him to wash it off. Rooster spit and blubbered, then laughed so hard he could hardly sit up.

We were breaking a gut in the loft. Percy said, "Ain't it crazy how a grown guy like Rooster acts so much like a little kid?" And it was.

Grandpa and Rooster had just traded roles, with Rooster being the teacher and Grandpa being the one who needed the help, when we spotted a car coming in the driveway. It was poking along about the speed you'd walk, and the driver had his arm hanging out the window, looking around as he drove. Rooster and Grandpa were screened from the road by the fence. It pulled up in front of the new house, and the driver climbed out and walked over to where the red "stop-work" notice had been tacked to the tree.

"Looks like a state car," Percy said.

"I think it's a bureaucrat," I said.

Percy muttered, "I'll go get Mom," then headed off down the stairs.

I took a last peek at Grandpa and Rooster in the tub. Grandpa's hair was all frothy with soap and Rooster was scooping a bucket of water to dump on his head. I didn't wait to watch him throw it, but slipped away and followed Percy down the stairs.

I found the bureaucrat standing at the top of the plank inside the opening that would be our front door.

"Well, hi there," he said.

I didn't answer him.

"This your house?" he asked. His voice was friendly enough but I still didn't say anything. After all I had heard about bureaucrats, I didn't intend to go out of my way to be friendly.

The guy had black curly hair and glasses and a kind of fuzzy moustache that bent down around the sides of his mouth. He was wearing a plaid shirt and some Hush Puppy shoes with big thick crepe soles. "I got a little girl must be about your age," he said. "Her name's Judy. What's yours?"

"Susie," I muttered.

"What's that, again?"

"Susie." I half whispered it again. Then in a louder voice I said, "I ain't a little girl."

He gave the side of his head a smack. "Oh gosh, I'm sorry. Big girl. Right?" He laughed and shook his head at his own stupidity. Then he said, "Well, Susie, I need to see your mommy or daddy. They around?"

I didn't answer again.

He waited a bit and I noticed his smile starting to wilt a little. "Are they up at your house?" he asked.

"We don't have a house," I said. "Are you a bureaucrat?"

"A what? Bureaucrat?" He threw his head back and laughed. "That's a big word for such a little girl." Then he realized he had made the same mistake again. "Big girl, I mean." He pulled at the corner of his moustache then rubbed his face the way men do when they feel their whiskers. "Nooo...I'm not a bureaucrat. I'm an inspector. I go around and help people when they're building their houses so they don't make mistakes."

Just then Mom and Percy came up the plank behind me. The inspector introduced himself as the one who'd tacked up the "stop work" notice on our tree. He asked if we'd seen it, which Mom said we had.

Then he said, "You've worked on the house since I left the notice, haven't you?"

Mom started to say something, but didn't. She just nodded her head.

The guy didn't act especially comfortable being the villain. He stood looking thoughtful for a moment, thumping his thumbnail with his finger.

Then Mom said, "My husband really needs to be here. He's got pretty strong feelings about his. He thinks we shouldn't have to have a permit clear out here."

"I'm afraid it's the law," the inspector said. "A few years ago you'd have been OK this far out, but now we have land use laws. You know what those are?"

"More or less," she said.

"They're to protect places like yours," he said. "They keep some developer from coming in here and putting in a housing project or something like that. But the gist of it is that there's no place in the whole state any more where you can build without a permit."

"I understand that," Mom said, "but my husband doesn't. You just need to come back when he's here."

"I'm real sorry about this," he said, "but there really isn't anything I need to talk to him about. He needs a permit, and that's about all there is to it. Just a matter of filling out an application and paying a fee and letting us have a look at your plans." He raised his finger. "Wait a minute—I think I've got an application out in the car." He went to his car and came back with a briefcase. He set it down on a pile of boards and opened it up and pulled out some forms. He straightened his glasses on his nose to read the writing, then handed the forms to Mom. "Have your husband bring this in to us with two sets of plans," he said. He shut the briefcase and sat it upright. "By the way—" he said. He hesitated and rubbed his thumb thoughtfully over his lips. "Do you have the other permits you'll need—electrical and septic and those?"

Mom looked at him as though she didn't know what he was talking about. "I don't suppose we do," she said faintly. "Where do we get them?"

The inspector started to tell her, but stopped before he'd gotten a word out. Standing there in his underwear and untied boots and with his dirty old felt hat pulled down over his dripping hair was Grandpa. He stepped up inside with the rest of us, and with a sugary sweet voice he said, "I don't recall sendin' you an invitation to this party."

I thought for a moment he was just kidding. But then, in the grimmest voice I'd ever heard Grandpa use, he said, "Mister, you get your buns movin' off our place or I'll take me my shotgun an' shoot 'em so full o' holes you won't sit down again—ever. Understand?"

"Wait a minute there," the inspector objected. "There's no need for that."

"You're darned right there ain't," Grandpa said. "There's no need for any of this."

The inspector started to say something else, but Grandpa cut him off. "See here how I'm dressed?" he said. He thumped his hairy chest. "These're my dressin' up clothes." He had his chin jutted out and his eyes zeroed in on the guy.

The inspector gave a little forced laugh.

"Funny-lookin', ain't they? An' this here's my Sunday hat." Grandpa pulled the old wet felt hat off his head and held it up for the guy to see. His hair was plastered against his head with water running in beads down his face to his neck. His old white, bony legs looked like gnarled tree limbs. He pulled his hat back over his head and said, "We're poor people, mister, an' our house burned down. Understand? It ain't here no more. Gone. I built that house fifty years ago, an' I'll tell you somethin': I didn't need no permit to do it—nothin'. Now you tell me—if a house that was built with no permit burns down, why in God's name do we need a permit to replace it? Huh? We got troubles enough around here."

The inspector started to say something again, but once more Grandpa cut him off. When Mom tried to say something, he cut her off too. "You may've noticed I'm a little wet," he said. "Notice that? There's a reason for it. You see, I been takin' me a bath. Right, a bath. And you know where I took this bath?" He paused a moment, but the inspector didn't say anything. "Well, I took it in the cow's trough over there in the barnyard. That's right—cow's trough—where the cows drink. Cow slobbers an' cow pies an' the whole shebang."

"Grandpa," Mom interrupted, "he doesn't need this. He's just doing his job."

"No—no. That ain't true," Grandpa objected. "That's the problem. He does need it. All of 'em do. Time somebody told 'em how it really is. They set down there in their offices makin' rules and chargin' fees, an' people like us don't even have a place to take a bath." He looked right at the inspector, who was closing up his briefcase and doing his best to hold his temper. "Darn it, man, don't you understand?" Grandpa said. "We ain't got a house. A house is like air or food. It's like water. Need a permit to get a drink next thing you know." He stepped around in front of the man. "And what we're doin' here is buildin' us a house. That's all—just a place to sleep an' take a bath. An' we're doin' one hell of a job of it. It'll be ten times the house that tin can down the road is, an' we don't need you desk jockeys out here pickin' our pockets an' tellin' us how to do it." He glared at the guy.

The inspector snatched his briefcase off the boards and turned to Mom nervously. "You've got the papers," he said. "Maybe you can talk some sense into him. I'm going." He brushed past Grandpa and went down the plank toward his car.

"Don't come back unless you're ready to shoot us, mister!" Grandpa yelled after him. "Cause you guys ain't wanted here."

The inspector threw his briefcase in the front seat, climbed in, and slammed the door. When he took off, he spun up gravel for fifty feet and just missed hitting one of our geese. It went honking out across the barnyard.

"Grandpa!" Mom said. "That was a disgrace."

Grandpa looked at her and an instant change came over him. He rubbed the bridge of his nose lightly, then smiled at each of us in turn, just like nothing had happened. "Wasn't I awful, though?" he said. "But I'll tell you somethin': I feel a *whole* lot better now. An' I'll tell you somethin' else. I don't think that thief'll be back again." He looked down and ran his eyes over his frizzy-haired, bony old body, then said, "Now I feel *real* clean."

Chapter 19

You've heard the expression, "He worships the ground she walks on"? Well, that's how Rooster felt about me. If I had asked him to go to the moon and spit in a crater, he'd have done it. And I think I know why. I think it started with the gifts I'd left for him beside the trail. He'd been beaten down and abused his entire life and hadn't seen much in the way of kindness. So when I sent my little bit his way, it bowled him over. And I think it wasn't the gifts that did it, because they weren't much. It was the fact that I gave them. He wasn't starved for things so much as he was starved for love.

It didn't take me long to figure out that Rooster's appreciation carried some side benefits with it. Having him grateful to you was equivalent to owning a slave. He liked nothing more than to follow me around, awaiting my command. Having spent all of my nine years at the bottom of the command ladder, I found this state of affairs to my liking, to say the least. If Mom asked me to give the cat the table scraps, I'd just give them to Rooster and point him in the right direction and, presto, he'd do it. If I wanted worms to fish with, I'd give him the shovel and a can and he'd have it wriggling full in no time. It was like that for everything, and the best part about it was that he loved it. It gave him pleasure, and who was I to deny him pleasure?

There was only one problem with this arrangement, but it was a big one: Mom.

"But he likes it, Mom," I told her. "It makes him feel good."

"I'm sure you can find plenty of other ways to make Rooster feel good," she responded. "It's not that I think you're abusing him or anything like that, Susie, but they outlawed slavery a hundred years ago." She clasped her hands in front of her chin, prayer-like, and bent down to my level: "Do your own work, Susie."

"But, Mom," I said, "you do it to me all the time."

"Oh, and how's that?"

I could tell by her smile and the way her eyebrows lifted that my line of reasoning wasn't going to get me very far.

"Well—" I said uncertainly, "you make me do your work."

"Uh-huh...and what else?"

"You make me dry dishes and feed the chickens and make my bed an' do a whole lotta things."

"Yes?"

"An' set the table an' get the mail."

"Uh-huh?"

The one-word responses I was getting were making me feel more and more uneasy.

"Now is it my turn?" Mom asked.

I gave a weak nod.

"OK, Susie-Q...and who is it that eats on those dishes you dry?" she asked. "And who eats those eggs the chickens lay, and sits at the table you help wipe off? And just in case you've forgotten, who is the mother here, and who's the little girl?"

That was it. It was over.

As I retreated, Mom said, "And I don't want you taking advantage of Rooster any more. Understand?" There was a pause as I opened the door, but as I stepped out she shot one last word at me. "Slave."

Mom was the rudder for our lives during these times, doing her best to keep me and all the rest of us on the straight and narrow. Surrounded by four family members and one adopted one who all had it in them to go over the edge any time they turned around, she was the one unfailing pull toward sanity. But it wasn't easy for her, and she struggled with it. Living in a glorified barn, with Dad tied down from before daylight to after dark each day with the monumental job of running a farm and building a house at the same time, she was hit with a load of new responsibilities that would have flattened most women. But she took it in stride. She'd be up before dawn fetching wood and water, building the fire, cooking two shifts of breakfast, keeping our rooms and Grandpa's bus spotless, doing the mountain of chores the men now couldn't handle, washing everything that needed washing, fixing what needed fixing, and when she could, taking her place alongside the men, nailing boards, setting posts, nursing sick animals. And through all this she kept up a poise and grace that were almost saintly.

But the row with the planning commission took its toll on Mom. She felt morally compromised by it, and as the conflict heated up, the first cracks began to show in her tranquility. One day not long after Grandpa had spoken his mind to the building inspector, Mom drove out to get the mail. When she came back she had a worried look on her face. "I think you'd better see this," she said to Dad. She handed him an opened letter.

Dad read it without saying anything, then put it in his pocket.

"What is it, son?" Grandpa asked.

"County," he said.

"Makin' threats?"

Dad gave an expressionless nod. "Same ol' stuff," he muttered.

Mom rubbed her eyes the way you do when you have a headache, then, looking out toward the mountains, she said, "It's not the same old stuff, Sam. You read what it said. They've got the law on their side."

Dad ran his palm back and forth across his whiskers, but he didn't say anything. Grandpa didn't either.

Mom stood and picked up the plates we'd been eating on and stacked the cups one inside the other. Her usual happy look was gone. Turning to Dad, she said, "We're going at it wrong, Sam. And we're getting ourselves into a big mess. We're breaking the law."

Dad didn't respond, but after Mom disappeared into the school bus with the dishes, he pulled the letter out of his pocket and read it again.

"What do you suppose they'll do?" Grandpa mused. "Throw us in the jug?"

Dad just shook his head.

A few minutes later Dad got up and went into the bus where Mom was, and he hadn't come out yet when Jon, Percy, and I headed down toward the cave hideout.

"What's gonna happen to us if we don't get that permit?" I asked the boys.

"Nothin' ain't gonna happen," Percy answered. "They can't do nothin' to us. They can't tell us what we can do on our own property." He was sounding more like Dad and Grandpa all the time.

"That's what you think," Jon said. "If anybody knows about gettin' in trouble, it's me. I seen people breakin' the law all the time back in Portland, an' bad stuff happens to 'em...really."

"Like what?" Percy asked.

"Like executin' 'em an' stuff like that."

"You mean they kill 'em?" I asked.

"Chop their heads off," he said. Then he said, "Do you know what the Indians did? They'd tie you up to a pole and heap up a bunch of dry limbs around it an' burn you."

"You're kiddin'," I said.

"Nope. Read it."

"White people don't do that, do they?" I asked.

Percy broke in. "They ain't gonna do that stuff to us, Susie. They don't chop your head off or nothin' like that unless you're a killer or drunk driver or somethin' like that."

"Or a rustler," Jon added.

But I was worried about it, and the next day when Mom took the checkbook and the permit forms and headed off to town to buy us a building permit, I was sure she'd just saved me from having the top foot of my body lopped off before I'd reached voting age. I was relieved. To ease Mom's mind, Dad had given in to buying a permit. Grandpa, on the other hand, was still dead set against it.

The thing was, Mom had made her point, and they knew it. They had taken their stand about as far as they could without getting into real trouble. Still, neither Dad nor Grandpa would stoop to making the trip himself. They said they'd send the crooks their money, but they'd be darned if they'd go down and deliver it with their own hands. "An' if they wanta talk to me," Dad said to Mom as she left, "tell 'em I don't know how."

Nobody was prepared for what happened next. It was like a bolt of lightning out of the blue, and it flipped our lives upside down so they never really got fully righted again. That afternoon when Mom pulled in from her trip to the planning commission, she parked the truck but didn't get out for a long time. She just sat at the wheel, staring straight ahead. Finally I went over and climbed up on the running board to ask her some dumb kid question. I don't remember exactly what it was. I think I asked if I could go down and play at the creek. Anyway, she glanced over at me and muttered "Okay," but her face was pale and stiff.

I stayed there at the window a bit, looking at her. "You all right?" I asked.

"Go play" was all she said.

Mom never acted like that. A lot of the time Dad was quiet, and his answers were notoriously short. Sometimes you almost had to pry words out of him. But Mom was never at a loss for words, and her answers were notoriously long.

Pretty soon Mom climbed out of the truck. She had some papers in her hand. About halfway across to the new house, Dad met her. I couldn't hear what they were saying, but all at once Mom just fell into his arms. I could tell she was crying. Dad was comforting her and patting her on the back. She had her face buried in his shoulder, so I couldn't see it, but I could see Dad's face plain as day...and he had the grimmest look I'd ever seen.

Now Grandpa joined them. Still holding Mom, Dad said something to him.

Grandpa just exploded. I won't repeat what he said, but it was probably the worst string of swear words that had ever been uttered on the ranch, in history. And he didn't just say them. He bellowed them. He pulled his old floppy felt hat off his head and threw it down on the ground, then he grabbed it up and slapped it against his leg so hard dust flew up.

I went up to Dad and asked what was wrong.

"Nothin'," he muttered.

Mom was shaking, she was crying so hard.

"Go play," Dad told me.

Chapter 20

It was so quiet you could hear forks clanking against plates. A fly buzzing the gravy sounded like a chainsaw. Rooster was the only one doing much eating. He sat at his end of the table shoveling down food as though nothing had happened. Mom's eyes were red, and Grandpa and Dad were grim. Even Percy and I were subdued. We still hadn't been told the details, but we'd heard enough to know that disaster had struck.

Percy asked, "Won't we ever be able to build the house?"

Mom shook her head without looking up, but Grandpa answered flat out, "You bet we'll build it."

Grandpa hadn't said any bad words for an hour or so, but you could tell by the way he ripped at his bread with his teeth and made the whole table shake when he cut his meat that he was sure as heck thinking them. "They throw them houses up downtown on lots no bigger'n paper plates. Hell, over in Portland they stack 'em one on top of the other. So now them dummies got the gall to tell us, just cause we sell off a few acres, we ain't got enough land left to build on? Criminently! They're a bunch of idiots down there, Susie. That's how I'd explain it." He hit the word "idiots" about ten decibels louder than the rest.

"Grandpa!" Mom scolded. She threw him a glance, then turned her eyes back down at her food.

Grandpa drove his fork into another piece of meat and jammed it into his mouth, attacking it with his teeth. Swallowing hard, he stabbed another hunk. "They are idiots," he said, waving the impaled meat around. "'Specially them boneheads over in Salem. They're city slickers—all of 'em. Live in them fancy offices an' air-conditioned cars, an' the only flowers they see're in pots. Probably never seen a real live crawdad or squirrel in their lives. So what do they do? They figure the whole world's as messed up as it is there in the city, an' figure it's up to them to dream up some new laws to straighten things out. What do they know? Hells bells, everybody knows mother nature's havin' a time of it these days. That's for sure...but not around here. Just look out that door. I don't see no problems out there. You see any problems?"

He snapped the meat off his fork and worked it over with his teeth like he was trying to inflict pain on it.

"We got birds all over this place. We got good air, trees, deer—everything. We don't need no city laws out here. We're doin' fine, thank you. Instead o' tellin' us what to do, them city boys should be out here seein' how it should be done. We're the ones knows how to take care o' the land. Thing that's endangered out here ain't nature—it's us!" He looked over at Dad for his approval. Dad was nodding.

Grandpa took his fork and herded his beans up into a clump on his plate, then made a crude effort to scoop them up that caught a few and scattered the rest.

"Anybody ever seen an animal around here that couldn't build itself a home if it wanted?" He swept his eyes around the table like he was just daring anyone to answer. "Well, I ain't, gosh dang it. We got every kinda animal under the sun makin' its home on this ranch. We got beavers dammin' up creeks and makin' lodges; got birds buildin' all kinds o' nests; got moles diggin' burrows—we got ants, moths, worms, snails—all of 'em makin' every kinda house there is—but not us! Now that ain't right." He thumped his fork down on the tabletop, then leaned back in his chair and, looking out the window. "Talk about the bears gettin' the shaft...."

It was quiet again as everyone let Grandpa's words sink in. Grandpa had a way of putting things, and whether he was right or wrong, he was hard to argue with. But Mom was sitting across from me, and I could see her head slowly wagging from side to side. "We can't blame anybody but ourselves for our troubles," she said, not even lifting her eyes. Then she looked over at Grandpa.

"The law's the law. We've been picking and choosing what laws to follow, and it's getting us in a mess." Then her voice dropped to a monotone. "We should have gone to them and found out what the rules were before we started. We should have gone as soon as the house burned."

"We done it just like we should've," Dad said. "If we'd've gone an' asked 'em like you say, they'd just've told us no." He motioned toward Grandpa with his spoon. "I don't agree with you, either, Dad. They're not idiots. They're a lot smarter'n you think. And I'll tell you somethin' else: they're all in cahoots—the whole lot of 'em. This wasn't no accident. They had it planned all along."

Mom gave Dad a sour look. "You don't really believe that."

"Sure," he said. "They been tryin' to get their mitts on this place as long as I can remember. You know as well as I do, them planners an' the guys from the Forest Service probably got their heads together an' set it all up. I'd bet on it. Bet they went in an' thumbed through their rule book an' said 'eenie-meenie-miney-moe', an' put their finger on some rule an' said, 'Let's use this one.'"

"Wouldn't put it past 'em," Grandpa cut in.

Then, in a tight, unnatural voice, Mom said, "I can't take much more of this kind of talk, thinking everybody's out to get us. It's just a bunch of sick excuses. If we'd worked with them from the start we wouldn't have a problem."

"Don't believe it," Dad interrupted.

"Why not? Why in God's name not?" Mom's voice rose to a pitch I'd never heard, and I saw her lips quiver. "You two have lived out here in the sticks too long. You're thinking about as well as the cows." She glared at each of them, expecting them to put up an argument, but they sat silent. She took a deep breath. "I can't believe they won't sit down and listen to our side of it. Maybe they don't know our house burned down. Maybe they just made a mistake."

"No mistake," Dad said, dryly. "They've known what they were doing from the start. It's how the government works. Hundred years ago the government was givin' land away. That's how we come to have this place...gave it to us. Now they want it back. Simple as that. Figure if they can give us enough grief we'll get discouraged an' sell."

"That's silly," Mom said. She was getting really angry now.

"Then what is it?" Dad demanded.

"A mistake!" She shouted the word. Then she grabbed control of herself and said it again, but more quietly. "A mistake."

It got still in the room again. I looked over at Percy. He was staring down at his fingers. Nobody said much more. We pushed our food around our plates a little, then excused ourselves, leaving only Rooster behind. He was still cleaning out the bowls. The whole matter was drifting right over his head. Good times and problems were all the same to him and he couldn't tell one from the other. He'd probably lived most of his life homeless. It was old hat to him.

The new house looked lonely as it stood empty in the sunset that evening. I could still remember how it had taken shape in front of us, board by board, over the summer, only to be brought to this unexpected end. I wondered to myself where we'd live if they wouldn't let us finish it.

I could see Rooster out in front of his cabin, sitting on one of Grandpa's lawn chairs. His dog was curled up in his lap, and the horseshoes were lying in the grass beside him. He and Grandpa played horseshoes every evening that Grandpa didn't go fishing. Tonight Grandpa hadn't gone fishing, but he hadn't come to play horseshoes, either.

The setting sunlight flooded through the rafters of the new house. It shone on the shakes where they were stacked, and on the heaps of sawdust and slab wood the sawyers had left behind. It shone on the piles of lumber that were now getting small as boards were lugged off and sawed and nailed into walls and floors and stairs.

I walked up the board ramp into the room we'd planned to be the kitchen. Dad's new Skil saw and power drill sat in the middle of the floor, with the extension cord draped through the window hole to the power box. The walls dividing the rooms from one another were bare studs with no covering on them yet. You could go from one room to the next without using the doors. I climbed the temporary steps to what was to be my bedroom. It was on the north side and had one big window that faced the snow peaks. I leaned there, looking out and wondering what was going to happen.

The next morning, Δbreakfast was more like a funeral than a meal, but some of the tension had melted. It was clear, though, that there'd been no agreement on how to move ahead.

Dad and Grandpa had been up since the crack of dawn doing their farm chores, and when breakfast was done, they were ready to start nailing up roof. They had no intention of stopping their building. Permit or no permit, they were going to build the house. But Mom was having none of that, and she announced to the group that she was going back to the planning commission to see if she couldn't convince them to change their minds.

"Well, I hope you come back with good news," Grandpa said. "I really do." Then he grinned his first grin since the night before, and you could tell that maybe he was getting back to his usual old self again. "I'll tell you how to do it." He wiped his nose with the back of his finger, which usually meant he was about to tease. "You throw a bottle o' booze in your pocketbook an' take that along. That's the way the big boys do it, a little somethin' to grease some palms with. Got a friend told me he left a bottle for the plumbing inspector. The guy just flushed the toilet an' said it looked okay to him an' signed 'em off without lookin' at a pipe."

Mom said she didn't believe those stories.

After breakfast, Mom left for town while the men headed to the new house to pound nails. Percy and I set off for the cave to meet Jon Pindar.

Painful as all the trouble with the planning commission was to our family, it was big news, and I gave Percy ten marbles and a deer antler to let me be the one to tell Jon about it. When we got to

the cave, Jon wasn't there. Percy sat down to whittle while I waited
on the big rock at the entrance, watching for him. I finally spotted
him fighting his way through the swamp grass at the edge of the
lake with the cavalry and sod-busters hot on his tail. He was
carrying a bow that was darn near as tall as he was. With a scream
I could hear clear up at the cave, he started killing white guys right
and left. He snatched imaginary arrows from his quiver, whipped
them into position, then twanged the bowstring at least an arrow a
second. Then the fighting went hand-to-hand. Jon was a human
buzz saw, kicking and punching and stabbing and tomahawking
and taking bullets to the shoulder like a hero. He backed the last
few steps to the cave entrance with his bow poised and the string
pulled back to his cheek saying, "Take that, you good-for-nothin'
baby-killers!"

"Wappato!" I shouted.

Jon like to dirtied his pants. When he spun around, his eyes
were as big as fists.

"Scared ya!" I hooted.

We traded "Did nots" and "Did sos." Just as I was about to
announce my big news from the planning commission, he pushed
past me like I wasn't there. He thrust his bow and a clutch of arrows
out to Percy to show them off, and that was the end of my
announcement. The bow was one of those fancy ones with pulleys
and all sorts of gadgets on it, and Percy went goo-eyed. He turned
it over in his hands. "Your dad buy it for you?" he asked.

"Rod and Gun cabin," he said. "Under the board."

My heart fell. "Well, it wasn't Rooster," I blurted.

"I didn't say it was," he said. "But if it wasn't, then who
was it?"

"How do you think I'd know?" I shot back. "All I know's it
wasn't Rooster. Somebody else musta put it there."

Percy said, "Susie...he's the only one it coulda been. He's the
only one around here who'd steal anything."

"No he ain't," I said. "He takes stuff outa garbage cans, but
that's because he's a bum. That ain't stealin'."

"Your sister's dumb," Jon said to Percy. "I think she's in love
with that ol' bum."

Percy was admiring the bow again. He turned it over in his hands and ran his fingers over the smooth surface. He said, "I bet you could shoot an arrow a mile with this thing."

"Shoots straight, too," Jon said.

Suddenly Percy pulled the bow up close to his eyes. "Hey, look!" he said.

We all pushed our heads in close. Scratched into the back side of the grip was the word "Turner."

Percy said, "He must've stole it from the Turners."

Jon grabbed the bow from Percy's hands and rubbed the name to see if it came off. "I didn't see that before," he said.

"Now what?" Percy asked.

"Now what, what?" Jon snapped. "So we know who he stole it from. That don't mean nothin'."

"Sure it does," I objected. "If we know who it belongs to, we should take it back or somethin'."

Jon rolled his eyes up to the sky as if he was asking deliverance from me. "Oh, sure. We'll just walk up there to the Turners an' tell 'em we found this bow'n arrow that Rooster stole, an' give it back. Mr. Turner's the meanest, stingiest man I've ever seen. He don't even buy stuff at our store any more. Says we charge too much. He'd have the police out here an' arrest Rooster so fast it'd make your head spin."

We stood silent a moment. Jon was right. "What if we just left it on their porch?" I suggested.

"You wanta get put in jail?" Jon said. "I mean, what if they caught you? I can just see it. There you are, sneakin' up with this stolen bow'n arrow an' they spot you. Whadda you think they'd think? They'd think you stole it. That's what they'd think."

"Anyway," Percy said, "the Turners have lots of money. They've probably bought a new one already."

"You guys don't care about helpin' Rooster or nobody. All you care about's this stupid bow an' arrow. It ain't yours. I have a mind to go up there to the Turners an' tell 'em you guys stole it. How's that grab you?"

Well, it didn't grab them very well. Jon backed me up against the rocks at the rear of the cave and threatened me with everything he could think of, from cutting my tongue out to driving a stake through my heart. Of course, he didn't scare me a bit, but he made me plenty mad.

The boys took the bow and arrows and headed off to shoot settlers. Under the threat of being considered a settler if I tried to follow them, I gave them one last piece of my mind, then stomped off like I'd won.

Back at the house, Dad and Grandpa were nailing boards to the rafters. I climbed up beside them, still feeling glum. I had no more than gotten up when I spotted Mom driving in. By the height of the dust plume she was throwing up and the way she jumped out of the truck and came jogging toward us, you could tell her luck with the planning commission had changed. She climbed the ladder and announced that in two weeks we could appeal, and if we made our case, we'd get our permit. She was so happy she crawled up and kissed Dad and Grandpa and me, all of us. Half floating, she danced off to the bus to fix lunch, and when she passed Herman the goat she gave him a kiss, too.

Dad and Grandpa leaned on their elbows against the roof. "Could be our luck's changin'," Dad said.

"Could be," Grandpa said. "Then again, could be they're just lettin' us say a few last words before they tell the firin' squad to shoot."

Chapter 21

It wasn't long after Jon and Percy decided to keep the Turners' bow and arrows that they dug their pit. I saw "Rooster" written all over it. It was about chest deep and right in the middle of the path to the cave. They laid pine boughs over it to hide it. Needless to say, I didn't think much of it.

"It ain't deep," Percy insisted. "An' anyway, we put soft stuff on the bottom."

"No way," I objected. "If Rooster falls in there he'll break a leg. Might even break his head."

"Come on, Susie," Jon muttered. "Rooster likes this kinda stuff. Besides, the Indians done it all the time. Any bad guys try to go up to the cave'n steal our stuff'll fall in."

"Rooster ain't a bad guy," I said. "Nobody likes fallin' in holes. How'd you like it?" I kicked a little dirt their direction and started to walk away. As an aftershot I turned and said, "This ain't play no more. You two're bein' mean to Rooster. An' I'll tell you somethin' else. If you don't fill that hole up, I'm gonna go right up there an' tell him where it is."

Well, they didn't fill it up, so just like I said I would, I took Rooster out and showed him where it was. The trouble was, he had a short memory, and the next day the boys coaxed him up the path right into it. I didn't see it happen, but when he came dragging home, he had a big scratch down one arm and a bruise on his cheek. I went right in and told Mom. Mom shared my opinion, of course. She had no patience for cruelty to bums or animals or anything else that moved, so she and Percy had what she called a "heart-to-heart" talk. Afterwards, he poked his finger in my chest and told me that if I stuck my nose into their play again he'd cut it off.

For the next few days playmates were hard to come by. Each morning I'd see Rooster tagging off behind the boys, and hours later he'd come dragging home looking like he'd been dipped in batter and rolled in dirt and pine needles, with a little blood mixed in. Finally I'd had enough. Before the boys could get to him each day, I'd coax him off and hide him away until they were gone.

It wasn't long after that that I decided to see if I couldn't break Rooster's stealing habit by making him return some of the things he'd stolen, beginning with the Turners' bow and arrow. A few years earlier Mom had actually used this strategy on me when I walked out of the grocery store with a Big Hunk candy bar in my pocket. I swore to her that it must have just fallen off the shelf and landed there, but she wasn't in a believing mood, especially considering that the end of the bar had been gnawed off. So she took me to the store manager to give me the opportunity to return what was left of it and confess my sin, which I did. It worked, too. I haven't stolen another Big Hunk since. And I figured if it could work on me, it could work on Rooster.

The next night, with snores rolling up from the direction of Percy's mattress, I poked a pillow and all the pants I owned down under my blanket to make it look like I was still in bed, then stuffed my flashlight in my pocket and snuck out. A big lopsided moon so bright that it cast shadows was sitting on the shoulder of Mt. Thompson. I could see to walk, even without the flashlight—but evidently not well enough. On my way to retrieve the bow and arrows, I walked smack into the boys' camouflaged pit. It made me furious. But to heap insult on top of injury, on the return trip I bumbled into it again. I broke my flashlight, skinned my elbow, and turned the night air from black to blue with a barrage of words I'd only heard Jon Pindar and Grandpa use up to that time. It was a bad start, and if I'd had any sense I would have called the whole thing off right then.

Back at the ranch, I roused Rooster and steered him out the driveway to the edge of the Turners' clearing. We ducked down long enough for me to recite Mom's "Big Hunk speech" as best I could remember it and to hand him the bow and arrows so he could return them personally. In the moonlight, the mobile home stood out like a wart on its expanse of gravel. There were no cars parked outside and no signs of life. It looked safe, and we crept in.

Sometimes it's hard to tell exactly when a good idea goes bad. But this time it was easy. It happened when Rooster caught his toe and fell over Mr. Turner's motorcycle, which was parked on the back deck. It sounded like a bomb had gone off. The cycle crashed to the boards and Rooster came down on top of it. The bow and arrows spewed out across the deck.

A light popped on inside.

"Somebody's in there!" I gasped.

Rooster was on his knees, fumbling around to get things picked up.

Another light flicked on, and I heard the front door open at the other end of the house. It slammed shut.

Footsteps came our direction from inside, then another light snapped on.

About then I grabbed Rooster's arm and said, "Run!"

Now someone was fumbling with the latch and the deck light came on. At that point it was each man for himself. I let go of Rooster, hurdled a pot of flowers and sprinted out across the gravel. I was back into the shadow of the trees when I heard Mr. Turner's voice roll out. "Hey! Stop, you thief!"

Then the air exploded with the sound of a gunshot. "Rooster!" I gasped, and spun around. Mr. Turner, wearing only his pajama bottoms, stood on the deck under the glare of the porch lights holding his rifle.

There was no sign of Rooster. Panic swept me, and for a moment everything froze: me, frozen where I stood; Mr. Turner, frozen with his gun; the mobile home, the moonlight, time—everything but my galloping panic.

Then up popped Rooster from behind one of the bushes out in the middle of the bark dust, and he was instantly running like I'd never thought he could run. He shot past me.

The trouble was, Rooster's endurance wasn't on a par with his speed, and back on the driveway, around the bend and out of sight of the mobile home, I caught him. He was bent over, huffing like a locomotive.

"Come on!" I pleaded, and gave him a yank.

Just then a sudden new sound filled the air.

"His motorcycle!" I gasped.

Like a couple of swimmers, we veered out into the trees and dived behind a log. Moments later a single beam of light swept around the corner and bounced through the branches. I heard gravel spinning out and the motor wound up to a shrill pitch.

Then I heard Mr. Turner wreck his motorcycle.

The air filled with a scraping clatter. The light beam pitched up into the starry sky, bounced around for a second, then snuffed out as Mr. Turner and his motorcycle skidded across the road, down over the ditch, and out into the swamp where the little creek came through the culvert. The engine made a gurgling sound, then choked to a stop.

Rooster and I popped our heads up for a quick look. For all we knew he was dead. But then a barrage of cuss words welled up from the swamp and we heard Mr. Turner sloshing up out of the water. We ducked down again. The chorus of swearing washed over us. Mr. Turner knew words that would have made even Jon Pindar turn pale—some directed at the motorcycle, some at the loose gravel, but most of them meant for us. I hardly dared to breathe. If he found us in this mood he'd tear us limb from limb. Even Rooster seemed to understand. Pressed up against the log, we followed the proceedings with our ears. Mr. Turner fired a few more volleys of choice words down the driveway, then sloshed back out into the swamp and dragged his motorcycle up from the water. Then, for what seemed like an eternity, he stomped on the starter—cussing and muttering the whole time, only pausing now and then to kick a tire.

Finally the motor gave a sick cough then sputtered back to life, and Mr. Turner, still wearing only his pajama bottoms and a good layer of swamp mud and riding what sounded like a very sick machine, putted down the shadowy driveway.

"I think he's goin' to the ranch," I moaned. "Do you think he saw who you were?"

Rooster thought a moment then gave me a big grin. "Bang!" he said.

Figuring we'd be safer if we kept away from the road, Rooster and I made our way back to the ranch through the woods. When we finally broke out into the open pasture there was no sign of Mr. Turner anywhere, and nothing to make us think he'd been there. Everything was quiet and dark except for the usual light from Rooster's window and the lopsided moon, now hanging straight overhead. The two of us drug back to our beds. It had been a long night.

The next morning at the breakfast table Mom said, "You got circles under your eyes, Susie. Not sleeping well?"

"Havin' bad dreams," I muttered, lying.

"Dreamin' about them bears?" Grandpa asked.

I nodded. "Stuff like that."

"Well, I swear you were sure sound asleep when Mr. Turner came," Percy said.

I almost choked on my bite of egg. "Mr. Turner?" I glanced over at Rooster, hoping he wouldn't say anything. He was poking food down as though the conversation wasn't even going on.

"Didn't you even hear him?" Percy questioned.

"Hear what?"

"Mr. Turner. He came up on his motorcycle lookin' for a robber."

"A robber?"

"Yeah."

"No," I said. "I musta been sleepin' too good."

"What were you doin' last night, Rooster?" Dad asked.

Rooster looked up at hearing his name. Chewing and grinning at the same time he scanned the room then turned back to his food again.

Across the table, Percy gave a nod in Rooster's direction and on his lips he silently formed the words, "It—was—him."

Later that morning Mr. Turner rode up to the house with a policeman. He had scrape marks down the side of his face and big bandages on his hands and both arms. He was walking with a limp. Dad and Grandpa and Mr. Turner and the policeman all went to Rooster's cabin, and they didn't come out for a long time.

"Whadda you suppose he did?" Percy asked.

"How would I know?" I answered. I felt rotten inside. Some lesson I'd taught him. I'd almost gotten him shot, and now I fully expected them to lead him out in handcuffs and take him (and maybe me, too) off to jail.

To my relief, when the men did come out, they weren't pulling Rooster along in chains, and they didn't come grab me either. They stood talking.

"He's a little kid in a man's body," the policeman said. "I could take him in, but I can't see where it'd do any good. He certainly doesn't seem to be dangerous."

Mr. Turner wasn't happy, though. He wanted something done.

Dad said, "How can you punish a guy who doesn't even know he's done anything wrong?" Mr. Turner started to object, but Dad cut him off. "Look," he said, "we'll keep an eye on him, but we can't tie him up. He ain't a dog."

"Lock him up at night," Mr. Turner demanded. "There's a lock on that door, isn't there? You wouldn't let your kids out running around at night like that, so why him? If he's got a little kid's mind, then treat him like one." He turned to the policeman. "I didn't move out here to get robbed blind. I mean it. If you won't protect me, then I'll do it myself."

"That's all fine and good," the policeman said, "but remember this, the penalty for robbery isn't death. You'd better put that gun away and forget about it or you're going to get yourself in trouble."

That afternoon Jon and Percy called me out behind the barn to tell me that "my buddy," meaning Rooster, had stolen the bow and arrows from the cave. They were livid.

For the next few days traps multiplied along the trail to the cave like rabbits. At first they dug more camouflaged holes. But then the digging stopped and new kinds of booby traps began sprouting up—bent-down limbs that flew up when a rope was tripped; hidden nooses that grabbed ankles; trip-strings that dropped nets out of trees; logs that dropped to cut off retreats; tin cans tied together in long strings to wrap around the victim's legs; fake paths that led into mud holes. The woods turned into a torture chamber—all custom-made for Rooster.

Getting him to blunder into the traps was the easiest thing in the world. But the saddest part was that Rooster never understood who it was that was setting the traps for him. I told him, of course, but my words never sank in. All he really understood was that every time he found himself snared in one, Jon and Percy were always there like heroes to pull him out. So instead of seeing them as the reason for his misery, he looked on them as his saviors. They'd come running to him, whooping and screaming and waving their weapons as if they were chasing off the bad guys, and while they fought their imaginary battle, they'd cut him loose or untangle him or lift him out (whatever the particular trap called for), and Rooster would fall all over them with thank-yous.

It made me sick to see.

There was one time during these weeks when the boys slipped from Rooster's favor, or at least Jon did. Early in the summer when the two of them visited Rooster's camp to look for stolen stuff, Jon had found a pretty locket and chain hanging suspended by a piece of string in Rooster's tent. He took it, figuring it was probably stolen. It was heart-shaped and hinged open. Inside was a photograph of a woman's face. It wasn't a good photograph, and not a good-looking face, either.

Shortly after that, Jon got a crush on a girl named Sarah Littlejohn, who came up to spend her weekends at the lake with her family at their cabin. As demonstration of his eternal love for her, he began wearing the locket with a picture of her replacing the one of the lady. Sarah was almost as obnoxious as Jon was, twice his size, and well-developed for her age, which multiplied his affection for her by two. Jon wore the locket with her picture in it everywhere he went.

One day Rooster spotted the locket around Jon's neck and, to our amazement, laid claim to it. He blurted "Mine!" and snatched at it. Jon spun away and poked it down inside his sweatshirt for safety, but Rooster insisted that it was his. It took some time to get him calmed down. Jon lied that Sarah had given the locket to him, and he even opened it up and showed him her picture, which didn't seem so much to satisfy Rooster as to confuse him. Both Percy and I told Jon that since it meant so much to Rooster, maybe he should give the locket back—that maybe it was a personal possession and that the lady in the picture was someone close to him. Of course, Jon would have nothing to do with giving the locket back. From then on, though, he kept it tucked down out of sight whenever Rooster was around. But Rooster never forgot the locket or that Jon had it, and any time Jon forgot to hide it inside his shirt, Rooster would raise a stink.

Chapter 22

he roof sprouted atop our new house in just days, and the siding went on even faster. Dad and Grandpa were up before dawn each morning and the sound of their sawing and hammering was our alarm clock. As the day for our hearing closed in, their pace speeded up to a near frenzy. Even fishing and horseshoes went by the wayside. Dad and Grandpa were working on a theory that what went up wouldn't come down. They figured that if they could get the darned thing looking more like a house than a pile of boards, the county guys would throw up their hands and just say, "The heck with it."

Needless to say, they and Mom didn't see eye to eye on the matter. Mom still clung to the idea that we were nothing more than innocent victims of an honest mistake, and that our best chance of getting a fair shake from the county was for the two of them to quit being bull-headed and start cooperating. The day they started building the porch, the strain between Dad and Mom finally blew up and for the first time in my nine years, I heard the two of them yell at each other. You could hear them through the wall, and when Dad came out the door he kicked a bucket halfway across the yard.

August was hot, anyway—hot as any of us had ever seen it. The heat alone was enough to make a saint cranky, and heaven knows, we weren't any of us saints. I was mad at the boys; the boys were mad at me; Mr. Turner was mad at everybody and put up a chain link fence around his mobile home to keep out the world; Dad and Grandpa were mad at the county planners; Mom was mad at Dad; and if all that wasn't enough, we were all well aware that down in Redbone the county people, in their own way, were mighty mad, too.

About my only happiness during this period came on an inner tube out in the middle of Russ Lake, when the cast on my arm finally reached the final stage of decay, slid off over my fingers, and settled out of sight to the bottom.

When the day of the appeals hearing came you could cut the tension with a knife, and Mom was the worst. The others managed not to cross her, but I wasn't so lucky. I set her off twice, both times having to do with my dress. I only had one dress and I'd worn it just once, to be flower girl in my Uncle Louie's wedding. It was a white, lacy thing with puffy sleeves and a charred spot from the fire down by the hem where it didn't show much. It was an okay dress, as dresses went, but the trouble was I hated dresses. When Mom told me I was going to have to look like a young lady for the hearing and wear the thing, I made the mistake of throwing a fit. Mom exploded in my face, and I had the dress on in no time flat.

The second explosion came ten minutes later when my dress and I were standing at the wrong end of the cow Dad had just finished milking. With her udder empty and evidently feeling the urge to empty her other systems, too, she arched her tail up and emptied her bladder all over my dress. I went dripping into the house feeling like a toilet bowl, and Mom blew up again. If Mom had been her normal self, she would have laughed and said something about diapers or my "new perfume" and let it go at that, but not this day. "I ask you to wear a dress once in a blue moon, and you can't keep it clean for five minutes!"

"Gosh, Mom...don't blame me," I objected. "It was the cow's fault. I was just standin' there."

But she wasn't impressed and told me that I knew darn well what came out that end of a cow.

I was still dripping bath water and buttoning my shirt as I mashed myself into the truck to leave. Rooster was standing off to the side with his pants zipped up, which meant he thought he was going to town too.

"You ain't goin' this time, Rooster," Dad said to him out the window. "All we're doin's goin' to a meetin'."

Rooster looked hurt and started to climb aboard anyway.

"Wait a minute," Percy said, and he unpacked himself from the seat and ran over to the barn. When he came back he had a play rifle he'd whittled out of a board. He gave it to Rooster then led him over to the new house, talking to him as they went. A big grin spread across Rooster's face and he sat down on the edge of the new deck with the play gun across his lap and his legs swinging like a little kid's.

"What'd you do?" Dad asked Percy when he came jogging back.

Percy said, "Just asked him if he'd guard the house while we was gone."

When we drove off, Rooster was sitting bolt upright on the porch with the gun in his lap, grinning like he'd just woke up in heaven and it was full of garbage cans.

The parking lot at the county offices in Redbone was full of shiny cars and pickups. Our old dusty truck looked embarrassed to be there. It was too long to fit a parking spot, so Dad turned it sideways across several spaces back beside the dumpster.

The hearings room was dinky. The appeals officer and two other men sat up front behind a blond table facing four rows of folding metal chairs. As we filed in, a guy with a telescoping metal pointer and an easel full of charts and maps was making the case to let his client tear down a house and put up a motel. There was a scattering of people in the chairs, all of them in their Sunday clothes and looking like they knew what they were doing. In the back row, Mr. Turner was seated.

"What's he doin' here?" I whispered to Percy.

"Beats me," Percy whispered back. "Maybe he's a witness or somethin'."

Up front, the guy with the pointer was quoting county codes like scripture. And when he finally folded shop and left, another guy took his place, then another. It was like watching a slow parade with too many politicians in cars and no floats or clowns. They each talked the same lawyer gibberish, trying to get the hearings officer to let their client build something where it wasn't supposed to be built or tear something down that should have been left standing. Before long, Percy and I started entertaining ourselves by squishing spit and firing off low-level bodily noises, which amused us but not those around us. It wasn't until after Mom had taken us out to the hall to give us our second "straighten up or else" speech that the officer finally called out Dad's name.

Dad wagged his finger to let the guy know who he was, then looked over at Mom. "You wanta do the talkin' or me?" he asked.

"You can," she said. She reached up and squeezed his hand and smiled for the first time all day. "Easy as hunting bear," she said.

Dad slid forward a lot like a little kid working his way up to the principal's desk when he's just been caught at his first big sin at school. He told the officer he couldn't afford a lawyer, so he'd have to do his own lying.

The officer chuckled and said that'd be fine with him. He read off a list of all the rules we had broken, then asked Dad to go ahead and make his case.

Dad knew about as much about making a case as he did about splitting atoms. He fidgeted, then said, "We just figured there'd been some sorta mistake. You see, our house burned down. Don't know if you knew that. Burned down this spring, an' it's just that we didn't know there was any laws against buildin' a new one. Kinda hard livin' with no roof over your head, you know?"

"I imagine," the officer said. Then he said, "Do you understand the problem here, Mr. Simpson? I have a feeling you don't."

"Guess I don't see where there is a problem," Dad said.

The officer cleared his throat and said, "You look to me like a do-it-yourselfer."

Dad nodded. "Pretty much everything."

"Including selling property?"

Dad nodded again.

"Well, that was your big mistake, Mr. Simpson. You should have worked through somebody who knew what they were doing. But I guess that's water under the bridge."

Then he proceeded to educate Dad on how land-use laws were designed to protect timber and farmland from development, and how the only reason we were allowed to farm on land that should be forestland was that we'd been doing it since before the laws were made. We were "grandfathered in," as he put it.

Dad nodded. He pulled his handkerchief out of his pocket, wiped his nose, and stuffed it back in.

The appeals officer leaned back in his chair and laced his hands behind his head. "But you see, Mr. Simpson, the trouble comes when you begin changing the use. Your property was zoned to be used as it had always been—as a ranch with a single-family dwelling on it. Now, if you decided to stop ranching and put in a motel, this would obviously be a new and different use that wouldn't be allowable. We wouldn't issue a permit to do that. You couldn't put in an amusement part or racing track or anything like that. Do you understand?"

Dad picked at his thumbnail a moment, then sniffed and said, "Well...I guess I ain't sure where you're comin' from, cause I ain't askin' to put in no amusement park. I ain't askin' for nothin' that wasn't there before. Just wanta rebuild my house that burned down."

"You miss the point," the officer said. "You are asking for something different. You're not asking for an amusement park, but you're asking to put two homes on a property that has always had just one. You see?"

Dad just stood there for a bit, not moving or saying anything. You could tell that the appeals officer's logic had thrown him for a loop. He gave his thigh a couple of half-hearted pats with his palm, then looked back at Mom and Grandpa, then back to the officer again. "I ain't sure what to say," Dad said. "If I was rich I'd just hire me a shyster like these other people an' let him throw some big words at you. But I ain't rich."

His voice raised. "If a guy don't have money he gets walked on around here."

The officer leaned forward in his chair and said, "Now, Mr. Simpson, there's no call to think like that. I can see this is all new to you, but money has nothing to do with it. You make a good argument and you'll get a good decision from me. It's that simple. The thing is, the burden of proof is on you. By law I can't overrule current zoning unless you can make your case." He gave a long pause, then said, "You know, Mr. Simpson, I have a feeling you and your family might appreciate a few minutes out in the hall getting yourselves organized. We have some of your adjoining property owners here to speak, anyway. How would it be if we took them first, then got back to you in a few minutes?"

Dad looked back at Mr. Turner, then to the officer again. "Why's he here?" he asked.

"It's standard procedure," the man said. "Adjoining owners are always notified."

Dad nodded, then turned and led us out.

In the hall the three grownups huddled. "Maybe one of you oughta do the talkin'," Dad suggested. "I ain't doin' too good."

"You're doing fine," Mom replied. "Just don't irritate him. You can see he's on our side, but we just haven't given him any good arguments."

With Percy peeking through the door relaying the goings-on in the hearings room, the grownups began trying to come up with the kinds of arguments the hearings officer wanted, while Mom wrote them down. But it was hopeless. It was like kindergartners trying to write the Gettysburg address. Mom used her eraser more than her lead, and our list stood still.

"How about the Bible?" Dad suggested. "Don't it say somethin' in the Bible about homes? I think Jesus said it...or maybe Moses."

"I think it was Shakespeare," Grandpa said. "But you're barkin' up the wrong tree if you start tryin' to build a case on the Bible. We know 'bout as much about the Bible as the man in the moon. Anyway, the only Bible these guys care 'bout's them code books they got in there. You find a verse'r two from one o' them books—then you'll have somethin'."

It went on like that for a good ten minutes or so—one person or another coming up with ideas the others didn't like. Mom wrote a few things down, but our list was puny. And to make matters worse, over at the door Percy was passing the news that the people from the Forest Service were doing their best to cut us off at the knees. It was clear they weren't on our side, and they had rules to support themselves.

"So, what's new?" Grandpa gritted. "Don't matter what we say, anyway. Them guys is in cahoots. We can make us a list as long as from here to hell, but when it comes right down to it, the only way we're gonna get a house is to build it like we're doin'...then fight the buggers off ."

We filed back into the room just as Mr. Turner was stepping forward.

The officer asked if he was Mr. Turner and he said he was.

"Go ahead," the hearings officer said.

Mr. Turner fidgeted with his rings, then said that he pretty much agreed with what the Forest Service guys had said.

"Is that it?" the officer asked.

Mr. Turner rubbed his chin like he was feeling his whiskers. "No," he said. "It's just that I'm worried about fire."

"Fire?"

"Yeah. They do a lot of burning up there, and I'm afraid it's just a matter of time before they start a forest fire."

"Good god!" Grandpa blurted out. "What a bunch of baloney." He started to stand up, but Dad pulled him back down.

"Please," the appeals officer said, looking back at Grandpa. "If you have something to say, we'll give you a chance in a bit. But don't deny others their turn." Looking back at Mr. Turner he said, "Go ahead."

Mr. Turner rubbed his chin again. "Well...there is another thing. They've got an old bum living up there with them who's about as retarded as they come, and he's been breaking into houses for months, now. He's broken into mine twice. It's gotten so bad I've had to fence my place and put in an alarm."

The appeals officer said, "That's too bad. I don't suppose it's too pleasant being robbed, but it doesn't have any bearing on why these people should or shouldn't be granted a variance. It's beside the point."

"If there was no house, nobody would live there. That's my point."

"Some neighbor," Grandpa muttered aloud. Mr. Turner didn't turn around, but by the way he stiffened you could tell he'd heard.

Then Grandpa leaned over and whispered to Dad, "I wish you'da never sold that property. We'da been better off livin' in a cave than next to this skunk."

The appeals officer gave Mr. Turner a long annoyed look, then asked him if he had anything else. When he said he didn't, the officer thanked him and without so much as glancing one way or the other, Mr. Turner walked toward the door. As he passed our chairs, Grandpa said in a voice you could hear all over the room, "When I get home I reckon I'd better set me some weasel traps."

Now the officer looked back at Dad and asked if he was ready. Dad told him he was as ready as he'd ever be and he made his way to the front where he fished Mom's list out of his pocket and unfolded it. Finally he said, "Well...I guess it goes like this. We didn't come up with much. But when it comes right down to it, we figured the main thing is that there's always been a house there— same land, same family—almost a hundred years." He stopped and waited, as though in that one statement he'd said all there was to say. But the officer just nodded. Finally, Dad said, "Yeah, an' I can take you out there an' show you where there's been two log houses built an' two more made outa sawed lumber. When one wears out, we put up a new one—same as when your clothes wear out. We're house builders in our family. Always have been."

The officer smiled. "And good ones, I'm sure."

"Darn good ones," Dad said. "We build a lot better ones'n that tin can the Turners drug in."

"I'm sure," the officer said. "The trouble is, Mr. Simpson, that tin can, as you call it, is the only legal home that can be put on that property. The fact that your family built all the preceding homes isn't relevant. What is relevant is that right now, at this moment, there is a house out there. Unfortunately for you, the Turners own it." The appeals officer tapped his thumbnail with his pen and said, "What other arguments have you come up with?"

Dad's arms drooped to his sides. He had his feet close together and was beginning to sway from side to side.

Dad shifted his feet to stop the swaying, then lifted the paper up to reading position again. "Well...we got a couple more here," he said. Then he left another long silence while he read the words on Mom's list. "Says here somethin' about 'caretakers'." He turned to Mom. "What was that, again—the part about caretakers?"

Mom was caught off guard. She stammered and after a false start, she said, "Uh, that was about the ranch needing somebody there to keep it up."

"Yeah," Dad said. "That's what it was. We just figure it wouldn't take long for the place to be a real mess without us."

"I suppose you have a real love for your farm," the officer said.

"Like an arm," Dad said. He looked back at Mom again, hoping she had more to add, but she didn't, so he went on. "Yeah, it's a big place. We keep it up good. None of them pesticides or poisons or nothin'. Do it all with a lotta sweat an' hard work."

The officer nodded, but he was obviously no more impressed by Dad's second argument than his first. "What else did you come up with?" he asked. "You said you had some more."

"Just one," Dad said. "Don't know it'll do any good, though. I can tell by lookin' that I ain't givin' you what you want."

"Don't try to read me," the officer said. "I'm listening."

Dad looked at the paper again, then poked it into his pocket. "We just thought it'd help if we told you why we sold that hunk of land to the Turners. Does that interest you?"

The man shrugged. "It might. Just tell me what you have."

Dad was swaying again, and you could see that not only was his confidence draining from him like a plug had been pulled, but he was getting mad, too. His neck and the backs of his ears were turning red. "Well, I don't reckon you'll understand this," he said. "By the looks of you, you ain't a poor man. Got a nice suit an' slick haircut an' all...but it ain't that way with us. We've scratched for what we have, an' when a poor man's house burns down it ain't like he can go out an' dig a wad of dough out of his piggy bank. If we didn't sell that land, mister, there wasn't nothin' but a tent in our future. Sellin' that land was the only way we was gonna have a house, an' that's the gospel truth. Now if that ain't enough reason for you to give us that permit, then there ain't nothin' I can say's gonna do it, an' that's for sure." He took a big gulp of air then puffed it out through his cheeks. "We need a house, mister."

The officer leaned back. "Oh, Mr. Simpson." He drew a big breath. "I was hoping you could do better. I'd like nothing more than to give you what you want. I really would. But it's going to be hard. You're not giving me much to work with. I mean, your reasons are certainly good ones, but they aren't the kind I need.

"Take this last one, for instance. You tell me I should issue this variance because you're having money problems. Just think what you're saying, now. You're saying that any time anyone gets hard up for money, we should change our zoning laws so he can sell his land off piecemeal. Well, everybody has money problems at one time or another. If we leave our laws at the mercy of people's finances, they won't be worth the paper they're printed on."

He leaned forward again. "You see, Mr. Simpson, the land is more than just a possession. The land's like air. Even those of us who might not live as close to it as you do are utterly dependent on it. This world can't exist without good cropland and good timberland and ranchland. And I'd hate to think of a world without lakes and rivers and places for recreation. And I don't mean just for today and tomorrow.

"You say your family has had that property for a hundred years. That's impressive. But what about the next hundred...and the next and the next? And who owned that land through all those thousands and millions of years before you? These land use laws assume that we have an obligation to our children and grandchildren to leave them an earth that isn't all fouled up—that isn't split up into billions of little lots or paved over."

"That's all good an' fine," Dad gritted. "But I'll tell you somethin'. Land ain't the only thing that's like air. So's shelter. You can save all the land from here to hell for growin' food an' trees. Hope you do. But when you start tellin' me I can't put a roof over my family's head, you've gone too far. You go ahead an' do your job. More power to you. But I got a job to do, too. I got a family to see after."

Suddenly there was a squeak as a chair slid against the floor, and Grandpa's figure came stalking to the front of the room. He plucked his hat off his head as he went, uncovering his smashed-down white hair, and in a voice that was so gooey-nice it wasn't nice at all, he said, "Hold it just a minute here. I got a little somethin' to say, too. If you ask me, this sounds a lot like a communist conspiracy."

"Whoa...whoa...." The appeals officer waved his hand. "There's no need for that."

"Says who?" Grandpa blurted.

"Settle down, mister," the officer demanded. "And could you tell me who you are?"

"'Scuse me," Grandpa said. "Harold M. Simpson. I'm the boy's dad. And by the way, the 'M' in the name stands for 'mad'."

Looking sternly at Grandpa, the officer said, "Your son has the floor right now."

"No...go ahead," Dad said. "I've done all the damage I know how. I ain't doin' no good, anyway."

With the stern look still on his face, the officer said, "Go ahead, then. But listen, I don't want any more of this communist conspiracy business. I'm here to listen to sound arguments, and even unsound ones, but no way do I have to listen to accusations like that. Understand?"

Grandpa tapped his wadded up hat against his palm, and bore his eyes down on the man. "I'll do my best," he said, "but let me tell you somethin'. You've put a burr in my fanny, and I ain't feelin' real nice right now. You see, we're good, hard-working people. We go by the laws an' don't hurt nobody or nothing...and that includes the land. An' we come in here today like good law-abidin' citizens to get some fair treatment. But we ain't gettin' it. You ever seen a pig try to fly, mister?"

The officer just gazed at him without answering.

"Well...ya ain't," Grandpa said. "Me neither. That's cause they can't. Put together wrong. The thing is, me an' my boy, here, can't fly neither. Some people got wings on their tongues an' some people don't. We don't. We come in here an' talk plain, simple, common-sense talk to you, but you tell us it ain't no good. You want lawyer talk. I'll tell you somethin': pigs can't fly, an' poor country folk can't talk like city-slickin' lawyers. So, dang it, get your pen an' write us one o' them buildin' permits an' let us outa here."

"Mr. Simpson...." The officer drew a breath then flopped both hands palm down on the table. "What can I say. I understand your plight. I do. I've presided over enough of these hearings to understand that some people do have trouble arguing their cases in person. But the fact is, I'm obligated to base my judgments on sound reasons, and you and your son haven't give me any. All I've gotten from the two of you is a sob story."

"Sob story!" Grandpa glared at the officer with his mouth hanging open. "Who do you think you are? You ain't God." He threw a glance at Dad. "We shouldn'ta come here. This thing's rigged. This ain't a hearin'. It's a lynchin'."

"Wait a minute, here," the officer boomed.

But Grandpa wouldn't stop. "You wait!" He pointed a bony finger at the man. "If you want somebody on that land out there who'll take care of it, that's fine an' dandy. But it ain't the Forest Service. It's us. Better understand that. I know you an' them Forest Service guys is in cahoots to get us out, but it won't work. We won't go."

From her chair Mom said, "Grandpa, please."

But Grandpa ignored her. "You guys can take your building permits an' stuff 'em up your noses."

"What?" The officer pounded the table.

"Up your noses," Grandpa repeated.

"Mr. Simpson..."

"Hush!"

The officer tried to say something else, but Grandpa cut him off. "You ever seen a shotgun from the front, mister?"

The officer bolted to his feet, "Are you threatening me?"

"Who...me? You said you wanted some facts, an' that's what you're gettin'—facts. Fact is, our house's goin' up, permit or no permit. Period. You let us alone an' you won't hear from us for another hundred years...an' that's the gospel truth. But if you an' your commie buddies poke your faces out there on our place again, we'll blow the boogers right outa your noses!"

"That does it!" The appeals officer's face was as red as a beet and he poked his finger at the door. "You and your clan get out of here right now, or I'll call the police."

Grandpa swept a deep bow, turned, and walked proudly down the aisle and out the door.

For a moment, nobody moved. It was as if the air had been sucked out of every sail in the room. Then Mom stood up and muttered "Sorry" to the officer, and herded us out.

When we got back to the truck, Grandpa was sitting in the front seat combing his hair in the mirror. He drew a neat part, then slicked it back. He was like an old rooster that had just strutted its stuff in the hen house and was now preening. As Mom climbed in the door beside him he poked the comb into his hip pocket and pulled her over against his shoulder. Mom gave him a weak smile, one that wasn't mad but wasn't pleasant either. She pushed away from his clutch and sat looking out the open truck window. It was a quiet trip back home.

When we drove in the yard Percy said, "Look!" and he pointed toward the front porch of the new house where Rooster was leaned up against a post, sound asleep, with the wooden gun still laying across his lap.

"He ain't even moved," Percy exclaimed. "He's sat there guardin' the house the whole time."

When the truck door slammed, Rooster's head popped up and he drew the rifle to his shoulder, then lowered it. A big grin split his face.

"I'll be," Dad marveled. "If he ain't the best guard dog I've ever seen."

Chapter 23

School started after Labor Day. I was in the fourth grade now, with a desk at the back of the room right in front of the World Book Encyclopedia and the pencil sharpener, and close to the door that led to the bathroom and recess (which I went through often and fast and usually first). It was a good desk with a lot of gum on the bottom but not many carvings on the top, and directly behind the fattest kid in the school, who formed what was darn near a wall between me and the teacher, which was a real advantage, considering my usual behavior.

The only thing bad about the fourth grade was that Jon and Percy had both graduated to the upstairs room. They were suddenly "big kids" while I was still a "little" one. This newly elevated status went directly to Percy's head and brought on an instant personality split. At home he was still the same old brother I'd always known—just a little bigger. But once we set foot on school property, he turned into a monster. He gave me clear orders to keep away, if I knew what was good for me. I had the same orders from Jon Pindar. All this wouldn't have been so bad, except for the fact that it threatened to totally wipe out the only side of school I liked—recess.

I told Mom about Percy's ridiculous behavior, of course, and asked her if she wouldn't do something about it. But to my horror, she sided against me. She said he was growing up and "asserting his independence." Then she asked if I hadn't noticed his voice.

"His voice?"

"Yes...the way it's getting lower. He's turning into a young man."

"I'm growin' up, too," I objected. "My voice's gettin' lower, too. Anyway, what'll I do at recess? There ain't nothin' to do. They won't even let me in the hideout this year. I already hate school...an' now I'm gonna hate recess."

The next day, coming home on the bus, I offered Jon and Percy a quarter each and all the marbles I owned to let me back into the group.

"They'll laugh at us," Jon said.

"Who'll laugh?" I asked.

"The eighth graders. They don't like little kids."

But the quarters and marbles were more than the boys could resist, and when I threw in a couple of leather belts I'd gotten from Grandpa that were a mile too big for me, anyway, the deal was done.

The bus dropped Percy and me off at the mailbox. We raced for the mail, then headed in the driveway. I kicked a pine cone along, and Percy was throwing rocks at birds. We'd just passed the Turners' place when the brush up ahead started rattling like somebody was thrashing it with an eggbeater. Then, a good-sized mountain of brown fur that looked all too familiar came pushing out. Percy and I dove down into the ditch like two soldiers hitting their foxhole.

"I think it's him!" Percy whispered with eyes the size of silver dollars.

The memory of that evening along the stream below Rooster's camp flashed in my mind like fireworks. My heart thumped in my ears so hard I could hear it, and I whispered, "What do we do?"

Percy just stared at me. We lay plastered to the bank, afraid to move for fear of being seen, but knowing at the same time that we had to take a look sooner or later to make sure it wasn't coming our way. Finally, about as slowly as something growing, we inched our eyes up over the berm.

The bear had its rump to us. It hadn't moved from where we'd first seen it. But even from that angle, we could see that where its left ear should have been, there was nothing.

Percy turned his head to me and whispered, "Listen. If he comes after us, we'll have to try to beat him to the Turners' house. Understand?"

I nodded.

He added, "But don't move unless I say."

We both held like statues, with Percy taking careful little peeps now and then. I shifted my feet and hands so they'd be in position for a fast start if Percy gave the "run" signal. In my head I tried to figure the best route to take to the Turners' and how I'd get over the chain-link fence if their gate was locked.

Finally, Percy whispered, "He's goin'."

I peeked up just as its heinie disappeared into the trees.

"Now what?" I whispered.

"Go on home, I guess," he said. But he didn't seem too certain. Then he said, "Maybe we'd better wait a little while."

Well, we waited more than a little while. Finally we eased up from our hiding place and inched forward. A slug couldn't have moved slower, and with every step we swept our eyes in every direction, just to make sure. When we came to the spot in the road where the bear had been, we both broke into the wildest sprint you've ever seen, and we didn't slow down all the way back to the ranch.

We found Dad and Grandpa nailing siding on the new house and Mom sitting in the shade snapping beans. We gave them a breathless blow-by-blow of what had happened.

Mom's snapping slowed down, then stopped. She looked over at Dad. "That bear's dangerous, Sam," she said.

"I know," he said.

"I was hopin' we'd seen the last of that ol' booger," Grandpa said.

"Probably down after apples or salmon or somethin'," Dad said. He pulled one of his gloves off and shook some sawdust out, and the kind of smile that told you he was about to tease or say something funny crept onto his face. "This is serious," he said. "An'

I don't mean to make fun of it, but how's this sound?" He chuckled out loud. "Whadda you say we get rid o' two problems at once. Whadda you say we catch ol' One-Ear an' tie him here by our door an' then see how itchy them county guys are to bother us."

Grandpa slapped his knees. "Couldn't you just see it?" he said. "Thing is, I'm afraid it'd be us ol' One-Ear'd bite an' not them."

"I don't know," Dad said. "We'd be pretty tough meat. Them county boys sit around down there gettin' fat an' lazy. They'd be a tender meal."

"No," Grandpa said, "I think we're right at the top of that bear's eatin' list. Tip-top. I reckon he likes us about as much as we like county men. You an' me'd make tough chewin', all right, but I'd bet a bundle he'd still gobble us up in no time flat if he had his druthers."

Dad said, "Anyway, I think you two kids'd better stick around close to the house for a while."

And Mom said, "Real close. In fact, I don't want you two out of sight of the buildings. And when you come home from school, one of us will meet you at the mailbox."

An arrangement like that would normally have drawn heavy objections from Percy and me, but this time we didn't mind at all. One go-round with a bear in a lifetime was plenty.

"Up to a little huntin', Grandpa?" Dad asked.

"Long as I don't have to climb no more trees," he chuckled. "Or did you mean huntin' county men?"

"That'd be fine, too," Dad said.

Mom set her kettle full of snapped beans down and said, "I don't like this talk about shooting people. Not even as a joke. It's not funny."

Grandpa hitched his nail apron straight then dug his fingers around in the nails for a moment. Looking over at Mom, he said, "You know what 'peckin' order' means?"

"Sure," she said.

Grandpa defined it anyway. "Means there's weak things an' strong things in this world, an' lest you like gettin' pushed around, you'd better be one of the strong ones. Thing is, peckin' order ain't always set up by fightin'. Fact, most o' the time it's set up by struttin' an' bluffin'. You watch the animals out in the barnyard. Ol' mister rooster out in the chicken coop don't hafta fight the whole flock to let 'em know he's in charge. Just struts 'round thumpin' his chest, an' the others get the message. Right? Ruffles his feathers an' flaps his wings an' does a little bullyin', an' that's about it."

He cleared his throat and spit down in the dust, then mashed it with his sole. "Us people got our peckin' order, too. You let yourself be on the bottom an' you get told what to do. Pull yourself up to the top...an' you do the tellin'. Now you take a rich man. He pulls himself up with his money. When you got money, you're at the top o' the peckin' order. Then there's them guys down at the county offices. They don't have no money. They got their laws an' that's all. So they go struttin' 'round with their fists full of them laws...an' the rest of us just fall in behind 'em like a bunch of ducklings behind mama duck. Now I don't know about you, but I don't like that. An' it seems to me that unless we wanta get gobbled up an' spit out by that bunch of shysters, we're gonna have to show 'em who's who. Ain't nobody gonna get hurt. No shootin'. Just a little struttin' and bluffin'.'"

"Grandpa," Mom said, "you're wrong. Shooting a bear is one thing, but you start waving a gun around a government man and somebody's going to get hurt or in big trouble. I mean it."

Grandpa held up his hands. "No...that ain't what I'm sayin'. Let me say it again. I ain't aimin' to shoot nobody. I'm just sayin' that if we strut around a little with our feathers ruffled an' wave a bear rifle under their noses, they'll whimper off like beat dogs. Wouldn't have to pull the trigger or nothin'."

Mom shook her head.

"I'm sorry if I rile you," Grandpa said. "I really am. You know how it is with me an' my mouth when it gets goin'...but remember this. There's some things in life that's just too important to back down from. An' that's right as rain. Them wimpy pencil-pushers think they rule this hen house, but I got news for 'em."

The next afternoon when Percy and I got off the bus, Grandpa and Rooster were waiting for us on the old Ford tractor at the mailbox. Grandpa had his rifle laying across his knees. "Orders from the boss," he said. "Bear patrol."

With Rooster standing on the hitch and Percy and me sitting on the fenders, we started for home. Not far from where we'd seen the bear the day before, and in sight of the Turners' mobile home, a car came up behind us.

"County men," Grandpa muttered. He stomped down on the brake and gave the wheel a hard turn that skidded the tractor sideways across the driveway and threw Rooster clear off his perch and almost did the same to Percy and me. Rooster wasn't hurt, but he gave his knees and elbows a good going-over to make sure. Grandpa apologized for the wild driving, then said, "Wait here." He climbed down holding his rifle and strode around front and sat back against the front tire with the gun cradled in the crook of his arm.

The car was stopped a couple dozen long paces down the road. There were two men in it. One of them was the inspector Grandpa had given such a hard time. The other was one of the appeals officer's two helpers. The inspector was at the steering wheel, and he opened the door and climbed out. Stepping from behind the open door he raised both hands like he was being held up and said, "Don't shoot—we've got women and children in here." He started to laugh, but when Grandpa's face stayed stony, his smile melted.

Grandpa spit, then worked up another mouthful and spit again. "Got a nasty taste in my mouth," he said.

The inspector looked in at the helper, then back at Grandpa, and made one more stab at humor. Motioning to the tractor, he said, "Nice car you're driving."

Without smiling, Grandpa said, "Poor man's Cadillac." He reached back and patted the radiator. "Got another one back in the hangar that flies."

The inspector gave another short-lived laugh, but Grandpa still hadn't cracked a smile.

Now the hearings helper opened the door on the passenger side of the car and climbed out. He started toward Grandpa with some papers in his hand.

"Hold it!" Grandpa ordered.

The man stopped in his tracks.

"By the looks of them papers, you got some news for us," Grandpa said.

"So to speak."

"Good'r bad?"

The helper looked back at the inspector, then at Grandpa again. "Bad, I guess."

Grandpa nodded. "How bad?"

"Look, I don't feel comfortable talking to somebody when he's holding a gun," the helper said. "Can't you put that thing away or something?"

Grandpa gave his head a long, slow shake. "Nope." He looked down at his rifle then back at the guy again. "Got cold hands," he said. "Keeps 'em warm. Better'n walkin' around with your hands in your pockets."

The man stood a moment, fingering the papers, then started forward again.

"Stop!" Grandpa ordered. The man halted in his tracks like a trained dog. "This is private property, mister," Grandpa said. He let a long silence lapse, then said, "We're a pretty good-natured bunch out here. Lotta happy people. Only news we allow's good news." Now, for the first time, he turned the barrel of his gun in his lap so it pointed in the general direction of the man, and his finger slid forward along the stock onto the trigger.

The color drained from the man's face.

Grandpa lowered his head in a warning way and, peering out from under his brows, he said, "Now, you tell me you got *bad* news...right?"

The man nodded.

"Don't want it, then. Don't want no bad news."

The man looked over at the inspector for help, but when it didn't come he said, "Why don't I just lay the papers here in the road, then? You can read them if you want. All I'm supposed to do is deliver them."

"Do they say we can't build our house?" Grandpa asked.

The guy nodded again. "You lost your appeal." He laid the papers down on the road, never taking his eyes off the gun. "Sorry," he said.

"You ain't half as sorry as me," Grandpa said. Then, with a flick of his wrist, he cocked his rifle. I could hear it from where I was, and the two county guys could sure as heck hear it, loud and clear.

The closest man froze in his tracks. "What're you doing?" He began backing up.

Suddenly Grandpa let out something like a cross between a turkey gobble and an Indian war whoop.

The two men scrambled into the car, yanked their doors shut, and spun in reverse back down the driveway. The car swerved right and left, skimming one ditch and then the other, until it disappeared around the bend.

At the top of his lungs, Grandpa shouted, "That's what we think about bad news out here in God's country. An' don't come back!" He pointed the gun up in the air and pulled the trigger. There was a click as the firing pin hit an empty chamber. He was grinning from ear to ear.

"Rooster...sir," he said, turning to Rooster.

Rooster pumped his head.

"Mister Rooster, would you care to hold my empty gun while I pick up a little bad news off the road?" He gave Rooster the rifle then strutted out and got the papers.

Rooster held the empty gun as Grandpa drove us on toward the ranch. When he passed the Turners' mobile home, Mrs. Turner was standing in the open front door.

"She musta seen it," Percy said.

"Good," Grandpa said, and he cupped his hand beside his mouth and yelled, "Know any good tin cans around here a guy can shoot?" He belted out a laugh and gave a big thumbs up.

Mrs. Turner ducked back inside and slammed the door behind her.

"She ain't too friendly today, huh Rooster?" Grandpa said.

Rooster grinned like a rotten-toothed Cheshire cat. Holding to his perch on the tractor with one hand, with the other he raised Grandpa's rifle clumsily to his shoulder and went "Bang!"

Chapter 24

Grandpa was edgy for several days after his run-in with the county men. Of course he wouldn't admit to it, but you could tell he was by the way he kept looking out the driveway to see if anyone was coming, and wondering out loud what the penalty was for "just sittin' there with a gun on your lap." The whole family, for that matter, was uptight. We were sure he'd overstepped the line, and we figured the police would be showing up any time.

But the police never came, and with each day that passed Grandpa's spirits rose as he realized that his feather rufflin' had worked.

Mom, as usual, was less than happy about what he'd done. "You're just lucky nobody got hurt," she said. "You had those kids sitting right there behind you. What if your bluff hadn't worked? What if one of those men had lost his temper? And what about poor Rooster? He's already in trouble. If he gets mixed up in something like this, the next step for him is jail."

But the rest of us thought Grandpa had been downright brilliant. In our play we kids switched from being the Indians against the white men to Grandpa and the Simpson kids against the county guys. Of course we always made Rooster the county man. We gave him an old notebook and one of Mr. Pindar's jaunty little dress-up hats with a feather in the band to wear.

"He looks just like one of 'em," Grandpa said, "'cept a lot prettier."

Rooster didn't look like anything but a bum with a hat and notebook, but we made a cardboard badge that said "county man" and pinned it to his shirt, and gave him one of Dad's broken tape measures to hang on his belt. It was play to us, but as usual, it was real life to Rooster. We set ambushes and roadblocks for him every place from the barn to the end of the pasture (which was as far as Mom would let us stray with the bear on the loose), and he loved it.

A week or so later we finally heard from the real county men. They sent us a letter telling us we were now "officially in violation of the law," and that they wanted the "illegal structure removed."

"Notice they ain't hand deliverin' 'em no more," Grandpa said. "We've seen the last of them boys. They're afraid of us."

"Shoot," Dad said, "I'd like to see anybody try an' take this house down now, anyway. Take dynamite." He wadded up the letter and dropped it in the garbage. "They can mail us letters till the moon turns blue, but there ain't no way this house's comin' down. No way."

If one new house wasn't enough, we kids decided to build a treehouse, our reasoning being, it'd be a good place to dump boiling water and boulders on county men if they tried to storm the place. We picked a big forked pine tree off the end of the new house and started toting boards over. The thought was we'd build it ourselves, but Mom said that anything we three kids put together would fall down sooner or later (probably sooner), and that the top of a tree was a long way to fall from. She wanted Dad to build it. Dad, of course, already had his hands full, but he said he'd at least put up the "holdin' up" parts for us. So he fastened a ladder to the tree with nails a team of horses couldn't have pulled out, and rigged up a platform that was just as strong. Then he gave us a saw and hammer and our own can of nails and told us to go at it.

Our problem was how to get our boards up to the platform. If it'd been just Percy and me, we'd have carried them up one by one. But Jon Pindar never liked the simple way of doing things, and he sure as heck didn't want to do anything that involved work if there was any way around it. So he gave it some thought and came up with a scheme to hoist them up.

"Got a rope?" he asked.

Of course, living on a farm, we had plenty of ropes, and we sent Rooster off to get one. Ropes were one of the few things Rooster could find on his own. He'd been sent to fetch or hang them up enough times he'd become a rope expert. A minute or two later he came dragging one back. Then Percy, who was the biggest and the best climber among us, shinnied up to a limb above the platform and threw the rope over it. But he had no sooner touched solid ground again than we saw the next problem.

"Rope's too short," Percy said.

Sure enough, one end hung to the ground, but the other was nowhere near it. Once again it was Jon who came up with the solution, and again it involved Rooster.

"This ain't dangerous, is it?" I asked.

"Safe as breathin'," Jon said.

He tied one end of the rope to the back of Rooster's belt with a good tight knot, and had him climb the ladder. As Rooster went up, the other end of the rope came sliding down. By the time he'd reached the top of the ladder there was enough rope on the ground for Jon to tie around some boards. When he had them tight, he yelled up for Rooster to climb back down the ladder. As Rooster came down, the boards hoisted up to the platform, where Percy was waiting to take them off.

"Presto!" Jon crowed.

The system worked like a charm, and it looked for a while like we'd have the boards all up without a hitch. The trouble was, with all the going up and down the ladder, it wasn't long before Rooster was running out of gas. Not wanting him to conk out before we were done, we decided to see if he couldn't hoist the rest of the boards up in one big batch. It was a bad idea. Rooster started down with the load tied on, but as it turned out, there were more boards on that end of the rope than there was of Rooster at his end, and instead of the boards lifting off the ground, Rooster lifted off the ladder. He floated up and away like Peter Pan, swinging in big arcs out above us the same way Herman the goat had done in the barn. His legs and arms flailed and his eyes were bugging out.

Jon and I were speechless.

Up above, Percy's head hung over the edge, swinging back and forth upside down, following Rooster.

When we'd recovered our voices, we tried to assure Rooster we had things under control, which, of course, we didn't.

Jon leaned over and whispered to me, "What if his belt breaks?"

Rooster's arcs were shrinking by now, but every time he swung past the end of the rope that was tied to the lumber, he'd snag an arm or leg and set into a spin.

Percy yelled down, "Try takin' a board out. Maybe that'll let him down."

It was the only idea any of us had, so Jon and I kicked and pulled till we'd worked one free, but nothing happened.

"Don't work!" I yelled.

At the end of the rope, Rooster had wilted. His arched, spread-eagled, flailing body had folded up like a pocketknife.

"Hurry up! Take out more," Percy yelled. "I think he's dyin'."

Jon and I pulled out one board after another, stepping back each time to see if that one was the one that'd do the trick. Finally, we took one out and noticed a little bounce to the pile, and with the next one the whole thing lifted skyward as Rooster settled to the ground.

Needless to say, we carried the rest of the boards up by hand. And as for Rooster, he had a red mark across his belly and a belt that was a good six inches longer than when he'd started. Each day after school for the next week or so, Jon Pindar would load his pockets with a good portion of his parents' candy supply and come over to build on the treehouse. We put a floor down and built walls and a roof, and Rooster was our constant sidekick, but always from solid ground. We never were able to coax him up the ladder again.

We felt bad about what had happened to Rooster, and remembering how well he'd guarded the house the day we'd gone to the hearing, and seeing how he'd put his life on the limb, so to speak, we decided to make Rooster our honorary treehouse guard. We built him a bench at the base of the tree to sit on and gave him one of Percy's stick rifles and one of Grandpa's hard hats to wear. We wrote "guard" on a piece of paper and taped it to the front of the hardhat and told him not to let anybody near.

"If anybody comes, just shoot him," Jon said. "They might be county men."

Rooster lifted his stick rifle up and went "Bang!"

"That's right," Jon repeated. "Don't let nothin' come. Somethin' comes, shoot it."

"Bears, too," I added. "You see a bear comin', you shoot him."

Rooster darn near popped his buttons, he was so proud. He sat back against the tree with his gun and hardhat, and he shot at everything that came anywhere near—dogs, cats, chickens, everything.

A few days later at school, I learned that Rooster was doing more than just guarding the treehouse. I still wasn't exactly popular with the boys and their big-kid friends, but that didn't keep me from following them around like a dog. On this day, I gave the password and crawled into the berry-bush hideout, where I found Jon, Percy, and two other big kids passing a fancy curved-stemmed pipe around, smoking up a storm. They weren't too happy about my arrival and did their best to make me fear for my life. But as somebody who'd already wrestled with a bear and played regularly with Jon Pindar, I didn't have much fear left in me, and I wouldn't budge. When they realized I was there to stay, for better or for worse, Jon said, "All right—you wanta stay, then you gotta smoke too."

"No way," I said. "I ain't makin' my teeth yellow. Besides, anybody finds out about this, you're all gonna be in big trouble." Jon gave the pipe a long draw then passed it to the boy on his left, who took a puff and passed it on. When it came to Percy, he gave me a long look, then put it to his lips and sucked in. I mean really sucked in. You could tell smoking a pipe wasn't something he'd done much of, because smoke came out every place but his ears. After a bout of coughing and with his eyes still watering, he held the pipe out for me to take.

I shook my head.

"Baby," Jon said.

"Baby yourself."

"Look," one of the boys said, "we don't give a hoot if you do it or not. Fact, I hope you don't. But if you're gonna be part of this bunch, you've gotta."

They all nodded their heads seriously.

"Just one puff?" I asked.

"As many as the rest of us," Jon said.

"Can they be just little ones?"

"Who cares?" Jon blurted. He grabbed the pipe from Percy's hand and shoved it into mine. "Just do it! You're wasting our whole recess."

I sat there thinking about it a little longer...then did it. I took the littlest puff I could, then whipped it on to Jon and spit till my mouth was dry. "That tastes like poop!" I said. I hung my tongue out over my front teeth and stroked my palm down it to wipe more of the bad taste off.

Trouble was, that wasn't the end of it. It was a long recess, and the pipe kept passing around the circle, and around, and around.

"Boy, this sure is fun," Jon kept saying.

"Sure is," the other boys parroted.

"How about you, Susie?" Percy asked.

"Most fun I've had in a long time," I lied.

Now, as the pipe made its rounds, Jon reached down in his pack and pulled out a portable radio. He spun through the dial a time or two till he found some rock'n'roll.

He sat the radio on the ground in front of him and started digging through the pack for something else. He set out a harmonica, several bottles of shaving cologne, a paperback book of dirty jokes, and finally a pack of cigars (which seemed to be what he was after).

"Where'd you get this stuff?" I asked.

"Rod and Gun Club cabin."

"No you didn't."

"Don't be stupid," he said. "I found it under that board, just like the other stuff."

"The pipe, too?"

"That's what I said."

"Rooster ain't takin' stuff any more," I said. "Anyway, he don't smoke. He wouldn't take smokin' stuff."

"I bet Rooster does a lotta things you don't know about," Jon said. "He probably even drinks beer."

"He don't drink beer or smoke or nothin'," I said, "an' he don't steal."

"Oh yeah?" Jon said. "Look here!" He dug down in his pack again and pulled out a little velvet-covered jewelry box. "Know what this is?"

"Maybe."

He flipped it open, and it was full of rings and necklaces. "Now, whadda you think about your ol' Rooster?"

My mouth hung open.

"This is big-time stealin'," Jon said. "These're real jewels, an' he didn't find 'em in no garbage can."

I didn't know what to say. I reached out to touch them, but he pulled them back.

"I suppose you think they're yours, now," I said. "Well, they ain't. None of this stuff's yours. Just cause you found it don't mean you own it...an' it don't mean Rooster stole it, either."

"Think not?" Jon said. He fished the locket out from inside his collar and held it defiantly out. "Came from the same place this did. He stole it."

"That locket ain't stolen," I objected. "Somebody gave it to him, and you know it. An' that picture that was in it—that was his mom or sister or wife or somebody like that."

"Wife!" Jon roared.

"Could be," I said.

Just then the bell rang. Jon poked everything back in his pack while one of the big boys snuffed out the pipe.

As I crawled out, my stomach felt odd. By the end of the school day I was feeling rotten, and by bedtime Percy and I had both thrown up more times than we could count.

"Must be the flu," Mom said.

"Could be somethin' they ate," Dad said.

"Probably them school lunches," Grandpa said. "They're enough to make anybody puke."

Chapter 25

P ercy and I gagged and heaved till almost morning. Mom moved her bed in beside us and spent the better part of her night holding pans under our chins.

"Boy, I don't know what you two got," she said, "But it sure is potent."

Some time before dawn I finally dozed off, and when I woke up, it was broad daylight. I was as weak as a baby. Over on the other side of the room, Percy was laying on his mattress fully clothed. His bedding was in a heap on the floor.

"Least we didn't have to go to school," I said.

"Whoopee," he muttered sarcastically.

Mom came in a little later with orange juice and jello for us to eat. We both gobbled it down and asked for more, but she told us to wait a while, just in case. "Your poor stomachs have had a rough night," she said. "No sense rushing things." Then she moved the two of us out to lawn chairs in the yard while she tore our beds apart to wash the blankets.

It wasn't long before Rooster wandered home from his rounds. He slid over to us clutching his garbage bag to his chest. He was wearing his usual shy grin and had his chin tucked down on his shoulder like a little kid getting called forward to say a poem. "Been sick?" he mumbled.

"Belly aches," I said.

He sidled up, wanting to help us out, but not knowing how to go about it.

"Want somethin'?" he finally muttered. He twisted his toe in the dirt.

"You can get us some cookies from the bus," Percy told him.

Rooster tromped off and came back with two handfuls. We split them up.

Rooster bobbed his head and grinned and hovered over us like a waiter in a fancy restaurant trying to earn himself a big tip, except Rooster's tip was the pleasure he got from pleasing us. His tiny eyes were as alive as I had ever seen them. He dug shyly at his fingernails. "Want more?"

"How 'bout some milk?" I asked.

"Me too," Percy said.

Rooster lit up like a candle. He headed off for the bus like he'd been shot from a gun. We watched him disappear inside.

"I feel sorry for Rooster," I said. "Remember that one huntin' dog Dad had when we were little kids? Remember how he got the habit of killin' chickens, an' how he'd plop a dead chicken down at Dad's feet like it was a pheasant or somethin', an' then stand there waggin' his tail, thinkin' he'd done something good?"

Percy nodded, "Yeah, an' Dad had to shoot him to break the habit."

"I know," I said. "That was sad, but Rooster's kinda like that dog. He's no thief. He's just got a bad habit...an' now he can't stop. Sometimes I even wonder if he ain't just takin' stuff so's we can find it. Know what I mean? Like a gift or somethin'."

"Could be, I guess," Percy said. "I don't know."

"Anyway, it's what I think," I said. "He loves doin' things for us. I mean, why else would he keep hidin' all that stuff in the same place all the time when we keep findin' it an' takin' it? It's like he knows we're gonna do it. I bet he's doin' it for us."

Percy shrugged then said, "At least I hope he don't take no more pipes or cigars...."

It was midafternoon when Dad and Grandpa brought the picking crew up to the house for a break. Mom had coffee and milk and lemonade for everyone, and hot apple pie right out of the oven.

The pickers were mainly transients and a few Indians from the reservation. They sat in the grass and ate without saying much.

"See any sign of bear?" Mom asked.

"All I've seen's apples," Dad said. He looked over at Mom. "But it's just a matter o' time. Creek's fillin' with fall-run salmon, an' you know how that brings 'em out. Between the apples an' the fish, this is bear heaven." He took a bite of pie and washed it down with a swig of milk, then set his glass down on the grass between his knees and said, "After what he's been through this ol' one-eared booger's probably gettin' pretty wary. We're probably worryin' over nothin'. Chances are, he's mighty shy 'bout now."

"Well, I'll rest a lot easier when he's dead," Mom said.

"We got our guns ready," Grandpa said. "He'll show up sooner or later." He flicked his head in the direction of the pasture. "Got company."

Jon Pindar was coming up through the grass, wandering back and forth scaring up grasshoppers. When he came to the fence, he spread the wires and crawled through.

"How you feeling, Jon?" Mom asked him as he came up.

"Fine," he said.

"You tell your mom she'd better keep an eye on you. There's a real nasty flu going around. You've probably been exposed to it."

Jon knew darn well what had made Percy and me sick, and he looked over at us with a little grin on his face. "I got a strong stomach," he said.

Then Mom said, "And you tell your mom something else. Tell her that bear's still roaming around here someplace. It's not safe to be walking through those woods all alone. When you're ready to go back, we'll drive you."

About the time Dad and Grandpa and the pickers were getting ready to go back to work, a truck from the power company came up the driveway and stopped by the new house.

"What could they want?" Mom asked.

Grandpa and the pickers were headed off toward the orchard. Dad slung his picking sack over one shoulder and went over to find out. A couple of guys had climbed down out of the truck and were leaning against the hood, talking, while a third one came toward the barn. He was looking up and following the wires along.

Dad came up to him and started up a conversation about the weather, which they both agreed was too nice for working. Then Dad asked, "Some problem with the lines?"

The man gave his head a vague shake, but didn't answer outright. He yelled back to the truck for the other two to bring a ladder. One of the men went to the back of the truck and pulled an aluminum extension ladder out.

Dad said, "Somethin' broke?"

"We have a work order to disconnect," the man said.

"Disconnect?" Dad's mouth dropped.

"Yeah."

"What for?"

The man gave Dad a sheepish look. "They really don't tell us all that stuff," he said. "We're just the grunts."

"Come on," Dad said, "they don't send people out to unhook people's power without givin' 'em reasons why."

"Something about an unauthorized structure," the man said.

"Speak English…." Dad demanded. You could see his temper rising like a rocket.

"An illegal building," the man said.

Dad and Mom looked at each other like they couldn't believe what was going on. Mom said, "They can't do that, can they?"

"Seems like they do whatever they want," Dad said. He turned to the man. "Look, mister. We paid a small fortune to get this power run in here. We paid for it with our own money. You can't tell me you guys can just waltz in here whenever you feel like it an' shut it off."

"I don't like doing it any more than you," the man said, "but I'm just doing my job."

"Everybody's just doin' his job!" Dad blasted. "Who in the dickens gave you these orders?"

The man didn't answer. The other two men came up with the ladder and tipped it up against the tree under the wires.

Dad stepped forward. "Ain't nobody gonna cut any wires less he's got some papers'r somethin'. These're my wires. I bought 'em, doggone it."

"Look, mister," one of the other men said. "Don't get upset. You've evidently got some sort of fight going with the county. It's not our fault. We just do what we're told."

"Well, if you're takin' orders from them, then you might as well take 'em from me, too...an' I'm tellin' you to put your ladder back on your truck an' git!"

Dad started to say something else, but the first man cut in. "Wait. Let me show you our papers. You say that's what you want. I'll be right back." He left for the truck.

The third man was wearing striped coveralls and a fluorescent baseball cap. He leaned against the ladder. "That's a nice-looking house. What'd they do, catch you for building without a permit?" He looked at us kids and then back to Dad and Mom. "I got a friend who had a problem with the county. Built an addition on his house without a permit. You don't need one if you're just changin' things around inside—new wall or something like that. Buy when you start putting on rooms or decks, they come running."

"Did they shut your friend's power off?" Mom asked.

"Gave him all sorts of hell. County's got all kinds of clubs to beat you with."

The other man had a belt of tools hung over his shoulder. He swung it around his waist and began buckling it on. "You can't fight the government," he said. "It's like fighting King Kong." He jerked the belt tight and tucked the end through the loop.

Just then the first man came back with a clipboard full of papers. He dug down through the stack and pulled one off and handed it to Dad. Dad ran his eyes down the paper then said, "This don't say nothin'. It's just a work order."

"That's all they gave us," the man said.

"I wanta see the paper from the county that tells you to do this. That's the paper I mean—the one that says why."

"This is all we have," the man said. He took the work order back from Dad. "Maybe you should give them a call or something."

The man with the tool belt around his waist tested the ladder to make sure it was solid, then started climbing.

"Wait a minute!" Dad said. "I said nobody was gonna shut off our power." And he grabbed the man's belt and pulled him down.

The man lit in a heap and jumped up like he was ready to tear Dad limb from limb. "What you doing?" he demanded.

"What any man'd do," Dad said.

"Don't touch me again!" the man said. "You touch me again and you'll have the police to answer to!"

Dad turned and ripped the ladder away from the tree and threw it to the ground.

"Set that ladder up!" the man ordered.

The man stepped toward Dad, but the other two grabbed him. The man in the coveralls said, "Look mister, we don't mean to make trouble. This is what they told us to do. We're just peons. Your squabble's with somebody else—not us."

"You heard what I said!" Dad warned. "Our squabble's with anybody that touches them wires. They're ours! We bought 'em!"

Two of the men picked the ladder up and began leaning it back against the tree, but Dad gave it a kick that sent it crashing down again. Rooster had come out to see what the commotion was about and had to jump back to keep from getting hit.

"Keep back, Rooster," Dad said.

Rooster stepped away.

"We don't want a fight over this," the first man said.

"You're gonna have one," Dad said, and he stepped forward threateningly.

"Sam—" Mom grabbed Dad's arm, but he shook her loose.

"Don't worry, lady," the first man said. "We're not paid to fight." He motioned the other two men back. They picked up the ladder and headed for the truck with it.

"Don't come back!" Dad shouted.

"Might not be us," the first man said over his shoulder, "but somebody will. You're fighting a fight you can't win."

We all watched silently as the three men slid the metal ladder into the back of their truck then piled into the cab. The big truck turned around in the grass and bumped out the driveway.

Chapter 26

Mom found huckleberry picking a joy. That was the word she used—"joy." I think the reason she felt that way was that of all the things a body could find to eat in the great outdoors, huckleberries were one of the few you didn't have to kill first. Of course, this pleasure she got from picking meant she did a lot of it, and since she was of the opinion that "those who ate food should help in the getting and cooking and serving and cleaning up," she was always dragging Percy and me along to do our part. Needless to say, the two of us didn't share Mom's enthusiasm. As far as the eating aspect of it went, we always pitched right in. We considered it our honored duty as kids to do our fair share in the eating of huckleberry pies and pancakes and muffins and all the rest. No problem there. But when it came to picking, it was a different story, and we found about as much joy in it as we did in weeding the garden or cleaning manure from the barn. In fact, we hated it.

On the day we had our final run-in with the one-eared bear, Mom brought the two of us, against our will, to do some picking in the burned-over hillside up at the head of Mallard Creek. As could be expected, we weren't especially inspired, and our buckets were a little slow to fill. Mom was working farther up the slope. Now and then her head would pop up when she straightened to work the kinks out of her back, but mostly she kept hard at her work. Finally, she stood up and yelled to us, "How's it going down there?" Well, she knew from past experience exactly how it was going.

"Bad!" I answered.

And Percy hollered up, "Huckleberry picking is girls' work."

Mom threw a berry in our direction, then said, "I'd better see a little life down there, or one brave and one squaw are both going to get the old Indian huckleberry torture treatment...from me."

"What's the Indian huckleberry torture treatment?" I asked.

"Huckleberries up the nose—a hundred in each nostril—squashed."

Of course that didn't scare either Percy or me, and we spent the next while plugging berries into our own nostrils, then blasting them as far as we could. It gave us purple noses, but it was more fun than picking.

A little later, Mom announced that her bucket was full and she wanted to know if either of us had any room left in ours. Of course, ours had nothing but room in them, and we climbed all over each other to get ours to her first.

"What have you two been doing down there—sleeping?"

"We had bad bushes," Percy said.

"They are bad," I said. "All they got's little bitty berries."

"Well, why don't you leave your buckets with me, and the both of you go over and help Rooster with his shoes before he burns them up."

Rooster had fallen into the water on the way up and was across the stream on a hummock of dry ground, drying his shoes over a fire we'd built for him. He was hunched over it with smoke billowing around him, and he was roasting one of his boots on a stick the way you'd roast a wiener.

"Geeze," Percy muttered.

We turned our buckets over to Mom and crossed the stream on a log. When we came up to Rooster, his dark eyes looked at us from out of the blue cloud.

"Get outa the smoke," Percy said.

Rooster grinned, with his hand cupped beside his mouth as usual to shield his snaggy teeth, but he stayed engulfed in smoke.

"You're gonna burn them boots," Percy said to him.

"Burn 'em?..."

"Yeah. You're gonna burn 'em. Take 'em off those sticks."

"Shoes'r wet," he mumbled.

"I know they're wet," Percy said, "but you leave 'em that close to the fire an' they'll burn. You won't have any shoes if you let 'em burn. Take 'em off."

Rooster took hold of one of the boots with his hand then jumped back, shaking his fingers. The boot fell into the fire. Percy kicked it out.

"You knew that was gonna be hot," Percy said. His impatience was showing in his voice.

"He didn't know," I said.

"Well, he should have, darn it." Percy looked back at Rooster and said to him, "You never think."

Rooster hung his head like a whipped dog. He had his burned fingers in his mouth.

I took a stick and poked it inside Rooster's other boot and lifted it away from the fire. I could see that the sole had melted away from the leather. "It's ruined," I said.

Rooster bit on his finger.

"Well, you can wear it with a hole in it," Percy said. "A hole don't matter."

Rooster nodded and grinned blankly. He was pleased that Percy thought he could wear it with the hole in it, and that the hole didn't matter. He reached down and picked up the burned boot.

"Better watch those eyelets," Percy warned. "They'll be hot a while."

Rooster nodded, blankly. His stockings were full of dirt and pine needles, with the tops slid down to his heels and the toes flopping out past the ends of his feet like wet washrags.

"Gonna feel real good with them pine needles in your socks," Percy commented.

Rooster sidled over a step or two closer to Percy, gnawing shyly on the end of his thumbnail. "Sorry," he mumbled.

"Don't be sorry to me," Percy said. "You're the one that's gotta walk in 'em."

Rooster looked down at the socks and gave one foot a feeble kick to shake it clean.

We put Rooster's boots back beside the fire again, but this time farther away, so they wouldn't burn any more than they already had. Rooster sat down cross-legged, poking in the dirt with his finger. The flames seemed to have a hypnotic effect on him, and it wasn't long before he was as still as a tree.

With Mom still across the creek filling our buckets and Percy sitting back against a rock whittling, I decided to wander upstream along the edge of the creek looking for old spawned-out salmon. By the time salmon lay their eggs, they're pretty much spent, and they move to the shallows to avoid the current. With luck and fast hands, you can grab them by the tail. It wasn't exactly the kind thing to do to half-dead fish, but it beat picking huckleberries, and I found it entertaining. I don't know how long I'd been at it or how many I'd gotten hold of, but I know my sleeve was soaked, and I was almost out of sight of the hummock when I heard Mom behind me. At first, other than the fact that she was speaking so quietly I could barely hear her, I couldn't tell anything was wrong.

"Come on—" she whispered.

"Time to go?" I asked.

"Come on," she said again, still whispering and motioning urgently. "Hurry!"

I noticed she had the gun. "What's wrong?" I asked.

She was getting a little irritated at me by then, and with a louder whisper she said, "It's the bear!"

I quit asking questions real fast and hurried back to the hummock behind her. Percy and Rooster were ducked down behind a log not far from the fire, looking downstream along the trail. Mom and I crawled in beside them.

"Where is it?" I whispered.

"Over there, now," Percy pointed.

Mom held her hand up for us to be quieter. A flick of motion in some bushes down along the stream caught my eye, but I still couldn't make out exactly where it was. Then the bushes rattled so hard you could have sworn they'd uproot. It looked like a little twister had hit them, and out from the leaves came the bear's big brown haunches. It backed out like a wind-up toy in reverse—one leg then the other, then the other—until it was in the open. Then with its nose up testing the air, it did a slow turn until we weren't looking at its rump any longer, but at its front, head-on.

Now I could see its eyes set close in its thick fur. I could see a strand of slobber dangling from the corner of its mouth, its squat, powerful legs and thick neck...and the terrible blank spot on the left side of its head where the ear was missing. For a long moment it clapped its eyes on us, the way a fighter does on an opponent in the middle of the ring before a fight—like it was ready to take us apart limb from limb, and softening us up with its gaze before commencing.

But then, with the same mechanical toy walk, it turned and wandered away, giving its attention back to the huckleberries.

"You gotta shoot it, Mom," Percy whispered. "We won't have a better chance."

Mom stared at him.

"Shoot him," Percy whispered, again. "You can't miss."

"He might charge," Mom whispered back.

Percy slid closer to her. "Then let me do it," he said. "I won't miss."

Their two minds were working in opposite directions. You could see Percy pulling forward, and Mom holding back—Percy understanding that this might be the best chance we'd ever have to make the kill; Mom remembering how Grandpa and Jon Pindar had each missed good shots and almost gotten somebody killed.

I glanced over to my left at Rooster. He was crouched lower than the rest of us, with his muscles quivering, like a scared animal. He had one boot pulled on but was holding the other one in his hand. His attention was totally riveted on the bear.

For the longest time nothing moved. Then the bushes exploded. The bear shot out across an open stretch of grass into the stream. Water flew up. A big old red-sided salmon flashed out across the riffle with the bear a close step behind, trying to make the pounce. Then another one flashed out from the opposite bank in the other direction. The bear forgot about the first fish and romped off after the new one.

"Let's get out of here," Mom whispered. "This is crazy." She had the barrel of the rifle up over the log.

"He's got the trail blocked," Percy whispered back.

Mom fingered the trigger and you could see her thinking.

The bear waded back to shore on our side of the stream and shook. It was standing broadside, now, and acting agitated.

"Shoot," Percy whispered. "Right up behind its front leg."

Mom had her eyes glued on the bear, but she didn't move—not even a muscle.

The thought suddenly came to me that Mom might have forgotten to load the gun. Grandpa had told us stories about that happening to hunters. I was reaching out to tap her arm to remind her when it happened. The bear wheeled around and in a split second it was romping up along the edge of the stream directly toward us. Whether it was attacking or just feeling its oats, I'll never know. But whatever the reason, the result was electric.

From out the corner or my eye I saw a flash of motion.

"Rooster!" I gasped. He was on his feet and sprinting headlong at the bear as fast as his old legs would move. In his one hand he was waving his shoes overhead like a weapon.

The bear skidded to a stop and reared half upright, then dropped to all fours again.

"Shoot!" I heard Percy shout. "Shoot!"

His words had barely cleared his lips when there was an explosion inches from my head. A shell flipped out in the grass in front of me, then another explosion, and another shell flipped out—this one glancing off my cheek. Rooster was only a step or so from the bear with his shoe poised when it fell in a limp heap on the ground. He stumbled to a stop and stood motionless over it, looking for all the world like he'd killed it with his own two hands. Then, with a stunned, confused look, Rooster turned to face us. Percy jumped up from where he'd been crouched and hooted and ran toward him.

Mom shouted, "Wait! He might not be dead!"

Percy stopped and looked back. "I gotta stick him," he said.

"Keep back!" she said. "I don't want anybody going close to that thing!" She looked toward Rooster. "Get back!" she ordered.

But Rooster didn't budge. He stood clutching his shoe, staring down at the bear.

"He might still be alive, Rooster," I hollered. "Come back!"

But then Rooster did an odd thing—one of the oddest things I'd ever seen. He dropped his shoe in the grass and knelt down beside the bear's head. Then he bent over close to its one ear and began talking to it.

"What's he doin'?" I asked.

Mom didn't answer, but only shook her head. She had a curious look on her face.

"Guess he's sad," I said.

"Guess so," Mom said.

We couldn't hear what he was saying, of course. He was too far away and talking too quietly. He didn't seem to be saying much, but now and then he'd make a slow gesture with his arms as though he was explaining something.

Percy had come back to where Mom and I were by now. "He was gonna fight him with his shoe," Percy said, reverently, "but now look at him." Then he said, "Can I go an' stick him now? We know he's dead."

"No," Mom said.

"It's safe," he argued.

"No. Wait for Rooster." She clicked the safety on the gun and stood up.

Rooster was still talking to the bear in the same quiet way and after we had waited a while and realized he wasn't going to stop, Mom said, "Why don't you go get him, Susie?"

"What'll I say?" I asked.

"Just tell him it's time to go."

So I went to him to tell him, but as I came closer I could hear what he was saying. I stopped and stood behind him, listening. His thoughts were halting and disconnected, but in his way he was telling the bear all about the cabin we'd given him to live in. He was describing his electric light and his tent and how the cabin had a door and a window.

I looked back at Mom.

She nodded for me to go ahead.

"It's time to go, Rooster," I said. "We gotta go home, now."

He looked up at me with his dull, dark-circled eyes. They were like two stones in his skull. The bear's head was laying outstretched in the meadow grass beside him with its tongue lolling out between its teeth. Its eyes were open but totally dead.

Then it struck me that Rooster's eyes were as drained of life as the bear's. The realization made me shiver.

"Time to go," I repeated.

Rooster picked his shoe up off the grass and climbed to his feet. Holding the shoe out for me to see, he said, "Shoe burned—see?"

"Yeah, Rooster," I answered. "Little hole won't hurt much, though. We'll buy a new pair."

Chapter 27

D
ad and Grandpa got home from wherever they'd been a little after dark. Percy and I met them at the truck and had the story about Mom and Rooster and the bear all told and embellished by the time they'd gotten to the door. A big grin was spread all over Dad's face, and Grandpa kept muttering, "Well, I'll be darned."

We trooped inside. Rooster was sitting on a chair with his shoes and socks off. Mom had his shoes hanging behind the stove.

"Got any bear meat around this joint?" Dad demanded. "We come for some bear stew."

Mom turned and pretended to be surprised. "Oh my—" she said in the most dainty voice she could muster, "We don't serve meat at this restaurant. Anyway, Mr. Rooster and I were just having tea."

"You mean there ain't no bear meat?"

Mom was working hard to hold a straight face. With her dainty voice beginning to break up, she said, "Most of our patrons who want bear meat bring their own live bear with them. Then Mr. Rooster, here, takes it out back and hits it over the head with his shoe. Did you bring a bear?"

Dad shook his head. "Nooo...had one. Had one when I left town, but I got hungry on the way home an' ate him." He walked to her and cupped his hands around her face and said, "Nice goin', Carrie." He gave her a kiss and hugged her so hard her feet lifted up off the ground. "Next time, though, don't hog all the fun for yourself."

"I think I owe her one o' them kisses, too," Grandpa said, and he put a hand to each side of her face the same way Dad had, and gave her a big one on the forehead.

"Well," Dad said, and he was being playful again, "if you haven't got any bear stew in this restaurant, maybe you could take Grandpa an' me out back an' give us shootin' lessons so's maybe some day we could go out an' get our own bear. Could you do that for us?"

Mom held her hands up. "No more guns for me," she said.

"Maybe you'd like to put a notch in your gun handle," Dad said.

Mom stepped over and put her hand on Rooster's shoulder. He turned his eyes up at her. Looking down at him, she said, "Maybe we'll cut one in Rooster's boot. Right, Rooster?"

Rooster grunted yes.

Mom gave him a pat on the shoulder and said, "I don't intend ever to touch that gun again."

"I'm just glad you had it when you needed it," Dad said. Then he looked down at Rooster. "Ol' buddy, I can't say's how I think too much of your judgment, but, by God, you're a good man. We love you. An' thanks. Takes guts to shoot a bear dead in his tracks when he's chargin', but goin' after one with your bare hands is a whole different thing. Whole different thing."

Rooster dropped his eyes shyly.

This being a Friday night, Percy and I were able to talk the grownups into letting us stay up late and go with them to bring the bear in.

"Let's all go," Mom said. "This is an occasion."

"Darn tootin'," Dad said. "This is an occasion." He turned to Percy. "Get us a few of them kerosene lanterns from the shop, son. Get one for each of us. We'll need some light."

While Percy got the lanterns, the men hooked the hay sled on behind the tractor. Mom found Rooster some dry socks and gave him a pair of Dad's knee-length rubber boots to wear. The boots were a couple sizes too big and made Rooster walk a little like an ape, but he was proud to have them on. He poked his pants legs down inside them and any time anybody was looking, he'd pose with his foot out like somebody in a shoe ad.

"You can wade right in the water with them things on," I said. "Won't even get your feet wet."

Grandpa trimmed the wicks and lit all the lanterns, and we filed out into the night. Mom and I and Rooster took our lanterns to the sled and sat down on it. Grandpa climbed on the tractor and started it up. Since the one working headlight on the tractor was now not working, Dad and Percy walked out front to show the way.

The night was clear and there were stars covering the sky like salt. Our little collection of lanterns moved through the darkness like an island of light.

"Anybody know a song?" Grandpa shouted over the sound of the engine.

Dad gave a thumbs down.

Mom started singing something, but she was the only one who knew the words...and it soon died out. "We need one everybody knows," she said. "Know any, Rooster?"

Rooster threw his head back with a laugh.

"Old McDonald." Grandpa suggested.

"Old McSimpson," Mom corrected, and she started it off. "Old McSimpson had a farm, eeeiii-eeeiii-ooo; and on this farm they had a bear, eeeiii-eeeiii-ooo; with a grr, grr here, and a grr, grr there—"

Everybody joined in, following Mom's lead.

Then Grandpa added a verse. "A Carrie," he said. "Old McSimpson had a Carrie!"

"Yeah!" Dad shouted, "With a boom-boom!"

So we put in Mom's name this time, with a boom-boom here and a boom-boom there.

We were getting into the swing of it, now, and everyone began thinking of new words. We added verses all the way down across the creek and on up the cat track into the forest. We had verses about apples and cows and Dad and Rooster, and even about the county men and the Turners. Rooster sang too—out of tune and out of rhyme and making sounds that were supposed to be words. But he had the spirit and more volume than all the rest of us except Grandpa.

When we finally came to the end of the cat track we were still a few hundred yards from the meadow. Our lanterns made a cavern of light in the trees.

Grandpa idled the tractor slower and said, "Now where?"

"I guess we could leave the sled and tractor here an' just drag the bear this far by hand," Dad said.

"You drug a bear lately?" Grandpa asked. "That ol' booger's gonna be heavy."

"Let's unhitch the sled, then," Dad said. "We shouldn't have any trouble squeezin' just the cat through. We can drag it back to here with the cat."

"Don't wanta ruin the hide," Grandpa said.

"We'll take her easy," Dad said.

So with new verses of "Old McSimpson" still popping up from time to time, as someone thought of a new character, Dad guided Grandpa and the tractor between the trees by lantern light until we finally came out into the huckleberry meadow. Percy and I took the lead, then, since we knew where the bear was. When we came to it, Grandpa backed the tractor up as close as he could, then shut the engine off and climbed down. For a while we all just stood looking down at the brown sprawl in the grass by lantern light.

"Big ol' sucker," Dad muttered. "Jus' makes you wonder what he was thinkin'." He set his lantern down and kneeled by its head. "Nobody stuck him," he said.

"I was gonna," Percy said, "but Mom wouldn't let me."

"Hasn't been that long," Grandpa said. "Bleedin' 'em ain't as important as what they say it is, anyway. I jus' wonder how many hunks o' lead we'll find in him? If it's the same one I tangled with, I'll bet you anything he picked some up from me. Couldn'ta missed all them shots."

"It's a shame," Mom said.

"What's that?" Grandpa asked.

"Oh...that we had to kill him."

Grandpa added that he thought so, too, then said, "It's a rough ol' life. This guy was jus' in the wrong place at the wrong time. Wasn't his fault. God knows, we gave him the message enough times, though." He looked over at Dad, then, and said, "Trouble is, this bear ain't the only thing around here that's gettin' sent that kinda message. Ain't easy listenin' to messages when you don't wanta hear 'em."

It took all of us to roll the bear on its side. When we had it turned, Grandpa slit each leg along the tendon and ran a rope through the cuts. Then he tied the legs together and fastened the end of the rope to the hitch.

"On McSimpson!" Dad shouted.

Grandpa started the engine, and running it just a notch above idling speed, he made his way out of the meadow and back into the trees. Mom and I led the way, now, and Dad followed along keeping a close watch on the bear to make sure it didn't get hung up on anything. When we finally got to the sled, we unhitched the bear, and with all of us heaving, we loaded it on and headed back. Grandpa pulled to a stop under our tree house. "Think that rope the kids have over that limb'll hold this bear up?" he asked.

Dad thought a minute. "Shoot, I don't know. Worth a try."

So they tied one end of the rope to the bear and the other end to the tractor hitch, and Grandpa chugged the tractor slowly forward. The rope came taut and the bear stretched then lifted up off the sled. Not being centered under the rope it commenced to swing. A bad feeling suddenly came over me. The image of Rooster swinging at the end of the same rope just days earlier flashed in my mind. I shook my head to clear it. But a sense of gloom settled over me. It must have settled over the others, too, because Grandpa said, "Sad in a way, ain't it, how a little tiny hunk o' lead can turn such a handsome animal into nothin' more'n a slab o' meat." He put his arm out and settled the bear's swinging then buried his fingers in its fur and said, "Make a nice rug, anyway."

Over the next hour or so, with a single electric bulb for light, Dad and Grandpa gutted and skinned the bear. When we finally left for bed, it was hanging with all the stuff of life cut away.

The next morning came up overcast, and for the first time in weeks you couldn't see the mountains for the clouds. It was cold as I dressed and when I went into the next room, there was a fire going in the wood stove. Dad came in carrying a bucket of milk.

"Fall's here," he said.

"I don't know about you," Mom said, "but I got cold in bed last night. I think we've got some work to do on this old barn if we're going to stay in it much longer." She had oatmeal cooking on the wood stove and a pan of cocoa in the kettle beside it.

"Go get Rooster for breakfast," Mom told me.

I sat close to the stove to tie my shoes, then went out to Rooster's cabin. His bed was empty. I stepped out onto his porch and called for him a time or two, but there was no answer. I circled the barn and the new house, calling as I went, and finally found him out by the treehouse sitting on his lookout stool. He was shivering and facing out across the pasture. The air was cold and damp, and the bear carcass hung from the rope beside him looking even more dead and naked than it had the night before. The hide lay in a heap on the sled, like a pair of woolly pants that had been kicked off at bedside. The head was attached to the hide and the tongue still hung out between the teeth as it had the night before. It was the deadest thing I'd ever seen.

"Time to eat," I said to Rooster.

He looked up at me.

"Guardin' the bear?" I asked.

He nodded.

"That's good," I said. "We don't want nobody to steal him."

He rubbed his hands together and pushed them down between his knees.

"Let's eat," I said again.

He stood up and fell in obediently behind me. He shuffled the rubber boots wearily along.

Then I stopped, and an odd feeling came over me. I'm not sure what it was. It might just have been the dreary weather or sleepiness. It might also have had something to do with the empty feeling the sight of the bear carcass had created in me. But I found myself turning to Rooster and I said, "I just wanted to thank you for tryin' to protect us from the bear again." I had the urge to say more or to say it better, but I didn't.

Rooster grinned his old snag-toothed grin, but his hand, which had always cupped up to cover his mouth on such occasions, stayed hanging at his side. He nodded shyly. I looped my arm through his and led him along the path and into the barn.

"Mornin', Rooster," Grandpa said.

As I led him around the table to his spot at the far end, everyone greeted him. He nodded and smiled at each greeting.

"How the boots workin'?" Percy asked.

Rooster stuck his leg out to show him.

"Feet still dry?" Percy asked.

"Feet dry," Rooster slurred. He reached down and patted the side of his leg.

I still had him by the arm, and I escorted him to his chair and pulled it out for him to sit. Mom placed a bowl of oatmeal in front of him, and a cup of cocoa.

"I put raisins in the oatmeal, Rooster," Mom said. "How's that sound?"

He smiled and nodded in the usual way, but, again, there was something different about it—or at least it seemed to me there was. I watched him pour milk on his cereal and clumsily spread sugar over it. He had never been good at spreading sugar and he dumped it in a little heap.

"How'd you sleep last night, Rooster?" Grandpa asked. "Have any good dreams?"

"Told me he dreamed about them good lookin' women again," Dad joked.

Rooster had a mouth full of oatmeal. He grinned at Dad's joke and milk ran out the corners of his mouth down his whiskers.

"I don't think he slept last night," I said. "I think he guarded the bear."

"Oh, Rooster," Mom said, "you didn't do that, did you?"

Rooster looked at Mom blankly with another bite in his mouth.

"That old bear doesn't need guarding," Mom said. "If there's anything we have that doesn't need protecting, it's that. Nobody's going to bother it."

"Rooster likes guardin'," Percy said. "Us kids made him the guard for the treehouse. He even has a place to sit."

Grandpa set his cocoa cup down with a thump and wiped his mouth with his sleeve. "I think Rooster's the most important guy around here," he said. "After all, he's put his life on the line twice, now, for us. Right? An' if he's good at guardin', I think it's time somebody besides the kids recognizes it. Don't you agree, Rooster?"

Rooster pumped his head a couple of times.

"How'd you like to be this family's official guard?" Grandpa asked.

Rooster thumped his chest with his palm. "Rooster guard bear," he said.

"Darn right," Grandpa said. "Like them rich people. A watchman. Yeah. One o' them guys that sits in a little buildin' by a rich man's gate to let in who we want, an' keep out who we don't want. Get you one o' them tall hats with a plume, an' a sword an' rifle with one o' them bayonets on it. Get you one o' them red uniforms." Grandpa paused to rub his nose with his fist. His face was grinned into wrinkles. "You guard the bear, the house, the cattle, the kids—cripe, Rooster, you can even guard me. I need guardin', too. That's your job around here. No more stayin' up all night, though. At night you're off duty. OK?"

Rooster turned his eyes around the room to each of us in turn. He was proud of his new assignment. You could see it in his face. He had his elbows on the table and his empty spoon poised straight up in the air, like a flag.

"One thing," Dad said. "No more fightin' bears with shoes an' clubs. We're glad you done it—but no more. Okay? We wanta keep you around a while. That kinda guardin' don't have much future in it."

"You just watch out for them county guys," Grandpa added. "Them county guys're the ones we need guarded against. Them power company guys, too. You see one o' them snoopin' around out here you can use your shoe or club or anything."

Mom pulled up her chair to begin eating. "Don't listen to these guys," she said. "I think it's fine to be guard, but I think we're about ready for some peace around here."

After breakfast the grownups set to butchering the bear. Dad and Grandpa would cut away a piece of the carcass, then pack it into the barn where they had a bench cleaned off to work on. There, they would trim the meat from the bone and grind it into hamburger with the hand meat grinder.

Rooster took his place on the stool under the treehouse. Each time Dad and Grandpa came out for another hunk of meat, he'd turn and watch them as they worked. When they went inside, he'd turn back toward the driveway and sit motionless for long periods, peering out blankly.

Over the night, the gun Dad had taken with him when we went out to bring the bear in had never been put away. This was a cardinal sin around our house. Guns never got left out or abused, but in this case it had just been overlooked. It was laying between the fender and the tractor seat on the metal toolbox. Shortly before noon Percy asked if Rooster could hold the gun while he guarded. I remember the time of day, because Mom had just gone in to make some lunch.

"Sorry, Percy," Grandpa said. "Can't do that. Guns ain't toys." Then he said, "Wait a minute." He went to his bus and came back with a .22. "Remember this?" he asked Dad.

"I thought you threw that away," Dad said.

"Should've." He handed it to Percy. "This thing fell down all the way to the bottom of the Deschutes canyon. It was your Dad's when he was a boy. Dropped it comin' up from fishin' an' stood there an' watched it bounce clear down an' splatter all over the rocks. I don't know why we even brought it back. Couldn't get a shell in it, much less shoot one." He turned it over in Percy's hands. "See here? Whole chamber's mashed in." He turned it again. "See where the stalk's split? Got it held together with screws."

"Can I have it?" Percy asked.

"No. I don't want you playin' with even a broken gun. Get bad habits. When we get you a gun it'll be a good one, an' we'll teach you to treat it like one. I don't see no harm in Rooster holdin' it, though. Today, anyway. If he's gonna sit out there in the cold all day thinkin' he's guardin' that bear, I don't see no harm in lettin' him feel a little bit important."

Rooster loved the gun. We didn't tell him it didn't work. As far as he was concerned, it was the real thing, and he was the real guard. He turned it over in his hands, then raised it clumsily to his shoulder. He seemed to know more or less how to hold it, but you could tell he had no idea how to line the sights up or aim it.

"It's yours...but just for today," Percy said.

"Don't let nobody steal the bear, now," I said.

He laid the broken gun across his lap and leaned back against the tree.

That was the last time any of us saw Rooster alive. It's hard, even to this day, to think about it, but as Percy and I left him to go to the barn and see how the meat-grinding was going, we didn't even look back.

The first we knew that anyone besides Rooster was out there was when we heard a door slam. Mom left her meat-grinding to look out the window. From the window there was a view southeast, out in the direction of Mallard Lake, but you couldn't see the driveway or the new house. And you couldn't see Rooster as he sat guarding the bear.

"See anything?" Dad asked.

"Not out here." She was moving toward the door to peek outside when we heard the shot. She hesitated. "That sounded like a gun," she said. She opened the door and stood with it swung wide.

"Who is it?" Dad asked.

"Power company again."

"Damn," Dad gritted.

"They have the sheriff with them," she said. Then she stepped on out, and as she did she gasped. "Rooster!" she screamed.

We all ran out.

Slumped on the ground beside what was left of the carcass of the bear was Rooster. He was laying across the broken .22 with just the barrel showing. One of the officers was crouched beside the police car with his arms extended and his pistol thrust out.

Another officer was making his way cautiously forward with his gun drawn, too.

We sprinted forward. The closer officer shouted for us to keep back. But no one listened. Mom stopped Percy and me beside the tractor and clutched us close against her. All three of us were crying. Dad and Grandpa knelt over Rooster.

As the officer came up, Dad looked up at him and muttered, "He's dead."

The officer's arms drooped limply at his sides and the gun hung from his hand like a rag. "He pulled a gun on us," he said.

Then Grandpa rose up off his knees to his full height and turned slowly to the man, and with his face twisted in agony and tears welling up out of his eyes, he said, "It didn't even work."

Epilogue

L ooking back on childhood is like peering through a fog, and the fog is time. But that year when I was nine and Rooster died, though I lived it many years ago, is as clear in my mind today as it was then—maybe more so, because I view it through the lens of experience.

Rooster's death marked the end of our efforts to build a new house. Not another nail was ever driven nor another board cut. Our will to struggle died with him.

There was a hearing held for the policeman who had shot Rooster, but it was only a formality. There was never much question that he had acted properly. He was found to have shot in self-defense, and was returned to his duties without punishment.

If there was guilt to be assigned, it most likely belonged to our family—and to Dad and Grandpa, in particular. They had simply had too many confrontations with the outside world—too many warnings, too many tirades, too many bluffs. They had built a reputation, and it had caught up with them. What were those policemen to think when they found themselves looking down the barrel of Rooster's gun, after both Dad and Grandpa had announced that they were ready to shoot intruders? Grandpa had even pointed a gun at someone. The truth was, the trigger had been pulled long before, and if it hadn't been Rooster who stepped in front of the bullet, then it would have been someone else.

Years afterwards, just before he passed away, Grandpa confided to me that his greatest regret in life had been the bull-headed way he had chosen to fight the county. "It was as dumb as tryin' to fight a bear with a shoe," he told me. "The best it could ever have led to was a good mauling." As it turned out, it cost Rooster his life.

We asked to bury Rooster on our land at the ranch. As far as we knew, it was the only home he had ever known. He thought so much of the little hut we had given him to live in that we felt he would appreciate being buried beside it. But like so many other things that seemed simple at first glance, there was red tape involved in this, too. So, instead, we held his funeral at the funeral home in town and buried him in the town cemetery. Our family, the Pindars, and the policeman who shot him were the only ones who attended

I cried hard at the funeral and for weeks afterwards each time I thought of him. Even to this day I can feel a tightness come into my throat when I find his image drifting through my mind, as it often does. His memory is embedded in me, like one of those little poems you memorize as a child. You think you have forgotten them, but then one day one comes filtering out as clear as a bell. You remember every word and comma of it, and then you can't get it out of your head.

That's how it is with Rooster. From out of nowhere I will picture him as if he were alive today—sitting beside his fire at his camp in the meadow with his day's salvage dumped out on the ground, sorting through it and sharing it with his dog. Or humping along the trail with his garbage bag over his shoulder. Or I'll see the dark, hollow eyes set deep down in his whiskered old face, and his rotten-toothed grin. Sometimes I'll see him swinging in great arcs, tied by his belt to the treehouse rope. Or charging down the dusky hillside toward the bear with his shoe in his hand—short of brains and short of judgment, but so long on heart and love for anyone who loved him that he was willing to die for them...and in the end, did.

Less than a week after Rooster was buried, I awoke one morning to the sound of a chainsaw. Dad was always cutting firewood, and as I lay in bed I thought nothing of what I heard. Dad was as glum as the rest of us. He was going about his work half-heartedly, and spending a lot of time just sitting. I guess he must have been doing a lot of thinking, too. Anyway, when I finally crawled out of my warm bed that morning and went to the window, I saw him sawing at the new house with his saw. He was cutting it to pieces.

I went to the living room to where Mom and Grandpa were sitting glumly at the table. I asked them what Dad was doing, but neither of them answered me.

By the end of the day Dad had reduced the new house to a pile of rubble. It was as though we were watching a final death—the death of our home, and of our dreams and way of life. Toward evening it began to rain, and Dad dumped kerosene on the heap of mutilated boards and lit it on fire. No one watched it burn but him and me. The others stayed inside. Dad and I stood under the eaves of the barn where we could keep dry and watched the flames billow up and consume the dry lumber and shakes, and then finally die down to a glowing pile of embers.

"Burns up a lot faster'n it took to build," Dad said. "Lotta pain in that fire."

The glow reflected against the side of the barn. It lit Dad's face and turned his skin a soft orange.

"It reminds me of when the other house burned," I said, speaking to him, but not really speaking to anyone.

Dad didn't respond at first. He was sitting on a round of wood, leaning back against the wall. His pitchfork was stuck in the ground near his feet. "Yeah," he sighed, "hadn't been for that fire there wouldn'ta been none o' this happened."

"Rooster would be alive," I added.

Then Dad looked over at me. "There's somethin' you never wanta forget," he said. "Things don't stand still. Gotta remember that. Stars're burnin', rivers cuttin' new beds, little girls growin' up." He smiled weakly. "Father Time comes sneakin' up behind you, an' next thing you know, things ain't what they useta be."

He reached out and took the handle of his fork and worked the tines out of the ground. He pulled the handle down into his lap. "Changes come, Susie. Ol' man ain't the same's the child. Ain't nothin' you can do about it, either. Snake can't crawl back in his old skin...an' people can't crawl back into the past."

He looked over at me again. "But sometimes that ol' snake skin's just too temptin'. Wanta crawl back in so bad. Only way you're gonna move on's to take a match an' burn it up."

The next morning when we awoke, the rain had stopped, but the clouds still hung low in the trees. That evening when I came home from school, I stood in the dampness looking out over the charred remains of our dreams. I felt hollow inside. In what was little more than a blink of time, a few small grains of the greater whole had gone away and left it poorer. The world moved along, but in its wake it was diminished by one bear, one homeless bum, and one of the last lingering tatters of a way of life. A thin line of smoke was slowly rising up from the ashes, leaning out to the east then losing itself in the misty air. The scorched remains of the foundation stones of our home lay like black bones.

Over the next months of fall and early winter, Dad and Grandpa built us a house inside the shell of the barn—a new skin inside the old. They put in a kitchen and a bathroom and two more bedrooms—one for Percy and one for me. They even built a pantry for Mom. From the outside, it looked just like the same old barn, but inside it was as nice a house as anyone could ever hope to have, complete with water and electricity and carpets and plastered walls.

Grandpa sold his bus that winter, too. He said he was getting tired of driving all the way to Arizona, and anyway, the sunshine was bad for his skin. With no help from anyone, which was how he wanted it, he did to Rooster's little cabin what he and Dad had done to the barn. He left the outside as it had always been, but made the inside into a nice little cabin for himself, complete with a kitchen and bathroom. Grandpa lived in that cabin until he was ninety-three.

The following spring one last thing happened which more or less brought this phase of our lives to a conclusion. It had to do with Jon Pindar, and indirectly it had to do with Rooster too.

One night in May, Mr. Turner caught Jon Pindar breaking into his house. He never would have caught him at all, except that Jon snagged the back of his leather belt on the top of the chain link fence as he started to jump down, and he hung there trying to kick loose till Mrs. Turner woke up and found him. Jon tried to lie his way out of it, but in his pockets he had all kinds of things he had stolen...and one of Mr. Turner's nice graphite fishing rods was laying on the ground right under him where he had dropped it. Mr. Turner wouldn't let him down off the fence until he confessed.

But that wasn't the half of it. Mr. Turner called the police out. The police started asking more questions, and with one thing leading to another, pretty soon Jon broke down and let everything spill out. It seems that over the past year or more he had been stealing things all over the area. He led the police to his caches, and they were stuffed full. As Mr. Turner said, "If somebody hadn't caught him, he would have stolen all of us naked within six months."

They took Jon away for a day or two and kept him in a sort of jail for kids—just to give him a scare, I guess—then put him back with his parents again. The experience had an impact, and I *think* it broke him of stealing. Other than that, though, it didn't change him a bit. In fact, getting arrested and all made him an instant celebrity at school. It gave powerful reinforcement to the reputation he had already built for himself. He had a red scar around his belly for a long time afterwards from the night he hung on the Turners' chain-link fence by his belt, and he showed the scar to probably every kid in school, right down to the first-graders. He loved telling how he got it. He also carried around a newspaper article about his exploits folded up in his wallet. He took it with him wherever he went.

I was furious about all this, of course. It was bad enough that he was stealing, but to blame it on a poor helpless person like Rooster was more than I could stand. Rooster went to his grave with his reputation blackened by what Jon had done, and now Jon was boasting about it. I was too mad even to beat Jon up. From that day on I never spoke to him again. As far as I was concerned, Jon was in another world, and I didn't want in.

But anger has a limited shelf life, and with the passage of years, mine has run its course. It is gone from me, now, and in its place I feel forgiveness.

I'm not sure what happened to Jon Pindar when he grew up. His parents went broke and sold the lodge a year or so later and moved up to someplace in Washington, where they managed a couple of laundromats. Somebody told me just a few years ago that Jon eventually became a long-haul truck driver. They said they knew it for a fact. Somebody else told me he had been killed in a car wreck. Another one of the kids from school told me she had heard that he was some kind of salesman over in the valley.

So I don't know the truth of what became of Jon Pindar, and I probably never will. But I am almost certain that the story about him being killed is wrong. Each year on the anniversary of Rooster's death, our family always went back to Rooster's grave to put flowers on it. It's a ritual we carry on to this day. We didn't have money to buy him a fancy gravestone, but we did get him a small one. It had his name engraved on it, and on top of it there was a little statue of a shepherd and a sheep. This past spring when we made our visit, I found, tucked down between the feet of the sheep, a metal film canister. At first I thought it had been put there by somebody who hadn't been able to find a garbage can to drop it in. I took it out, intending to throw it away. But when it rattled, I opened it and poured out into my palm a small note and the locket and chain Jon Pindar had found in Rooster's camp and worn all that time as though it was his own. The note simply said, "I'm sorry." It was unsigned. When I snapped the locket open, the photograph of Sarah Littlejohn was gone, and in its place was the original picture. Jon must have simply covered it with Sarah's photo.

I handed the locket to Mom. "It was Rooster's," I said. "Jon took it."

Mom looked at it closely. She shook her head slowly. "I wonder who the lady is?" she said.

"I think it's his mom or somebody," I said.

We put the note and locket back into the canister and dug a small hole beside the headstone in the grass. We put the locket and canister into the hole and covered it. I had a strange but good feeling, then—like the one you get when you close the last page of a moving book—sad but fulfilled. And it had less to do with Rooster than with Jon Pindar. I suppose the locket could have been put there by someone else, but in my heart I believe it came from Jon. If our family had had a hard time crawling out of its old snake skin, it must have been a hundred times harder for Jon. Nothing could make me feel better than to know that maybe he has finally made it.

About the author:

Ron Cogdill is a retired teacher and coach who lives outside Estacada, Oregon, in the Cascade foothills, with his wife, Nancy, and three children, Ben, Brynn, and Jeremy. These days he spends his hours farming Christmas trees and looking out over the slow-filling sheets of paper in his typewriter at the river, where the once impressive salmon runs are now vanishing.

To order additional copies of

Slow Dust Rising

Book: $16.95   Shipping/Handling: $3.50

Contact: ***BookPartners, Inc.***
P.O. Box 922
Wilsonville, OR 97070

E-mail: info@bookpartners.com
Fax: 503-682-2057
Phone: 503-682-3235
Order: 1-800-895-7323